INTERPRETING AUDIENCES

The Media, Culture & Society Series

Series editors: John Corner, Nicholas Garnham, Paddy Scannell, Philip Schlesinger, Colin Sparks, Nancy Wood

The Economics of Television

The UK Case

Richard Collins, Nicholas Garnham and Gareth Locksley

Media, Culture and Society

A Critical Reader

edited by Richard Collins, James Curran, Nicholas Garnham, Paddy Scannell, Philip Schlesinger and Colin Sparks

Capitalism and Communication

Global Culture and the Economics of Information

Nicholas Garnham, edited by Fred Inglis

Media, State and Nation

Political Violence and Collective Identities

Philip Schlesinger

Broadcast Talk

edited by Paddy Scannell

Journalism and Popular Culture

edited by Peter Dahlgren and Colin Sparks

Media, Crisis and Democracy

edited by Marc Raboy and Bernard Dagenais

Culture and Power

A *Media, Culture & Society* Reader

edited by Paddy Scannell, Philip Schlesinger and Colin Sparks

INTERPRETING AUDIENCES

The Ethnography
of Media Consumption

Shaun Moores

SAGE Publications
London   ●   Thousand Oaks   ●   New Delhi

First published 1993

 SAGE Publications Ltd
6 Bonhill Street
London EC2A 4PU

SAGE Publications Inc
2455 Teller Road
Thousand Oaks, California 91320

SAGE Publications India Pvt Ltd
32, M-Block Market
Greater Kailash - I
New Delhi 110 048

British Library Cataloguing in Publication data
Moores, Shaun
  Interpreting Audiences: Ethnography of Media
  Consumption. – (Media, Culture & Society Series)
  I. Title II. Series
  302.2308

ISBN 0–8039–8446–4
ISBN 0–8039–8447–2 (pbk)

Library of Congress catalog card number 93–085117

Typeset by Megaron, Cardiff, South Wales
Printed in Great Britain by The Cromwell Press Ltd,
Broughton Gifford, Melksham, Wiltshire

46124

Contents

Acknowledgements

This is my first book. It's taken shape rather more slowly than I had originally anticipated – across two jobs, three countries and four different institutions. To those who taught me during that period in London (Brunel University) and Brighton (University of Sussex), to former colleagues and students in Cardiff (Polytechnic of Wales) – and to some newer ones in Edinburgh (Queen Margaret College) – I'm grateful for your advice and criticism. My series editor, Paddy Scannell, has been a constant source of encouragement ever since undergraduate days at the Polytechnic of Central London. I would also like to thank Stevi Jackson at Strathclyde University in Glasgow for her friendship and support throughout the writing of *Interpreting Audiences*.

1
Approaching Audiences

Since the late 1970s, what might broadly be described as an 'ethnographic turn' has taken place in studies of media consumption. New ways of investigating and interpreting audiences have emerged – attempts to chart the sense that media consumers make of the texts and technologies they encounter in everyday life. This book's main aim is to provide an overview of these recent developments in qualitative audience research. It is written principally for students who are looking for a starting point from which to engage with one of the fastest growing areas in contemporary media studies – and although my intention has not been to produce a 'how to do it' guide to audience ethnography, I hope that the book will encourage its readers to carry out research projects of their own. I should declare at the outset that my perspective on the material under review is, at least in general terms, supportive. I believe that a critical ethnographic practice best equips us to map out the media's varied uses and meanings for particular social subjects in particular cultural contexts. Such a method departs and differs from other approaches, in both academic and industry-led research, which have failed to deal adequately with the dynamics and diversity of media reception.

I begin the book with a brief introductory chapter that performs a number of preliminary tasks. It offers an initial assessment of the key contributions made by qualitative work on audience consumption over the past fifteen years – preparing the way for a more detailed examination in the chapters to follow. I also consider the characteristic features of ethnography as a method of cultural investigation, stressing its potential for giving voice to everyday interpretations 'from below' while recognizing its own status as an interpretative activity. In addition, there is some discussion of the opposing, alternative perspectives on media reception hinted at above – because to understand 'the ethnographic turn' in audience studies as a significant intervention, it has to be seen in relation to these other approaches. This is not simply a matter of highlighting different views of the same pre-given object from a range of theoretical and institutional positions. It may well be that competing discourses are actually addressing different things, constituting the category of 'the audience' in various forms. A good place to start is therefore with the most basic of questions concerning our object of study.

What is an Audience Anyway?

There is no stable entity which we can isolate and identify as the media audience, no single object that is unproblematically 'there' for us to observe and analyse. The plural, audiences, is preferable – denoting several groups divided by their reception of different media and genres, or by social and cultural positioning – yet even this term presents conceptual difficulties. Exploring the etymology of the word, Janice Radway (1988:359) has noted its original usage to refer to an individual act of hearing in face-to-face verbal communication (to 'give audience'). Only later was it employed as a collective label for the consumers of electronically mediated messages. These two sets of circumstances are, of course, far from being equivalent. In the former, the producer and receiver of sound are co-present in the speech situation. They share a common physical space. If a valid comparison might be made with the theatre audience – where a specifiable group of people are gathered together in one place to give their attention to a live performance – the parallel with watching television or listening to the radio is less clear. Here, consumption is geographically dispersed across a multitude of settings and frequently in competition with other practices as a consequence of its embedding in day-to-day social life. It becomes harder to specify exactly where media audiences begin and end. The conditions and boundaries of audiencehood are inherently unstable.

So given the lack of an easily identifiable thing to be researched, how is it that we have come to accept the category of 'the audience' as a self-evident fact? An important reason for the word's naturalization has undoubtedly been the vested interests of media institutions (as well as many academic researchers) in imagining the existence of such a fixed object to measure or monitor. John Hartley (1987:125) has made this point forcefully, claiming that 'in all cases the product is a fiction which serves the needs of the imagining institution. In no case is the audience "real", or external to its discursive construction.' Indeed, his position presents a radical deconstructionist challenge to the whole enterprise of audience research – including the work of reception ethnographers. When the very existence of an object of inquiry is thrown into question, all efforts to 'know' it are immediately undermined. My own position, however, is not so pessimistic about the possibilities for an empirical investigation of media consumption. I shall maintain that there is a reality outside of and beyond the discourses which constitute the audience as a category to be known. That reality, as I have already argued, is a dispersed and embedded set of everyday practices which always finally eludes attempts to fix and objectify it – something more than just an 'invisible fiction'.

On this epistemological point, it is worth turning to Ien Ang's recent book, *Desperately Seeking the Audience* (1991). She is sympathetic to Hartley's ideas about discourses constituting their objects, building on his insights with an incisive critique of the TV industry's research methodology – but she retains a crucial distinction 'between "television audience" as discursive construct and the social world of actual audiences' (Ang, 1991:13). That social world defies full categorization. Moreover, its elusive character is a constant thorn in the side of industry researchers even as they devise increasingly sophisticated technical means of surveillance. If – to borrow Dallas Smythe's famous argument – TV institutions are in the business of 'delivering audiences to advertisers' (see Smythe, 1981), then it is essential for them to define and quantify what they are delivering. Their requirement has been met with the development of 'audience measurement' techniques (the set meter, the diary, and now the 'people meter') which are used to compile ratings figures. The procedure is one of head counting and the purpose is to artificially convert the many situated instances of consumption – ultimately unknowable in their totality – into manageable, calculable units. As ways of comprehending the lived experience of actual audiences, these methods would be doomed to failure. Within the logic of the ratings discourse, though, an 'audience commodity' is created to be traded for financial gain. Its fictionality does not necessarily hinder its economic functionality.

The ethnographer, in contrast, conceptualizes media audiencehood as lived experience and approaches his or her object with very different sorts of interests. There would be no sense in denying that, as academic researchers, reception ethnographers also have some degree of personal investment in delimiting a category they can investigate (there are careers to be made and books to be written on 'the audience'!) – but an ethnographic method is nevertheless preferable to industry techniques precisely because it holds out the hope of representing consumption practices 'from the virtual standpoint of actual audiences' (Ang, 1991:165). It promises, at least, to subvert the institutional point of view by speaking that which is unspoken in the ratings discourse. This means attending to the media's multiple significances in varied contexts of reception as opposed to focussing on quantification through measurement. I am not suggesting that ethnographies can magically give us direct and unmediated access to the real – they are discourses too. What I am saying is that they have greater potential for engaging with the production of meaning in everyday life. In the next part of the chapter, I go on to talk further about the prospects and problems for qualitative field research on media consumption.

Ethnography as a Method of Cultural Investigation

Although the use of ethnography in media studies – as a method for investigating the social world of actual audiences – may still be relatively new, there is a long history of such work in the disciplines of anthropology and sociology. Whether researchers have sought to document the customs and beliefs of 'exotic others' overseas or to look at practices and settings closer to home, they have evolved a now established array of qualitative techniques – most notably the extended period of participant observation 'in the field' and the unstructured conversational interview with informants (for a fuller introduction to technical issues, see Burgess, 1984:78–122). Their objective has often been to understand a culture 'from the native's point of view', trying to get to grips with people's subjective apprehensions of the social environment. Ultimately, of course, this desire for complete knowledge of 'the other' is an unattainable fantasy. As commentators like James Clifford (1986) and

Paul Atkinson (1990) have pointed out – advancing a line of argument that echoes Hartley's in certain respects – ethnographic discourses are necessarily 'partial truths' and the cultures they purport to describe are always to some extent the product of the researcher's imagination. These critiques force us to reflect on the materiality of ethnographies as 'fictional' modes of writing and on the subjectivity of the observer as interpreter (Walkerdine, 1986, is one of the few to have touched on such matters in audience studies – see Chapter 3). However, this does not mean that we should disappear down a self-reflexive cul-de-sac, leaving behind the original path of cultural description. To elaborate an adequate account of media consumption, I propose we hang on to an interest in recording the experiences and interpretations of others – and a conviction that there is something outside of ethnographic discourse which is worth our while researching. It is quite permissible to recognize the partial nature of our knowledge without losing a determination to reconstruct the consumer's point of view.

Having said that, a comparison between recent qualitative studies of media reception and the tradition of anthropological and sociological research mentioned in the previous paragraph might lead us to wonder whether there is anything very ethnographic about 'the new audience ethnography' (see Nightingale, 1989). With few exceptions, the studies I will be discussing in the coming pages have relied mainly on audio-taped conversations with viewers, listeners and readers which may not last much more than an hour each. The inquiries can sometimes incorporate short periods in the company of media consumers, with academics attempting to share in the routine cultural experiences of those being investigated – but these are clearly not the same as the lengthy spells of participant observation carried out by pioneers in field research. There are good practical reasons why this has been the case, not least the difficulties of gaining prolonged access to contexts of consumption – usually the private sphere of the household. Nevertheless, sessions spent talking about television in the sitting rooms of eighteen south London homes (Morley, 1986) are evidently quite different from two years living amongst the Trobriand Islanders (Malinowski's *Argonauts of the Western Pacific*, 1922/ 1978, is widely recognized as a founding text of modern anthropological ethnography).

My own feeling is that despite these clear differences reception studies can still properly be called ethnographies. It is true they are not based on extensive fieldwork in distant lands, but they do share some of the same general intentions as anthropological research. There may be a similar concern, for instance, with questions of meaning and social context – and with charting the 'situational embeddedness' of cultural practices (see Marcus & Fischer, 1986; Silverstone, 1990). If the means of investigation are not always identical, then the aims of the inquiry can be. I ought to make it explicit, though, that I am advocating an ethnographic perspective of a certain kind – one which is committed to critically analysing culture as well as describing it. In attending to the meanings produced by social subjects and to the daily activities they perform, qualitative audience researchers have frequently sought to explain those significances and practices by locating them in relation to broader frameworks of interpretation and to structures of power and inequality. This is the mark of what I referred to in the opening paragraph of the book as a 'critical' ethnography (following Harvey, 1990). It is an approach which takes extremely seriously the interpretations of the media constructed by consumers in their everyday routines. At the same time, it is not afraid to interrogate and situate their spoken accounts.

To begin to illustrate my arguments and give substance to my support for an ethnographic approach, I now want to pick out what I see as the four main concerns and contributions of qualitative audience studies over the last decade and a half. Firstly, there has been an intervention into debates about the power of media texts to determine the meanings made by their readers. Secondly, reception ethnographers have attempted to account for the articulation of media genres to diverse 'taste publics'. Thirdly, and relatedly, they have shown an interest in the day-to-day settings and dynamic social situations of consumption – focussing in particular on the domestic context and on familial relations. Finally, there is a growing body of work on the cultural uses of a range of communication technologies in the home. This research looks not just at TV and radio, but also at other elements in the domestic media 'ensemble' (video, computers, satellite, etc.). It is concerned as much with the significance of the technological 'hardware' for consumers as with the meanings of the sounds and images conveyed.

5-7

Textual Power and the Determination of Readings

Questions about the extent to which media messages influence the thoughts and actions of their receivers have always been at the centre of communications research. Ever since the emergence of industries for the large-scale production and distribution of cultural goods, academics have asked about the effects of those products on consumers. The earliest efforts to provide an answer led to an understanding of the audience as a 'mass' that was passively subject to ideological manipulation or to moral decay (depending on which side of the political spectrum the critique of mass culture came from). Then later, especially in American behavioural science, the emphasis was placed on empirically verifying the media's influence on individual audience members. The problem here was the way in which investigations were framed. *To find out* To inquire about the power of a given message – say an election broadcast or an advertising campaign – is certainly worth while, but as Stuart Hall (1982:61) has pointed out, 'effects studies' confined themselves to immediately observable changes in human behaviour and left the formal structure of media output wholly untheorized. They were also unable to deal with the wider effectivity of economic and cultural processes.

With the formation of an alternative, 'critical', paradigm in media studies from the end of the 1960s – the intellectual impetus for which came principally from European social theory – there was a radically different framework within which media/audience relations could be approached. There was a new vocabulary of concepts too. Cultural theorists drew on semiotics and began to talk about the message as a 'text', as a complex and structured arrangement of signs rather than an empty vehicle for the transmission of information or opinion. In this jargon, receivers became 'readers'. They were seen to be involved in – and for a number of analysts, constituted by – a construction of meaning. The stress here was on signification not direct behavioural change. That switch in emphasis, though, did not result in a move away from the fundamental issues of power and influence. In fact, some of the first models of text–reader relations developed in the 1970s might be compared with Marxist inflections of the old 'mass society' thesis (for example, with Adorno & Horkheimer, 1944/1977) – because they continued to regard audiences as almost entirely subjected to the ideological work performed by media institutions. Probably the most striking example of 'textual determinism' at that time was the perspective on films and film spectatorship advanced in the pages of a British journal, *Screen*. Contributors brought together semiotics with Althusserian Marxism and a distinctive brand of French psycho-analytical theory associated with Jacques Lacan (see Chapter 2). The mixture was a heady theoretical cocktail in which readers were reduced to a set of textually inscribed 'subject positions'.

A more fruitful model of texts and readers was being put forward, partly as a critique of 'screen theory', by members of the Media Group at Birmingham University's Centre for Contemporary Cultural Studies. In their analyses of television and its audiences, they recognized the power of the text to propose and prefer particular ideological readings – but also, and crucially, they invited us to understand readers as active 'decoders' who will not necessarily accept the encoded meanings and positions which are on offer. Depending on the socioeconomic and cultural placings that media consumers already occupy, the text's preferred interpretation may in certain instances be negotiated or even refused altogether. The CCCS's encoding/decoding theory, then, opened up a gap between readings inscribed in the text and the actual social subjects who interact with it. What finally determines meaning is a 'dialogic' encounter between the two – and it is this continual conversation between texts and readers that qualitative audience research initially set out to explore. In the following chapter, I will be reviewing David Morley's landmark study, *The 'Nationwide' Audience* (1980a). His project was designed to sketch a provisional map of different 'interpretative communities' by carrying out interviews with TV viewing groups drawn from various educational and occupational backgrounds. The commitment to empirical inquiry marked out Morley's approach from almost all critical academic work in that period on media reception – as well as from literary theories which were beginning to reinstate the reader in studies of narrative fiction (see Freund, 1987).

Outside of the critical paradigm, however, a 'uses and gratifications' perspective had emerged in mainstream communications research (I should say 're-emerged', since its origins can be traced back to the 1940s). It reversed the question posed by effects studies – asking 'what people do with the media' instead of 'what the media do to people' – and because of its interest in the active consumer there might appear at first sight to be overlaps with the Birmingham Media Group's model of decoding. Both approaches do indeed reject any view of audiences as passive and highlight what they see as the productivity of consumption, although the differences between them outweigh this apparent similarity. Whereas Morley, Hall and others at the CCCS were working towards a sociologically grounded semiotics of the text–reader dialogue, gratifications researchers concerned themselves with how individuals use the media as resources 'to satisfy their needs and achieve their goals' (Katz *et al.*, 1974:21). One is a social theory of subjectivity, power and meaning construction – while the other is a psychological conception of human personality which focusses narrowly on the media's functions for the individual. There is also a tendency on the part of gratificationists to overplay 'audience freedom' and ignore issues of ideology completely. Recent talk about 'reaching out' for a possible convergence of mainstream and critical schools in audience studies (Blumler *et al.*, 1985) must therefore be treated with caution.

Patterns of Preference and Contexts of Consumption

The Birmingham Centre's encoding/decoding theory and its *Nationwide* research project made a vital breakthrough in debates about the media and their audiences – taking into account the relative power of text and reader in cultural struggles over meaning. At the same time, there were some significant absences in that work which had to be addressed. Two of these in particular provided a springboard for reception ethnographies in the 1980s. It was necessary to supplement readers' responses to the ideological problematics of a specific television text by raising a more fundamental issue about the relevance, or salience, that media genres have for different reading publics. Put simply, there was limited value in inquiring how viewing groups selected by the researcher decoded a TV programme without first establishing whether those people would usually be watching at all. A sense of the social patterning of tastes and preferences was required. The other important shortcoming of Morley's study had been its failure to deal with the social settings in which consumption normally takes place – the immediate physical and interpersonal contexts of daily media reception. In the case of TV, entry into the domestic realm of family viewing was needed if we were to see how context shapes interpretation and choice.

As will become evident in Chapter 3, the most interesting qualitative studies on the theme of genre and taste have been carried out by feminist cultural critics. Several of these projects have attempted to 'rescue' the denigrated media forms that are traditionally associated with feminine audiences – so-called 'women's genres' such as soap opera and romantic fiction. By treating sympathetically the pleasures available in the text and the competences demanded of the reader, their work has shown the highly skilled and discriminating nature of fans' interpretations and preferences. There are no 'zombies' or mindless 'addicts' here – only consumers whose gendered abilities and enjoyments have been devalued by those with more legitimate 'cultural capital' (Bourdieu, 1984). Ethnographies which seek to positively re-evaluate the position of such subordinated reading publics can sometimes run the risk of celebrating popular experiences uncritically. The dangers of 'going native', of stumbling into the pitfalls of populism, are great. Equally great, though, is the importance of mapping diversity and distinction in media consumption. It enables us to open up a politics of cultural taste and value, shaking the foundations of established aesthetic judgements and giving voice to previously mocked or silenced social pleasures.

Issues of gender and power have also informed recent research on the household contexts of viewing, listening and reading. In fact, work of the sort mentioned above – on the significance of TV serials or literary romances for female audiences – inevitably began to ask how the reception of those fictions is implicated in the dynamics of family life. Probably the best example of this would be Radway's excellent book, *Reading the Romance* (1987). She explains that, in the course of doing the fieldwork for her book, the study gradually became 'less an account of the way romances as texts were interpreted than of the way romance reading as a form of behaviour operated as a complex intervention in the ongoing social life of actual social subjects – women who saw themselves first as wives and mothers' (Radway, 1987:7). Her interest, then, was in consumption as a 'social event' located in a familial setting. She came to see the act of reading in these women's lives as an important, if limited, bid for independence. It marked a temporary escape from the physical and emotional demands of domestic labour (see Chapter 3 for further discussion). Of course, by no means all households are organized around the model of domestic femininity lived out by the consumers in Radway's research. The structures and relations of the home are culturally varied. Her general analytical principle holds good, however. In exploring practices of media reception, we must pay attention to the environmental conditions in which meaning and pleasure are constructed.

That same principle passes through a number of ethnographic projects from around the world which have set out to examine TV viewing as a situated social event. The writings of James Lull in the United States, of Hermann Bausinger and his colleagues from the Institute for Empirical Cultural Studies at Tübingen in Germany – as well as Morley's own follow-up to the *Nationwide* research, *Family Television* (1986) – all share Radway's concern with interpreting embedded acts of consumption. With differing degrees of emphasis, each looks at what we might call 'the politics of the living room' (Cubitt, 1984). For instance, if the tastes of household members vary, whose preferences take precedence where there is a clash of viewing choices? What happens when the football is scheduled at the same time as the long-running serial, or the news is being shown on the other side from the pop music show? How are these potential confrontations, across divisions of gender and generation, resolved within the power relations of the home? Taking such questions seriously means treating TV use as a barometer for gauging the household's cultural climate – just as some researchers have studied family food consumption for similar reasons. What emerges from the growing body of literature in this area is a report of conflict in the sitting room, with disputes over what, how and when to watch.

Communication Technologies in the Home

A valuable extension of inquiries into audience engagements with the media's texts and genres can be found in current attempts to approach communication technologies themselves as texts to be read (see Haddon, 1991, for a general statement of the cultural studies perspective on technology as text). A new wave of research is now addressing their significance as objects of domestic consumption. Like the sounds and images which constitute the 'software' of mass communication, its 'hardware' might equally be seen as a collection of signs that have multi-accentual social meanings – capable of being decoded and appropriated in a plurality of ways within the context of household cultures. The remote control device for changing channels, the time-setting switch on the video recorder, and the satellite dish attached to the outside wall of the house are all examples of contested cultural symbols. In everyday family interactions, the possession, utilization or interpretation of these things appears to be constantly fought over. It is in this particular field of research that my own qualitative work is situated (for instance, Moores, 1985, 1988, 1991, in press a). Employing oral history techniques in addition to ethnographic methods, I have been concerned with charting the initial entry and incorporation of new media technologies into the private sphere. Later, in Chapter 4, those projects will be discussed in some detail and considered in relation to recent studies like the one carried out by Roger Silverstone and others at Brunel University. Their intention – in the first phase of a larger investigation into 'The Household Uses of Information and Communication Technologies' – was to account for the interconnected meanings of several domestic media objects (see Silverstone *et al.*, 1989).

We should remember, of course, that in analysing the household consumption of communication technologies we are not simply dealing with the micro-politics of family life. What distinguishes media objects from many other domestic artefacts is their capacity to join the private world of the home with larger public worlds beyond the front door. Raymond Williams (1974) expresses it well when he says that broadcasting has helped to constitute a form of 'mobile privatization'. During the early twentieth century, the tendency towards a home-centred way of living was accompanied by technological developments – in motor transport as well as electronic communications – which put the household in touch with places that were distant in time and space. Radio, and then television, offered senses of 'knowable community' in an increasingly atomized society. The shape of these symbolic communities has often corresponded to the boundaries of the nation state. In the case of British broadcasting, social historians like Paddy Scannell and David Cardiff (1991) have tried to show how media technologies played an important role in actually 'putting the nation together' (although they primarily support their argument with an investigation of BBC policy and programming rather than audiences – and it may be that Scannell and Cardiff have overestimated the true extent of 'national unity'). Moving towards the end of the twentieth century, as new advances are being made in cable and satellite technology, I would suggest that the media's 'territories of transmission' are now becoming more markedly transnational in character. Indeed, one of the major challenges facing reception ethnographers in the 1990s is to trace the potentially shifting points of identification for consumers where 'the local' meets and intersects with 'the global' (Ang, 1990a; Morley, 1991). The box in the corner of the living room can be a site of convergence between routine day-to-day existence and much broader cultural transformations.

Leading on directly from that discussion of the media as domestic technologies, I conclude the book with a chapter which consciously seeks to blur the edges of audience studies by reviewing a range of theoretical and empirical perspectives on cultural consumption and the practices of everyday life. The embedded nature of media reception means that, in the end, we have to widen the scope of our inquiries to take in the whole gamut of texts, objects and daily activities – asking about the ongoing and intricate processes through which social subjects articulate their lived cultures. Alongside viewing, listening and reading, we might place eating, shopping or ways of dressing. Across all of these categories, the aim must be to look for patterns of identification and differentiation (for identities and differences in the construction of lifestyle). Pierre Bourdieu's ambitious survey of class tastes in 1960s France – aptly entitled *Distinction* (1984) – is in my opinion the best starting point we have. Although there are gaps in both his theory and method, Bourdieu comes closer than any other contemporary researcher to developing a comprehensive sociology of consumption. In Chapter 5 I also consider the currently fashionable work of Michel De Certeau (1984). He has chosen to stress the creative tactical resistances of the subordinate in 'making do' with the commodities of a capitalist system, providing a useful and interesting contrast to Bourdieu's political pessimism, but I will argue that appropriations of De Certeau in cultural studies have tended to exaggerate and even romanticize the oppositional potential of the popular (notably Fiske, 1989a, 1989b). By presenting an exposition and critique of these various positions – examining commercial market research and writings on youth subculture too – I work towards a framework for understanding consumer practices.

2

Ideology, Subjectivity and Decoding

What Stuart Hall (1982) has called 'the rediscovery of ideology' was central to the formation of a critical paradigm in modern media studies. It signalled a return to some of the fundamental questions about material and mental production which had long occupied Marxist cultural critics, but which had been missing from mass communications research since the 1940s. The analysis of ideology, as John Thompson (1988:370) succinctly puts it, is concerned with 'the ways in which meaning and power intersect . . . ways in which meaning may serve, in specific social-historical contexts, to sustain relations of domination'. If the writings of Marx and Engels – and most importantly the thesis that in every epoch it is the ideas of the ruling class which are the ruling ideas – provided a crucial point of departure for critical media inquiry, their work nevertheless lacked a fully elaborated model of signification. There was no explanation in the Marxist classics of exactly how social meanings which may serve the interests of the dominant are made. However, a perspective known as semiotics had emerged out of Saussure's linguistics and was extensively redeveloped by the French cultural commentator, Roland Barthes, for precisely that purpose (see his *Mythologies*, 1973). In the 1970s, especially for British intellectuals interested in issues of ideology and mass communication, there was the hope of combining these two traditions of thought and building a materialist account of meaning construction.

Another perceived absence in the original works of Marx and Engels – one which had to some extent been identified and rectified by twentieth-century 'Western Marxists' like Antonio Gramsci and Louis Althusser – was an adequate theory of subjectivity. Beyond stating that consciousness is determined by social being, the classics once again had little to say. To account for the mechanisms by which consciousness (not to mention the unconscious) is socially shaped, several academics in British media and cultural studies began looking to psychoanalysis as a way forward. As we shall see shortly, it was in investigations of the cinema that this tendency became most marked. Aspects of Freud's own writings, such as the notes on voyeurism and scopophilia, were taken up in film criticism (see, for instance, Mulvey, 1975) – but a more influential figure was Jacques Lacan. His psychoanalytical theories, which claimed to 're-view' Freud through the lens of structural linguistics, promised to show how subjectivities are constituted in discourse. By extension, it was believed a Lacanian perspective could be used to unpick the process through which spectators are 'positioned' as viewing subjects in film. While there can be no doubt that subjectivity is a key concept for any

ideological analysis, I will explain how Lacan's writings and their application
to media consumption have proved highly problematic. Above all, they led to
a form of textual determinism which left no room for negotiation or resistance
on the part of audiences. What we require instead is a dynamic and
'interdiscursive' model of relations between media texts and the situated social
readers who decode them.

'Screen Theory' and the CCCS Critique

The film journal, *Screen*, was one of the first ports of call for French
poststructuralist theory – and particularly for Lacanian psychoanalysis – on
its arrival in Britain during the 1970s. Amongst the journal's regular
contributors and on its board of editors at that time were enthusiastic
advocates of Lacan's work such as Colin MacCabe and Stephen Heath. They
were interested in studying the formal structures of cinematic representation,
asking how those representations construct certain ways of looking and
knowing for spectators. MacCabe, Heath and others were also arriving at
some rather grand conclusions about the role of film in the reproduction of
capitalist social relations. Not content with the close analysis of texts, their
readings were accompanied by broader assertions about the cinema's
ideological functions. In order to follow these arguments, it is first necessary to
understand something of the theoretical standpoints which underpin them. I
shall therefore attempt to outline Lacan's account of human subjectivity – but
I begin with a few basic principles of Althusserian Marxism, because they
helped to define the more general political parameters of *Screen*'s project.

Althusser's essay, 'Ideology and Ideological State Apparatuses' – written in
the late 1960s and appearing in English translation by 1971 – had a profound
impact on sections of the British academic Left (see Althusser, 1984). At the
start of this essay, he proposes that there are a number of key institutions in
civil society (for example the school, the family and the mass media) whose
purpose is to sustain and reproduce the presently unequal relations of
industrial production. For the most part they perform their task by ideological
rather than directly coercive means, by engineering consent to the existing
social arrangements. According to Althusser (1984:24), these institutions or
'ISAs' have to be seen as part of the state machinery because, he says, they
work in a 'teeth gritting harmony' with the repressive apparatus of state
power. While there are problems with such a functionalist explanation, it is
not too hard to appreciate the attraction that his work must have had for film
theorists. With communications and cultural organizations being listed
amongst the major ISAs, media studies seemed to be offered a place in the
vanguard of revolutionary struggle, and the editors of *Screen* accepted the
challenge. There were further inviting formulations in the second part of
Althusser's piece – centrally, his suggestion that ideology is a 'representation'
which hails or 'interpellates' individuals as subjects. This clearly prompted
questions about the ideological operations of cinema as a system of
signification and its mechanisms for interpellating the spectator-subject.

The Althusserian notion of hailing was, in fact, the result of his own engagement with psychoanalytical theory (see 'Freud and Lacan' in Althusser's *Essays on Ideology*, 1984). Lacan's ideas appealed to those who were trying to develop an anti-humanist Marxism because he dismissed any conception of the subject as a fixed and unified human essence that stands unproblematically at the centre of thought and action. Instead, Lacanian psychoanalysis is concerned to emphasize the 'de-centred' nature of subjectivity – its necessarily provisional and precarious status, and its production within an external system of signs. We are not, so the argument goes, able to act freely upon the world or to express ourselves freely through speech. Rather, it is the other way around. The social world acts upon us and we are only constituted as subjects in the very instance of speaking, as we enter into the 'symbolic order' of language. And for Lacan, this cultural construction of subjectivity actually entails a crucial 'misrecognition'. When speaking, we get caught up in a fiction or illusion that we really do have fixed and unified selves – whereas, Lacan suggests, our subjectivities are constantly in process and always divided. The fiction is recreated every time we occupy a 'subject position' in discourse, as the personal pronoun 'I' is uttered or another person is addressed as 'you' (Benveniste, 1971). We imagine that we are the source of meaning and identity – when in reality we are subject-ed to the differences of language (see Lacan, 1977; and for the best of several recent commentaries, Sarup, 1992).

'Screen theory' was an application of these Lacanian insights to an analysis of film as discourse. The aim was to uncover the symbolic mechanisms through which cinematic texts confer subjectivity upon readers, sewing them into the film narrative through the production of subject positions. Exponents of this theory saw the realist mode of representation employed in classic Hollywood cinema as the main target of their criticism. In 'Realism and the Cinema' – one of the most influential essays published in *Screen* during that period – MacCabe (1974) proposed that 'the classic realist text' works by constructing an illusion of transparency in which, supposedly, spectators imagine themselves to be gazing directly on to a 'real' scene when the reality of the situation is that they are watching a movie. Hollywood film, so it was claimed, denies its own material existence as text – and in so doing, constitutes a fiction of centred vision and unified subjectivity for the reader. Like speakers who misrecognize the relationship they have to language, spectators come to feel as though they are the source of 'the look'. Their gaze, however, is subjected to and controlled by the vision of the camera. In these circumstances, argues Heath (1977/8:58), the reading subject is left no option but to 'make . . . the meanings the film makes for it'.

Realist representation, at least in the opinion of these film theorists, was an irredeemably bourgeois cinematic 'language'. For them it performed an important ideological function, contributing to the reproduction of the existing social order. It did so by constituting the subject in an imaginary unity and by constructing 'the real' as obvious and beyond question (there are further connections here with Althusser, 1984:49, who contends that ideology is the imposition of 'obviousness' and states, somewhat playfully, that 'one of the effects of ideology is the practical denegation of the ideological character of ideology by ideology'). Against such a narrative strategy, MacCabe and Heath were seeking to promote what they saw as a revolutionary film-making practice. Their antidote to bourgeois realism was to be found in an avant-garde tradition of cultural production that goes back to the work of Bertolt Brecht, Sergei Eisenstein and others in the 1920s and 1930s (for a broad historical review, consult Willett, 1978). This tradition operated around not an illusion of transparency but a 'foregrounding of the machinery' of representation. Jean-Luc Godard's films are in this vein, and provide a good example of texts that continually highlight their own material existence as image and sound. In screen theory, the practice was judged to be radical because it promised to disrupt the imaginary relations between spectators and representations – repositioning the reading subject as divided and in process.

A contrast, then, between classic Hollywood cinema and so-called 'Brechtian cinema' was at the heart of screen theory. In a retrospective piece written several years after he left the editorial board of *Screen*, MacCabe (1985:9) summed up the contrast clearly:

> insofar as a film fixed the subject in a position of imaginary dominance through the security of vision . . . it fell immediately within bourgeois ideology, insofar as it broke that security it offered fresh possibilities. . . . The disruption of the imaginary security of the ego by a problematising of vision was linked to Brecht's emphasis on the breaking of the identificatory processes in the theatre as the precondition for the production of political knowledge.

Looking back, it seems hard to believe now that these issues around realism and the avant-garde were so central to debates about media representation in the 1970s. In its heyday, though, screen theory did come close to being the new orthodoxy in critical media studies. At a time when Left intellectuals were quite correctly listening out for novel thoughts on ideology and mass communication, *Screen* seemed to be making the appropriate noises. However, for all the good political intentions and the apparent theoretical sophistication (I have done my best to summarize the arguments succinctly), there are a number of major problems with the propositions that were advanced. Some of the shortcomings are immediately evident, like the strangely inflated importance attached to the medium of film during an era in which the cinema as an institution is in general decline. Others require closer inspection – and I want to set out a series of objections here, drawing in particular on the critique that was offered by members of the Media Group at Birmingham University's Centre for Contemporary Cultural Studies. They were by no means the only academics in dispute with screen theory (see, for example, Garnham, 1979; Robins, 1979) but it was the CCCS critique that proved especially relevant for the formation of qualitative audience studies in the 1980s.

The first main limitation arises out of that distinction made by MacCabe between the classic realist text and 'the revolutionary text' – between a reactionary realism and a radical avant-garde. This categorization led inevitably to a wholesale dismissal of commercial cinema. Indeed, within MacCabe's terms, almost all popular media texts were consigned to the ideological dustbin without a proper consideration of 'the popular' as a field of possible contradiction or contestation. Even realist drama with progressive political content was criticized for its inability to disrupt the reader's identification (note the contributions of MacCabe – and McArthur also – to a discussion about the BBC television series, *Days of Hope*, in Bennett *et al.*, 1981a). In a parallel move, texts that broke with the narrative conventions of classic realism were automatically held up as models for revolutionary cultural production. As Hall (1980:162), then the CCCS's director, pointed out : 'a rather simple . . . identity has been forged between the practices of struggle in ideology and the practices of the avant-garde'. There are obvious difficulties, too, in trying to build a political cinema around techniques of modernist art which the working class has consistently treated with contempt. In Britain, at any rate, there is little evidence of popular demand for Brechtian drama (although see McGrath, 1981)!

A belief that avant-garde strategies are the only proper means of ideological intervention in the cinema was perhaps a logical consequence of adopting Lacanian perspectives on language and subjectivity which have severe limitations of their own. Psychoanalysis certainly explains something of the procedures by which individuals are constituted as speaking subjects 'in general', but it does not attend to the cultural specificity of discourses – nor does it address the relationship of those discourses to wider social structures. Lacan's conception of the 'symbolic order' remains extremely abstract and ahistorical. Screen theory claimed to have resolved this by bringing together psychoanalysis and historical materialism. The ambitious fusion, though, was never satisfactorily completed. Hall (1980:159) put the point well when he concluded that *Screen*'s notion of the text's effectivity does not depend :

> on the ideological problematics within which the discourse is operating, nor on the social, political or historical practices with which it is articulated. Its 'productivity' is defined exclusively in terms of the capacity of the text to set the viewer 'in place' in a position of unproblematic identification. . . . It follows that all ideological struggle must take place . . . at the level of 'the subject' and is confined to disrupting the forms of discourse which recapitulate those primary positions.

In screen theory, debates about ideology were conducted wholly around questions of form over and above those of content or context. Ideology was held to be 'in' the placing of the subject (the instance of 'suture' – see Heath, 1977/8). Meanwhile, the substance and social location of the film text remained outside the terms of analysis.

One further problem – and the most significant for research discussed later in this book – is the textual determinism of screen theory. It appeared there as though the subject is always-already successfully interpellated, or positioned, by the text. David Morley (1980b:166–7) – still a research student at Birmingham in the late 1970s – argued that in the work of MacCabe, Heath and others, the text is 'not so much "read" as simply "consumed/appropriated" straight, via the only possible positions available to the reader – those inscribed by the text'.

The Birmingham group strongly contested *Screen*'s model of text–audience relations, putting an emphasis on readers as active producers of meaning and on media consumption as a site of potentially differential interpretations. For Hall and Morley, the meanings made in the encounter of text and audience could in no way be directly 'read off' from the characteristics of the text. Instead, a crucial space needed to be opened up between the subject positions 'on offer' and the actual social subjects who interpret or decode media forms.

Charlotte Brunsdon (1981), also involved in research at the Centre, explained that:

> We can usefully analyse the 'you' or 'yous' that the text as discourse constructs, but we cannot assume that any individual audience member will necessarily occupy these positions. The relation of the audience to the text will not be determined solely by that text, but also by positionalities in relation to a whole range of other discourses . . . elaborated elsewhere, already in circulation and brought to the (text) by the viewer.

While recognizing the text's construction of subject positions, the Birmingham group pointed to readers as the possessors of cultural knowledges and competences that have been acquired in previous social experiences and which are drawn on in the act of interpretation – the 'repertoire of discourses' at the disposal of different audiences (implicit here, I sense, is a retreat from Lacan's complete de-centring of subjectivity and a welcome return to some measure of human agency). Reading was not to be theorized as an isolated relationship between one text and its inscribed reader. There could be no reduction in which the reader is seen only as the occupant of a single textual positioning. In the interaction between text and subject, 'other discourses are always in play besides those of the particular text in focus – discourses . . . brought into play through "the subject's" placing in other practices – cultural, educational, institutional' (Morley, 1980b:163). Reading, in this formulation, is decidedly 'interdiscursive'.

The Encoding/Decoding Model

Before going on to look in detail at empirical research carried out at Birmingham on the interdiscursive character of interpretation, it is important to set out the alternative model of text–reader relations that informed the CCCS Media Group's critique of screen theory. The catalyst for much of the Birmingham group's work in the 1970s – which concentrated far more on TV representations and their reception than on film spectatorship – was an early paper by Hall, 'Encoding and Decoding in the Television Discourse' (1973). Hall's essay attempted to account for the active consumption as well as the production and textual organization of media sounds and images. His encoding/decoding model also sought to successfully combine semiotic and sociological concerns – connecting up approaches to the study of meaning construction with perspectives on cultural power and social relations. For Hall, the communicative process had to be taken as a whole – with the moment of programme making at one end and the moment of audience perception at the other. Operating within the routines and conventions of professional practice, producers encode a 'meaningful' message to be read by viewers. This message is a structured text which is itself a determinate moment in televisual communication. Hall recognized that media 'language' is not a straightforward 'tool' for transmitting ideas, or a transparent 'window' on the social world, but a necessarily refractive sign system. In TV news and current affairs, for example, events and issues have to be 'made to mean'. They are therefore subject to the symbolic work of encoding, constantly being shaped into established textual forms. This is only part of the process, though, because audience members are engaged in semiotic labour too. They bring their interpretative frameworks to bear on the message and, to use his words : 'the codes of encoding and decoding may not be perfectly symmetrical' (Hall, 1973:4).

There are two principal reasons for this potential asymmetry. Firstly, it is in the nature of signification that all texts are – to some extent and with varying degrees – polysemic. That is, they are always open to more than one possible reading. Visual signs in particular can have several associations at the level of what Barthes (1973, 1977) has called 'second order' or 'connotative' meaning. However, Hall (1973:13) – like Barthes – was quick to qualify this semiotic fact of textual openness by stressing a sociological point about the ideological forces which serve to constrain and close down the range of available readings:

> 'Polysemy' must not . . . be confused with pluralism. Connotative codes are not equal among themselves. Any society tends . . . to impose its segmentations, its classifications of the cultural and political world, upon its members. There remains a dominant cultural order. . . . This question of the 'structure of dominance' in a culture is an absolutely crucial point . . . there exists a pattern of 'preferred readings'.

Hall believed that the 'professional code' of TV news production – though it does on occasion depart from dominant definitions of social reality – works in the main to prefer 'hegemonic' meanings. This may not be the conscious stated intention of broadcasters (they will usually claim to present a 'balanced' view) but it is, according to Hall, the general ideological inflection of most news texts.

The theory of communication which fits closest with Hall's conception of TV discourse – and one he has drawn on explicitly at other times (see, for instance, Hall, 1982) – is the social semiotics of Valentin Volosinov. In a book first published in 1929 in the Soviet Union, *Marxism and the Philosophy of Language* (1973), Volosinov put forward his influential arguments concerning the 'multi-accentuality' of the sign. He stated that there are no fixed meanings in language because the sign is continually the site of a class struggle, an arena for the clash of differently oriented 'social accents'. In a move against the version of structural linguistics ('abstract objectivism') which was coming into vogue in Volosinov's day – and still is in some circles – his theory located the sign in living social interaction : 'In order to observe the process of combustion, a substance must be placed into the air. In order to observe the phenomenon of language, both the producer and receiver of sound and the sound itself must be placed into the social atmosphere' (Volosinov, 1973:46). So, in the context of class relations, signs such as, say, 'the nation' or 'the people' are not wholly closed around a single hegemonic connotation. They constitute a sphere in which meaning is dialogically contested. Yet, as Hall would say, these competing accentuations will be 'structured in dominance'. Indeed, Volosinov (1973:23) noted that the leading social class will always endeavour to reproduce the conditions of its dominance by proposing certain meanings as taken-for-granted and obvious – by trying 'to impart a supraclass, eternal character to the ideological sign . . . to make the sign uni-accentual'.

A second reason for the possible non-correspondence of encoded and decoded meanings in the process of televisual communication – following on directly from Volosinov's argument about the varied social 'accents' given to the sign by its users – is the interrogative and expansive nature of reading practices. To reiterate a key tenet in the critique of screen theory, the social subjects who decode a media message are not the same as the text's implied or preferred readers, and those subjects can therefore interact creatively with the text as they make productive use of the symbolic resources they bring with them. In an essay published in the CCCS's journal, *Working Papers in Cultural Studies*, Umberto Eco (1972:115) had talked about interpretations of the TV message being dependent upon the reader's 'general framework of cultural references . . . his ideological, ethical, religious standpoints . . . his tastes, his value systems, etc.'. Eco's formulation has to be understood as quite distinct from a psychological theory of selective perception, where each individual is seen to be making his or her own private readings. While there will, of course, be individual differences in interpretation, Hall (1973:15) was insistent that perception is rarely as personal or privatized as one might think. Audience research should be in the business of locating 'significant clusters' of meaning. It should be charting the lines that join these clusters with the social and discursive positionings of readers – inking in the boundaries of various interpretative communities.

Concluding a paper which took up this task of distinguishing different audience 'subcultures', Morley (1974:12) suggested that :

> what is needed is the development of a 'cultural map' of the audience so that we can begin to see which classes, sections of classes and subgroups share which cultural codes and meaning systems . . . so that we can then see how these codes determine the decoding of the messages of the media [and] what degree of 'distance' different sections of the audience have from the dominant meanings encoded in the message.

Hall had already tentatively identified three 'hypothetical' positions from which decodings of television texts may be constructed. In doing so, he was making use of – and elaborating on – the notion of 'meaning systems' that the sociologist, Frank Parkin (1972), employed in his study of social class and political order. In the first of these positions, the viewer interprets within the 'dominant code' and reads the preferred meaning which has been encoded 'full and straight'. The second is one in which readers adopt a 'negotiated code' that 'acknowledges the legitimacy of the hegemonic definitions . . . while, at a more restricted, situational level . . . operates with exceptions to the rule' (Hall, 1973:17). The illustration of a negotiated reading offered by Hall is that of the worker who is adaptive to messages about the national requirements for wage restraint in a period of economic recession, but who is opposed at the same time to any lowering of his or her pay and living conditions. General acceptance of the dominant definitions and a rejection of their local implications co-exist despite the apparent contradiction. In addition, he referred to a third, 'oppositional', position where the message is decoded 'in a globally contrary way'. This corresponds to Parkin's 'radical' meaning system, and will usually incorporate a political form of class consciousness. Hall's hypothesis about the differential interpretation of TV messages plainly called for an empirical investigation into text–reader relations, and the following section is a discussion of the Birmingham Centre's *Nationwide* project – research which applied these theories to the specific analysis of a TV programme and responses given by viewers. I ought to stress before moving on that the encoding/decoding model is not without its problems (see the final part of this chapter), but its considerable value was in providing a dynamic conception of media communication when many other academics and critics were still pursuing a stale formalism.

Nationwide: Text–Reader Relations

The BBC's *Nationwide*, which occupied a slot from six to seven o'clock in the British early evening schedule during the 1970s, became the focus for a research project at the CCCS on the encoding and decoding of TV discourse. The programme was initially selected for close attention by members of the Media Group in 1975–6 – and that work was developed and written up as a monograph by Brunsdon and Morley (1978). Their study concerned itself with the programme's distinctive ideological themes and with the particular ways in which *Nationwide* addressed its viewers. In the second stage of the project, Morley (1980a) went on to supplement this textual analysis with a qualitative survey of readers' interpretations. Conducting interviews with viewing groups from different levels of the education system and from various occupational backgrounds, he sought to draw precisely the kind of 'cultural map' of the audience that could flesh out Hall's preliminary notes on decoding.

Sandwiched between the main national news from London and the peak-viewing family entertainment period, *Nationwide* adopted a magazine format with human interest stories from the regions and a 'down to earth' look at the major events of the day. Unlike another of the BBC's current affairs programmes, *Panorama*, which sets out to deal with the complexity of a public issue, *Nationwide* had a more direct commonsense tone – asking about the implications of complex issues for 'ordinary' viewers. This style was personified by its regular presenter, Michael Barratt, a 'no nonsense man of the people' (Brunsdon & Morley, 1978:8). By means of what the Birmingham group termed a 'populist ventriloquism', the programme attempted to speak for its viewers in a language they were assumed to share. In fact, for the most part, items featured the routine activities of people going about their daily business – rather than the grand affairs of public life : ' "Nationwide" doesn't cover areas remote from everyday life (like a "Panorama" special on Vietnam) but visits the places many of us have visited, takes us into the living rooms of ordinary families, shows us . . . couples coping with inflation and their new baby' (Brunsdon & Morley, 1978:11). An important ingredient in this ordinariness was the regional flavour of the stories. If the text presented its readers with a mirror in which to recognize themselves, then the image was one of a nation constructed from its many parts – unity in difference. As Brunsdon and Morley (1978:92) summed up :

> 'Nationwide' constructs a picture of 'the British people' in their diversity. We are constituted together as members of the regional communities which make up the nation and as members of families . . . our shared concern with domestic life is grounded in 'Nationwide's' common sense discourse.

In the follow-up study – published as *The 'Nationwide' Audience* (1980a) – Morley explored the degree to which actual social subjects accepted or rejected the programme's preferred reading of events and issues, and the extent to which they were 'hailed' by identifications on offer (although surprisingly little effort was made to pursue the region/nation theme). Video recordings were shown to a total of twenty-nine groups containing either managers, students, apprentices or trade unionists – who were then invited to comment on the material they had watched. Each of these viewing groups was already established because of the participation of their members in some form of education or training, and the decision to carry out group interviews was taken deliberately so as to chart collectively reached interpretations of a TV message (but see Lewis, 1983; Jordin & Brunt, 1988, for critical discussion of the group interview method). Some saw an extract that had been scrutinized by Brunsdon and Morley (1978) in the earlier monograph – others viewed a special on the chancellor's annual budget which assessed the economic consequences for three 'typical families'. Through an analysis of the talk that followed, Morley began to trace the groups' patterned responses both to the text's ideological problematics and to the *Nationwide* mode of address.

So, for example, he found that a group of bank managers were dismissive of the style in which *Nationwide* presented its budget special – 'it wasn't sufficient . . . it's entertainment . . . if I'd wanted to find out about the budget I'd probably rely on the next day's newspaper . . . something like "The Telegraph" ' – and yet they appeared to share the programme's ideological framework to the extent that it was 'largely invisible to them because it is so closely equivalent to their own view' (see Morley, 1980a:105–8; also Philo, 1990:183–4, who expresses doubts about this reading of the interview data). For a group of shop stewards, however, the opposite was the case. While on the whole they were willing to endorse the text's populist rhetoric – 'it takes the issues of the day and it is quite entertaining' – they forcefully rejected what they understood to be *Nationwide*'s sympathies towards middle management and its failure to tackle fundamental economic questions : 'there's no discussion of investment, growth, production, creation of employment' (see Morley, 1980a:112–18). There are evident difficulties in dealing with these two dimensions of interpretation at the same time, particularly when it comes to classifying the sorts of response I have quoted above. Reactions to the programme's presentational style and mode of address have more to do with patterns of taste and cultural disposition than with degrees of distance from a preferred meaning. One is a matter of genre preference, the other is a stance taken in relation to specific ideological propositions or framings – and Morley was later to recognize the problems such a separation causes for research design (see the last section of this chapter). For the purposes of the *Nationwide* study, he was ultimately constrained by the model of decoding positions inherited from Hall and Parkin. That model led him to focus, therefore, on the propositional aspects of a TV message and to attempt a 'ranking' of group decodings within the pre-established grid of dominant, negotiated and oppositional readings.

Management groups, along with apprentices and schoolboys, were seen to inhabit the dominant code and to accept the text's encoded meanings. Negotiated readings were made by teacher training and university arts students. Trade union groups, depending on their members' roles as either officials or shop stewards, produced versions of negotiated or oppositional decodings. Meanwhile, the black college students interviewed by Morley made oppositional readings of another kind (raising further questions about the adequacy of his classificatory system and research sample). 'In a sense they fail,' he said, 'to engage with the discourse of the programme enough to deconstruct or redefine it' (1980a:142–3). They actually showed little interest in the text and found it extremely hard to recognize anything of themselves in the *Nationwide* image – not so much rejecting the programme's preferred view of the world as refusing to read the message at all.

Probably the most significant conclusion to be drawn from the research is that viewers' decodings of a TV current affairs text cannot be reduced in any simple way to their socioeconomic location. That location will certainly limit the array of codes and discourses which are available – the interpretative 'repertoires' to hand – but Morley's interviews demonstrated how groups occupying broadly the same class position can offer quite different responses. Comparing the readings of apprentices, trade union/shop steward groups and black further education students, he noted that the discourses in play are in the first case 'a tradition of mainstream working class populism, in another that of trade union and Labour Party politics, in another the influence of black youth cultures' (Morley, 1980a:137). It is necessary, then, to inquire into the specific linkages of social placing with discursive or institutional positioning. The point was stressed by Morley in a further piece, in which he summarized the findings of his study:

> we cannot analyse communications separately from . . . the structures and divisions of the social formation. On the other hand, we must attempt to avoid a crude

sociological reductionism which would take these factors to determine decoding practices in a mechanistic way (e.g. all working class people, as a direct result of their class position, will decode messages in manner X) ... we need to investigate the ways in which structural factors are articulated through discursive processes. (Morley, 1981a:56)

Despite all its shortcomings – several more of which I will be identifying in due course – *The 'Nationwide' Audience* has justifiably come to be regarded as a landmark in the development of critical media theory and research. It is clear, in retrospect, that Morley's work was an important turning point at which attention began to be switched from the narrow examination of textual forms towards an empirical exploration of audience engagement with texts. Although media representations themselves still require detailed analysis, and although the talk generated by respondents presents the researcher with a second 'text' requiring interpretation, Morley was able to confirm Hall's proposition that consumers are not passive recipients of encoded meanings and identities. Even those viewers who made sense of the *Nationwide* message within the dominant code performed active, if partly unconscious, semiotic labour. Their general acceptance of the programme's preferred reading was the outcome of an interdiscursive encounter – rather than a result of them being 'blank sheets' for the text to write on.

Interpreting TV News and Current Affairs

Since the publication of Morley's study, a number of other academics – principally in Britain and Scandinavia – have followed his lead by carrying out qualitative research on viewers' interpretations of news broadcasts or current affairs and documentary programmes. I now want to consider some examples of work done in this tradition over the ten years after *The 'Nationwide' Audience* first appeared. These examples might best be seen as part of what John Corner (1991) has termed the 'public knowledge' strand in audience inquiry – a strand of research marked by general concerns with the media's power to define issues and meanings in the information sphere. Corner distinguishes such work from that which falls within the bounds of what he calls the 'popular culture' project. The latter is a type of ethnographic investigation concerned primarily with questions of taste and pleasure in the sphere of entertainment (Chapter 3 deals with developments in that area, although the separation here should not be taken to imply a mutual exclusivity of information and entertainment as categories of media output – see Dahlgren & Sparks, 1992). Several of the 'public knowledge' studies discussed in the next few pages demonstrate an additional, particular interest in the cognitive and linguistic aspects of viewer response. In fact, they tend to concentrate rather more than Morley's book did on readers' basic under-standings and ways of speaking about TV news and current affairs. They are often less successful in relating viewers' ideological orientations to social and cultural variables. All the same, I would suggest that their insights can be treated as complementary to the conceptual and empirical advances made by the Birmingham group.

Justin Lewis (1985; see also Lewis, 1991) conducted interviews with fifty 'decoders' after they were each shown a recorded ITN *News at Ten* bulletin. The transcript material revealed a remarkable gulf between the news stories as they were told by the broadcasters and accounts of those items as they were retold to Lewis by the majority of his respondents. One item was about a politician who had been under attack from members of his own party – but had now strengthened his position following a standing ovation at his party's conference. Lewis found that only twelve out of fifty viewers referred to the fact that the politician had recently come in for criticism. Instead, around four-fifths of the interviewees commented on the content of the conference speech – yet 'in terms of the story's encoded meaning . . . the brief clip of his speech was completely irrelevant' (Lewis, 1985:210).

Decoders also made varied sense of an item to do with employment statistics. For some, the key point was the ratio of jobs being created to those being lost – while for others, it was a story about a regional imbalance in levels of unemployment, or about the decline of jobs in manufacturing industry as opposed to growth in the service sector. Lewis tried to explain the different readings with reference to 'channels of access' that open up only certain parts of the TV message to interviewees. These are the extra-textual narratives drawn on by viewers in their attempts to understand the news and, if Lewis is a little vague at times about the nature of these channels, he nevertheless notes a correspondence in this instance with the geographical location and cultural circumstances of many respondents. For people living during the early 1980s in Sheffield – the declining northern city where he conducted his research – the regional distribution of employment was likely to be an important theme (still, it doesn't help to account for differences of interpretation across the sample). The narrative structure of news itself was seen by Lewis as a further factor contributing to the variations in decoding. He argued that stories were often badly told in the first place, and even took the unusual step of proposing his own alternative script for the item concerning the politician (see Lewis, 1985:233). I say 'unusual' because the researcher's main worry here appears to be whether a clearly understandable and unambiguous message is being successfully transmitted. Such anxieties are not strictly in keeping with the more directly political framework adopted by Morley, for whom reception analysis was a way of exploring connections between meaning construction and social structure.

A study that comes rather closer to reproducing the original design and intention of the Birmingham project is the recent work of John Corner, Kay Richardson and Natalie Fenton at Liverpool University. Their book – *Nuclear Reactions* (1990) – reports on research in which they charted decodings made by varied viewing groups who were asked to watch documentaries offering very different perspectives on the issue of nuclear power ('public issue' investigations of this sort may be a pointer to future developments – for another example, see the 'mixed genre' media research on women and violence carried out by Schlesinger *et al.*, 1992). Groups were selected by Corner and his colleagues to represent a range of interests and political positions – for instance, local Labour or Conservative party members, environmental activists or nuclear industry workers. The programmes they were being invited to respond to included a BBC2 documentary that focussed on the health risks associated with nuclear energy, a promotional film commissioned by the electricity generating authority, and an independent video production which simulated the consequences of a major disaster at a British station. Each was distinguishable in terms of its formal style as well as its substantive content.

Not surprisingly, group responses to the programmes revealed some significant divergences of opinion and disposition. So, to take a specific case, we could compare the commentaries given by employees at Heysham power station with readings made by 'Friends of the Earth' campaigners. The researchers found nuclear industry workers to be antagonistic towards an imaginative scenario presented in *From Our Own Correspondent* (the independent video production) – 'it's highly political . . . absolutely unbelievable' – yet the same group of employees appeared blind to the contrived character of a scripted interview sequence in the industry's own promotional film. In contrast, environmentalists were strongly critical of that 'staged' current affairs interview in *Energy : The Nuclear Option* – which involved hiring a TV presenter already known for the tenacity of his questioning : 'he's somebody that the public sees as impartial so to use him in a partial setting I don't think really works'. When it came to the simulated disaster in *Correspondent*, though, they felt that dramatised scenes were acceptable because 'that's the sort of thing that gets to people . . . it brings it into your backyard' (see Corner *et al.*, 1990:69–78, 96–7).

This attempt to catalogue and contrast the interpretations constructed by differently placed groups of media consumers is a valuable and necessary part of any reception study. In itself, however, it isn't a sufficient justification for doing qualitative audience research. As I have pointed out earlier, there needs to be a move beyond description and a commitment to explanatory analysis. Morley's explanation of patterned decodings in *The 'Nationwide' Audience* had revolved around a complex argument concerning the relationship of socioeconomic location to institutional and interdiscursive positionings – and it required those material and ideological features to be grafted on to a hierarchy of dominant, negotiated and oppositional readings. *Nuclear Reactions* undoubtedly falls short of that Birmingham project in terms of grand theoretical ambition, but the authors do seek to delineate certain 'frameworks of understanding' which they believe are informing the stances taken by viewers. The category identified most often in their respondents' talk is what they refer to as the 'civic' frame – defined by a quite genuine search for overall fairness in broadcast output:

> Such a sought 'fairness' is massively problematised by its inter-articulation with ideas of balance and of truth, but it is the single most powerful regulator of interpretative assessments we found and it frequently provides the parameters

within which a critical scrutiny of forms is carried out by the viewer. (Corner *et al.*, 1990:107)

Apart from the civic, of course, there are other potential framings that can be activated in the sense-making process. Corner, Richardson and Fenton speak additionally of the 'evidential', the 'political' and the 'personal'. A good illustration of the last evaluative category in this list is the following response to the BBC2 documentary that focussed on health risks. It comes from a woman in Friends of the Earth who resists the civic and evidential frames chosen by her fellow group members to judge the programme:

> they [the programme makers] were just appealing to very basic fears, not particularly good facts but just people's basic fear instinct. I'm not very well up on the facts and so on of nuclear, but I know basically I'm scared of it, you know, and that's how it came across to me. I thought it was great. (quoted in Corner *et al.*, 1990:74)

The authors of *Nuclear Reactions* describe the method of investigation they adopt as 'ethnodiscursive' – because it pays particular attention to these framing styles in respondents' accounts – and, in a previous piece on documentary decodings, Corner and Richardson (1986) had been more interested still in examining the linguistic features of interview talk. The smaller scale of their earlier study prevented them from reaching any significant conclusions on the social patterning of interpretation, and they turned their efforts instead to analysing how interviewees said what they said about a TV text. On that occasion, Corner and Richardson chose to tape one-to-one sessions with viewers and to organize discussion around specific sequences of a programme. This, they suggested, gave them scope to deal with the subtleties of 'interpretative processing'. In the talk that was produced, they once again pointed to several different expressive stances taken by decoders towards what was seen and heard.

Documentaries regularly draw on naturalistic forms of representation (see Collins, 1986), and the recorded broadcast played back to respondents by Corner and Richardson was a good example of this textual strategy. Its topic was the so-called 'fiddling' by unemployed workers living on a Liverpool housing estate. After a reporter's brief introduction, the impression was created of residents simply speaking for themselves – volunteering seemingly unsolicited testimony and enacting what appeared to be normal episodes from daily life. In relation to the realist aesthetics of the programme, viewers offered either 'mediated' or 'transparent' accounts. As Corner and Richardson (1986:149) explain, 'our general term for interpretations that are intention/ motivation conscious is "mediation reading"; as against "transparency reading" where comments are made about the depicted world as if it had been directly perceived reality'. One involves a recognition that the documentary is a construction – an interpretative possibility which was denied to the consumer by screen theorists like MacCabe – while the second treats TV as if it is an unproblematic window on the world. There were also examples of 'displaced readings', where interviewees speculated on the interpretations that absent viewers (for example, 'my mother' or 'people from Basingstoke') might make. Calling for future work to pursue and extend their provisional typology of readings, they claimed that the study :

> brings out some of the key processes involved when the combinatory forms of documentary 'saying' and 'showing' interact with viewers' social dispositions and attitudes . . . the range of 'mediated' and 'displacement' accounts given, and the frequent tacking between these and the more 'transparent' uses made of screen depictions, seem to us to open up new perspectives on the transformation of media form into meaning and significance for the viewer. (Corner & Richardson, 1986:159–60)

Work done by the Swedish media researcher, Peter Dahlgren (1988), deserves to be mentioned here because his interests overlap with those of Corner and Richardson. Like them, he sought to understand the features of language use in talk about TV. Dahlgren dealt not only with the types of speech produced in a formal interview situation – he monitored the informal chatter to be heard in numerous other settings too. This was done by entering into conversation about the news at social gatherings like dinners or parties, and while travelling on trains or speaking to neighbours. He resorted to these less obtrusive methods in the belief that there is a fundamental dichotomy between 'official' and 'personal' modes of talk. In the former, the style is that of the dutiful citizen engaged in public dialogue, while the latter is an example of what micro-sociologists would call 'back stage' speech. The personal mode may be harder to access or subject to analysis – but if audience studies are to get to grips with the circulation of news narratives in day-to-day life then they must surely take note of Dahlgren's distinction. Whether it is the sometimes trivial associations made by viewers between TV items and elements of their own experience, or the cynical expression of estrangement from news discourse (see Dahlgren, 1988:295–7), researchers need to record and reflect on these mundane interpretative activities.

Fellow Scandinavian, Klaus Bruhn Jensen (1990), is someone else who has recently been exploring the everyday conditions of news reception – and his conclusions have serious implications for any media theorists who are too quick to celebrate the polysemy of the text, or the ability of audience members to construct negotiated and radical readings of TV programmes. Looking back at elements of the data gathered for a book called *Making Sense of the News* (Jensen, 1986), he argued that 'oppositional decodings are not in themselves a manifestation of political power . . . the wider ramifications of opposition at the textual level depend on the social and political uses to which the opposition may be put in contexts beyond the relative privacy of media reception' (Jensen, 1990:58). Thus, while it may well be the case that news is employed by certain viewers as a resource for the critical examination of social issues, few ever carry this through into active participation in the political process apart from infrequent voting at elections. As one of his interviewees remarked : 'Well, I can vote. As far as taking it further, I don't know. I guess the opportunity will have to arise . . . I feel I'm just the average person out here' (Jensen, 1990:67). It is, in part, the domestic context of viewing which leads to

the gap Jensen identifies between audience decodings and political action –
and the question of consumption contexts is one of those I touch on next in
returning to ask about the shortcomings of *The 'Nationwide' Audience* and
Hall's encoding/decoding model.

Reformulations for Audience Ethnography

Earlier in this chapter, while discussing the innovative work performed by
members of the Birmingham Centre, I deliberately sought to highlight the
advantages of their encoding/decoding research. I hope to have shown that
these advantages are considerable – especially when Hall's interactive model
of media communication is compared with the textual determinism and
aesthetic formalism of screen theory. As we have just seen, the CCCS's
Nationwide project helped to establish a distinctive 'public knowledge' strand
in reception ethnography – inspiring several other studies of viewer interpretation in the area of TV news and current affairs. I have also suggested that
The 'Nationwide' Audience represents a more general watershed in critical
media theory because of its insistence on empirical audience inquiry.
However, the Birmingham group's conception of text–reader relations had its
problems too. I alluded briefly to some of them in my account of Morley's
findings, but it is now time to expand on and add to those objections. The
purpose here is definitely not to encourage an overly dismissive view of the
encoding/decoding framework. Rather, my aim is to explain how its
limitations gave rise to a revised agenda for many reception researchers during
the 1980s. In a short postscript on the *Nationwide* study, Morley (1981b)
himself admitted to frustrations with that particular framework and indicated
a wish to widen the focus of audience inquiry. His major proposal was for a
move away from the theory of decoding which had emerged out of Parkin's
notes on 'meaning systems' – towards a genre-based, contextual model of
media consumption in everyday life. He may well have been too hasty in
jettisoning much of the previous agenda – questions to do with the ideological
or 'definitional' power of specific TV texts. The fact remains that such
reformulations were to prove highly influential in the development of an
'ethnography of reading'.

So this final section of the chapter points the way forward to the concerns of
the next by addressing a set of problems and proposals for research on
decoding – but before moving on to matters of consumption, we need to tackle
a few difficulties associated with the concept of encoding and the notion of a
text's preferred reading. To begin with, Hall's notes on the encoding and
preferring of meaning tend (unintentionally?) to imply a necessary intention-
ality on the part of the broadcasters. No doubt there will be occasions in news
coverage when certain social interests are consciously favoured – at a time,
say, of perceived national crisis or civil unrest (see Masterman, 1984, on the
BBC's suppression of references to police brutality after a picket line incident
during the British miners' strike). In routine practices of media production,

though, the operations of ideology have much more to do with a taken-for-granted reproduction of dominant definitions and an adherence to accepted professional conventions than they have with the deliberate biases of broadcasters or the institutions in which they operate.

Another difficulty arises when we try to determine the exact status of a preferred reading and the concept's applicability across various types of media output. Where is it and how do we know if we've found it? Can we be sure we didn't put it there ourselves while we were looking? And can it be found by examining any sort of text? Attempting to answer these teasing questions takes us quickly into a theoretical minefield. One possibility would be to treat the preferred reading as if it was a property of the message – something contained in the text – and assume that it is accessible to researchers who conduct a close inspection using the correct methods of semiotic analysis. This is the assumption made by Hall, and by Brunsdon and Morley in their initial study of the *Nationwide* discourse. By the time he wrote his postscript on the project, Morley (1981b:6) was a good deal less confident – wondering whether it might be the 'reading which the analyst is predicting that most members of the audience will produce'. An understandable degree of uncertainty crept in where previously the researcher had been sure about identifying the text's preferred meanings.

Indeed, two later critics of the encoding/decoding model, Tony Bennett and Janet Woollacott (1987), went so far as to argue that there is no 'text itself' available for inspection outside of the 'reading formations' in which meaning is activated. Presumably they would view the academic activity of semiotic analysis as just one more of these reading formations – no more privileged than any other interpretation. To seek 'the text itself' is, they believe, 'to chase a chimera' (Bennett & Woollacott, 1987:264). Now in a way they make a good point, and Bennett and Woollacott have in effect turned Morley's admission of uncertainty into a full-blown scepticism. It is true that the researcher relies on constructing an interpretation of a programme like *Nationwide* as much as the 'ordinary' viewer. For Morley – as a reception ethnographer – the situation is doubly problematic because he is also faced with reading 'ordinary' viewers' interpretations of what he supposes to be the text's preferred, encoded meanings. All of this is to say that the academic's account will be partial. David Sless (1986:38) describes the dilemma well when he writes: 'In the study of communication there is no omniscient vantage point from which all things are visible. We cannot look down from heaven and see everything . . . throughout semiotic research we are earthbound' (assessing Brunsdon and Morley's monograph, Sless shows how they are themselves occupying an oppositional or radical decoding position).

However, having recognized the obstacles illuminated by Bennett and Woollacott, I would not want to use those as an excuse for dissolving 'the text' altogether or for rejecting out of hand the notion of a preferred reading. A healthy measure of modesty concerning our analytical insights may be the order of the day for media researchers and students, but there is a world of difference between admitting that the text is only accessible via an interpretative act and denying the very existence of a message to be read. I want to hang on to the idea that texts exceed the interpretations which are made of them by consumers (Brunsdon, 1989, advances a similar argument). It appears to me that Bennett and Woollacott are in danger of collapsing the whole communication process into what they call the 'reading formation'. While I am committed in this book to an approach which comprehends media consumption as an active practice, I am unwilling to follow Bennett and Woollacott's position to its logical conclusion – thereby disregarding the constraints imposed on polysemy at the moment of textual production. To ditch the preferred reading model completely is a grave mistake. Of course, the concept might be better suited to some forms of representation than others – better suited, for instance, to understanding news and current affairs than it is to analysing TV soap opera. Popular fictional drama can exert a strong ideological force, yet it rarely offers audiences the same sort of substantive propositions to contend with.

This acknowledgement of genre variation – coupled with the realization that a 'preferred reading' analysis, though still valid, is best applied to the propositional aspects of a (usually non-fictional) media message – leads us neatly into Morley's plans for a reformulated reception ethnography. He came to feel confined by Hall's grid of dominant, negotiated and oppositional decodings. It had been drawn up exclusively for the purpose of gauging whether readers 'agree, or disagree, or partly agree with the ideological propositions of the text' (Morley, 1981b:10) – and was far less able to cope with basic dimensions of audience response such as how relevant or irrelevant a particular text or genre is for decoders. To illustrate the limiting nature of the Hall/Parkin model, we could take a case from the *Nationwide* study to which I have already referred. The black further-education students, who failed to connect or identify at all with the programme's concerns, are a perfect example of a viewing group that falls outside the 'rankings' employed by Morley. On reflection, it was premature to ask about the proximity of their interpretations to the text's preferred meanings because in normal circumstances they would not even have chosen to watch. Their exposure to the text was solely a consequence of it being artificially supplied to them by an academic researcher.

Here we must begin to doubt Morley's claim, embodied in the title of his book, to have charted *The 'Nationwide' Audience*. As John Hartley (1987:126) alleges, and with justification: 'Morley's audience is . . . produced by his project'. Hartley, remember, rejects any attempt to map media consumption empirically (see Chapter 1) – and so has no investment in proposing more adequate means of investigation – but for reception ethnographers, a heightened sensitivity to programme-type preference was surely required. Future studies clearly had to pay attention to the kinds of material that interest different cultural groupings in the first place. This entails going beyond the dominant, negotiated and oppositional positions adopted by selected viewers who are presented with a single current affairs text – and looking at patterns of taste across a range of genres:

by translating our concerns from the framework of the decoding model into that of genre theory, we may be able to develop a model of text–audience relations which is more flexible, and of wider application . . . it would involve us in dealing more with the relevance/irrelevance and comprehension/incomprehension dimensions of decoding rather than being directly concerned with the acceptance or rejection of substantive ideological themes. (Morley, 1981b:10)

Audience ethnographies, in Morley's opinion, had to start plotting the 'purchase' of media genres on various categories of readers. This was to inquire 'who likes what?' – to supplement his previous cultural diagram of decoding so as to show an organized diversity of taste publics. The task would be to match up distinctive generic preoccupations, narrative styles and modes of address with the socially distributed forms of cultural competence that readers possess. Our focus, then, remains on interdiscursive relations – but on the connections between subjectivity and pleasure, not immediately those between subjectivity and textual power. Brunsdon (1981:36) gives a useful example of what is at stake in the shift to 'genre theory':

Just as a Godard film requires the possession of certain forms of cultural capital on the part of its audience . . . an extra-textual familiarity with certain artistic, linguistic, political and cinematic discourses – so too does soap opera. . . . It is the culturally constructed skills of femininity – sensitivity, perception, intuition and the necessary privileging of the concerns of personal life – which are both called on and practised in the genre.

That the diversity of tastes and competences is an organized one – that it is socially patterned – needs to be stressed. The skills required to comprehend and get enjoyment out of watching an avant-garde movie and a soap opera are likely to be located in consumers with quite different social, institutional and discursive positionings. Indeed, these two types of text usually appear at quite different points in the TV schedule, indicating an assumed split in the composition of their respective reading publics. On British television, we would expect to find a season of Godard films being screened late at night on Channel 4 (a station committed to minority arts coverage for a predominantly middle class viewership high in 'educational capital'). Continuous serials, on the other hand, are broadcast either early evening on ITV and BBC1 – or else in their traditional daytime slots, where they were originally placed on radio to attract an audience of housewives for soap powder commercials (see Hobson, 1982).

The historical circumstances in which 'soaps' first emerged are actually symptomatic of the industry's wider relationship to its audiences (I touched on this near the beginning of the book). TV institutions, at least those in the commercial sector, tend to see taste publics as commodities that can be 'delivered' to advertisers – who, in turn, treat them as potential markets for other commodities. The industry is interested in 'measuring' viewer preferences only in so far as it enables the manufacture of demographic data on what it is claiming to deliver. A theory of genre or an ethnography of taste sets out from elsewhere. Its challenge is to specify the interdiscursive articulations through which salience and pleasure are produced. To the 'who likes what?'

question, then, it adds a 'why do they like it?' Under Pierre Bourdieu's influence, it also went on to ask 'how is what they like valued?' Readers' enjoyments and competences are accorded greater or lesser 'worth' in what Bourdieu (1984) calls the 'cultural economy' – and as we might expect, the resulting hierarchy of programme preferences is generally skewed in favour of the dominant social groups. For anyone who is worried about whether the research reformulations being discussed here mark a retreat from politics, the answer is now clear. However, the precise object of our criticism changes. We go from an agenda that foregrounds the power of the text to a new politics of cultural distinction.

In fact, those issues of taste and distinction were taken up in relation to an additional shift in the research agenda – a new concern with how the media are consumed in the 'natural' settings of daily social life. As well as showing his interviewees a video recording of a text they might not otherwise have watched, Morley realized there was a further artificial feature of the *Nationwide* study. Even if all members of the viewing groups had been regular followers of the programme, the context in which they were invited to interpret it was somewhat untypical. People rarely view TV at college or at work in a 'classroom' atmosphere with fellow students or employees (unless they happen to be on a media studies course!). Watching TV is routinely done in the private sphere of the home – a place where we spend the major part of our leisure time – and Morley came to the conclusion that future projects must investigate this household environment of media consumption. While writing *The 'Nationwide' Audience*, he had already begun to wonder about 'the differences which might arise from a situation in which a programme is decoded in an educational or work context – as compared with its decoding by the same respondents in the context of the family and home' (Morley, 1980a:27). We shall see in the next chapter that reception ethnographers who did venture into the household setting were to concentrate on family viewing itself as a dynamic set of cultural practices. Alongside the politics of preference outlined above, there evolved a parallel 'politics of the sitting room'.

3
Taste, Context and Ethnographic Practice

If a central aim of reception ethnography is to understand the lived experiences of media consumers – to see things, as Ien Ang (1991) put it, 'from the virtual standpoint of actual audiences' – then it has to engage with the situational contexts in which the media are used and interpreted. In the present chapter, I employ the term 'context' to refer specifically to what we might call everyday micro-settings. By this, I mean the routine physical locations and interpersonal relations of reception. These local settings are themselves embedded within and intersected by the wider structural formations of a society (the macro-context) – but in order to give the concept some analytical purchase I propose that we distinguish between the two. The *Nationwide* decoding study can be said to have focussed on the latter, asking how divisions of class determine readings of a TV programme. It failed, however, to deal with the former – with the usual domestic circumstances of viewing. A large proportion of the work I look at in the coming pages attempts to address that immediate social context where media messages enter into lived audience cultures. It constitutes an emerging 'anthropology of everyday consumption'.

I start with an account of pioneering studies that were carried out on either side of the Atlantic – James Lull's research in the USA on the 'social uses' of TV in family life, and in Britain, Dorothy Hobson's investigation of how young mothers at home relate to media output (Lull, 1980; Hobson, 1980). Although their respective theoretical and political points of departure were somewhat different, both shared a belief in the importance of ethnographic inquiry and both opened up valuable questions to do with the contextual dynamics of viewing and listening in the household environment. I have suggested in the previous chapter that David Morley's The *'Nationwide' Audience* laid the foundation for reception ethnographies in the 1980s and through into the 1990s, but it could be argued that Lull and Hobson were equally significant figures in the development of a qualitative tradition. They had already begun to explore some of the issues highlighted by Morley in his critical postscript – and their ground-breaking work on media and daily life was to leave an unmistakable mark on Morley's own later book, *Family Television* (1986).

Towards an Anthropology of Everyday Consumption

In the early ethnographic research done by Lull and Hobson – and across much of the subsequent writing on audiences and everyday life – there has been a strong emphasis on broadcast output and the household contexts of its reception (in the main, a concern with TV viewing in families). That emphasis is, I think, justifiable for a number of reasons. The increasingly 'privatized' character of cultural activity in the current historical period means inquiries into household leisure are essential. Also, despite competition from a range of other communication technologies in the home, television remains the 'leading object' (Silverstone, 1991) in most domestic media ensembles. Nevertheless, what is strikingly absent from these advances towards an anthropology of consumption is any qualitative empirical work on the public settings of cinema spectatorship. This can be explained, at least in part, by the continuing influence of textual semiotics and psychoanalytical perspectives in film studies – often serving to isolate it from new directions in media and cultural analysis (see Lapsley & Westlake, 1988, for an introduction to film theory which could have been published a decade before). John Ellis (1982) has touched on the public experience of movie-going and the physical surroundings of the cinema hall, contrasting these with the conditions of TV reception. Unfortunately, little effort has been made to pursue Ellis's useful comments. A recent collection of autobiographical pieces written by film fans (Breakwell & Hammond, 1990) gives some idea of the kind of material we could expect to produce with more sustained ethnographic attention – and any such future initiatives would provide a welcome addition to the literature.

For now, though – having qualified my rather broad claim to be dealing here with 'media and daily life' – I discuss the domestic context of consumption with reference first to Lull's essay, 'The Social Uses of Television' (1980). Assisted by a team of observers, Lull had collected data during a three-year period on TV viewing practices in over 200 households in California and Wisconsin. These families were contacted through schools, clubs and community organizations – and researchers visited their homes on several occasions, spending afternoons and evenings in the company of household members. They 'ate with the families, performed chores with them, played with the children, and took part in group entertainment, particularly television watching' (Lull, 1980:201). In fact, his project is one of the few audience ethnographies to have relied chiefly on long periods of participant observation (in-depth interviews with each resident were also recorded). The advantage of the method, for Lull, was the access it promised to give to everyday routines. He believed that after a relatively short time, the 'presence of the investigator in the habitat of his subjects ... need not severely disrupt the natural behaviour of the family unit' (Lull, 1980:199). There are certainly instances cited from the field notes which indicate a witnessing of quite intimate domestic moments, but we should be careful not to make too hard and fast a distinction between 'naturalistic' and 'artificial' modes of inquiry. While participant observers in a cultural setting can gather rich data, all types of social research are in a sense artificial because they necessarily involve an intervention into the lives of those being monitored. Precise degrees of disruption to the people and places under ethnographic surveillance are debatable. Valerie Walkerdine (1986), for example, is far less optimistic than

Lull concerning the possibilities for an unobtrusive recording of viewers' behaviour (see my remarks on her work at the end of this chapter).

Drawing on illustrative material from the study, Lull constructed a 'typology' of social uses. Two main varieties of TV usage in the home were identified – structural and relational. Under the category of the structural, he included the employment of the medium as an 'environmental resource' – 'a companion for accomplishing household chores and routines . . . a flow of constant background noise which moves to the foreground when individuals or groups desire' – and as a 'behavioural regulator' that serves to structure domestic time, punctuating daily activities and duties (Lull, 1980:201–2; see Scannell, 1988, for a further examination of the temporal arrangements of broadcasting). However, Lull's paper concentrated far more on the different relational uses to which TV is put by its viewers. This category covers the positions occupied by the medium in the interpersonal dynamics of family life, 'ways in which audience members use television to create practical social arrangements' (Lull, 1980:202).

Perhaps the most fascinating accounts of familial relations appear under his subheading 'affiliation/avoidance', and I will quote Lull's telling of these mundane domestic dramas in full because they are exactly the sort of active negotiations around the TV set that we might recognize from our own observations and experiences. One is a case in which TV offers a married woman an infrequent opportunity to display open physical affection towards her spouse. In this particular family, Lull (1980:203) reports that:

> the husband and wife touched each other only twice during the seven day period. The first time the man playfully grabbed his wife and seated her on his lap while his daughter, acting as a kind of medium, told a humorous story about something that had happened at school that day. The other occasion for physical contact during the week took place one night while the couple watched television. The man was a hard working labourer who nearly always fell asleep when he watched television at night. He dozed as he sat in a recliner rocking chair with his shoes off. He snored loudly with his mouth open. His wife, who had been sitting on the floor in the same room, pushed herself along the floor until she was close to his chair. She leaned back until her head rested against his bare feet and smiled as she created this rare moment of 'intimacy'.

A second situation Lull (1980:204) describes – resulting here in avoidance rather than affiliation – revolves around generational ties and tensions: 'A blue collar family . . . was grateful for television since it occupies so much of the grandparents' time in the evening, thereby keeping them away from their home which is located just three doors away. This young couple preferred not to be bothered by their parents. Television limits unwanted visits.'

'Communication facilitation' was the term given to another of the relational uses observed by Lull and his research assistants. For children, then, popular programmes and characters supplied 'known-in-common referents' which enabled them to clarify issues when talking to adults. Similarly, broadcasts were often found to spark off collective discussions within the household (dispelling the widespread myth that TV has destroyed the art of conversation?). Lull did realize, though, that the communication TV facilitated could be caught up with expressions of power by some family members. As he noted, the programme decision-making process 'provides incessant opportunities for argument' and is a primary site for interpersonal dominance struggles (Lull, 1980:206). Indeed, this theme of how programmes get selected was followed up in a paper published elsewhere (Lull, 1982) – with the conclusion that it is fathers who are usually responsible for controlling the TV set. Morley's study of domestic reception practices was to produce parallel findings on paternal authority and power over viewing choice (Morley, 1986 – and see below).

At this point, before turning to Hobson's work and in anticipation of reviewing Morley's *Family Television*, it might be appropriate to compare the theoretical underpinnings of Lull's social uses approach with the perspective of British cultural studies. To do so, we also have to consider the breaks and continuities between Lull's ethnographic project and the 'uses and gratifications' model in mass communications research. Back in the opening chapter, I briefly mentioned what I believe to be the main problems facing gratificationists – namely, their focus on 'the individual' as the basic unit of consumption and their understanding of media utilization within an overly functionalist framework that foregrounds personal psychological needs. Lull writes in the language of the functionalist school – he says, for instance, that 'audience members create . . . practical actions involving the mass media in order to gratify particular needs' (Lull, 1980:197) – yet his notes on family viewing depart significantly from older 'uses' typologies (McQuail *et al.*, 1972, is the best known of these). They deliberately seek to foreground families as the proper units of reception and to locate TV use in the social dynamics of households. In drafting his own typology, Lull privileged interpersonal contexts over individual viewers and began to raise questions about the differential distribution of power amongst consumers in the domestic setting. What he was prevented from doing – as a direct consequence of the intellectual baggage he inherited – was explaining those power relations with reference to, say, a theory of patriarchy or a feminist critique of the family. Cultural studies insists on making such connections. For someone like Hobson, issues of media and daily life are of interest precisely because they can inform a critical challenge to existing social structures. Lull's introduction to an edited collection of his essays enthusiastically acknowledges developments in British cultural studies and talks about the possibility of building a 'shared agenda' with qualitative research in American communication science (Lull, 1990). My feeling is that any convergence, if it were to prove possible, would ultimately depend on a shared recognition of the political dimensions of the everyday (see Ang, 1989, for a useful interrogation of other recent 'convergence' claims).

Hobson's paper, 'Housewives and the Mass Media' (1980), is firmly situated within the critical school of contemporary cultural studies. Along with Morley and Brunsdon, she had been a student at the Birmingham Centre – and was a key member of the Women's Studies Group there. Her analysis of radio and TV reception actually grew out of a larger project she was undertaking on the experiences of young working-class women caring for small children in the home. That research can be seen, too, as part of a concerted effort by female students at the CCCS to force feminist scholarship on to the map of cultural theory (several interventions in this area are published in Women's Studies Group CCCS, 1978). Hobson understood the family to be, fundamentally, a place of women's subordination. Her work was based on taped conversations with housewives in which she inquired about patterns of domestic labour and (to the extent that they experienced it at all) domestic leisure. Whereas the *Nationwide* decoding study had treated audiences as a number of subgroupings defined principally by class position, Hobson's major contribution is to have stressed the gender-specific meanings of the media in household contexts. In particular, she cleared a pathway for investigations of gender and genre – for future writing on feminine reading pleasures.

Housework is, as the saying goes, 'never done' – but it is frequently invisible to those who don't do it, often not recognized as work at all. Few employees could be expected to tolerate the conditions under which such labour is performed. It is an unpaid, low-status job carried out in isolation from other workers in the same position. In a piece called 'Housewives : Isolation as Oppression', Hobson (1978:85) had quoted the words of an interviewee who expressed a strong sense of the physical and psychological restriction felt by many women in the study – 'I said to him [husband], you'll have to teach me how to drive and then I can go out. I wouldn't mind so much then, it's just . . . here the only connection you have with the outside world is the radio and the telly.' Interestingly, broadcasting is identified by this woman as her 'lifeline' contact with the world beyond the walls of the private sphere – and it was the central importance of mass communication in the daily practices of these young mothers that led Hobson to write 'Housewives and the Mass Media'. As she stated at the beginning of that essay : 'radio and television . . . are never mentioned as spare time . . . activities but are located by the women as integral parts of their day' (Hobson, 1980:105).

During the mornings, before TV was switched on, radio provided the main accompaniment to household chores (when she conducted her research in the late 1970s, there was no equivalent of British TV magazine programmes like *Daytime UK*, *After Nine* or *This Morning*). The women tuned in regularly to Radio 1, the BBC's popular music station. Hobson (1980:109) argued that the records played on air supplied them with a poignant reminder of leisure time before they were married – 'radio is . . . a substitute for the world of music and discos which they have lost'. And it was not just the records attracting them to Radio 1. Her interviewees saw the disc jockey as a replacement for 'missing company' in their lives. Comments were made about the good looks of one of the presenters, who would be well known to audiences through publicity photos or TV appearances, and Hobson (1980:107) suggests that 'it is not too far fetched to see the DJ as . . . playing the role of a sexual fantasy figure in the lives of the women who listen'. The general point, though, is that we only comprehend the appeal of the text when we pay attention to the settings in which it is routinely consumed. Radio helps to combat the loneliness felt by the housewives as a result of their confinement to domestic space. Despite its usual status as background sound, the medium is a means of managing the many frustrations of isolation in the home. If some of the themes Hobson touches on are familiar from the gratifications paradigm (e.g. using the media for substitute company), the difference is in her recognition of the politics of context. These housewives are more than just individual listeners with psychological needs – they are subjects whose practical actions have to be understood in the light of social positionings and concrete material circumstances.

Radio broadcasts also made available a series of punctuation marks in the work routine (note the overlap here with Lull on the structural use of mass media as 'behavioural regulators'). Switching on the wireless sometimes marked the first boundary of everyday life : 'Six o'clock I get up [*laughs*], er, put on the radio full blast so that me husband'll get up' (Anne, in Hobson, 1980:106). Programmes and regular features are, in turn, given names which acknowledge the place they have in household rituals – for example, *The Breakfast Show* or *The Coffee Break*. While Hobson was doing her ethnography, the DJ on Radio 1's morning programme even ran a 'Tiny Tots' spot at eleven o'clock. This involved playing a special record for children and teaching them a nursery rhyme while 'mums' were invited to take a rest and put their feet up (in the same slot, the station now has a rather different feature called 'Our Tune' – see Montgomery, 1991). Unlike the highly segmented temporal organization of industrial labour, housework is characterized by its 'structurelessness'. There is no production line and no factory hooter to announce the start or finish of a shift – and therefore the 'boundaries provided by radio are important in the women's own division of their time' (Hobson, 1980:105). The regularity of the schedules, as well as the constant time-checks, enabled these housewives to sequence domestic duties and give shape to daily existence.

When it came to speaking about TV viewing preferences, the women clearly separated out those types of programme that they positively enjoyed watching from the genres which they preferred to avoid:

> television programmes appear to fall into two distinct categories. The programmes which they watch and enjoy are comedy series, soap operas, American television films, light entertainment and quiz shows. . . . The programmes which are actively rejected deal with what the women designate the . . . 'man's world', and these predominantly cluster around the news, current affairs programmes, scientific programmes, the subject matter of politics or war, including films about war, and, to a lesser extent, documentary programmes.(Hobson, 1980:109–10)

For Hobson's interviewees, then, there were 'two worlds' of TV – a gendered demarcation of interests and involvements. They could relate to a feminine realm of fictional programmes that connected with the personal and emotional concerns of everyday family life – or else offered a fantasy alternative to their own daily experiences. What the women disliked was TV content which they understood to constitute a masculine domain, associated with the factual reporting of current affairs or with action and adventure. The news, according to these housewives, was either boring or depressing. Many said they would rather leave the room while their husbands had the evening bulletin on. One, Lorna, recalled an incident surrounding a particularly gruesome TV documentary:

> I don't like it [the news], I don't like to hear about people dying and things like that. I think about it afterwards and I can't sleep at all. Like when I watched that thing, 'World at War', and I watched it once and all I could see were people all over the place, you know, heads and no arms and that and at night I could not sleep. I can't ask him to turn it over 'cos he likes it, so I go in the kitchen till it's finished.(Hobson, 1980:111)

With reference to the cultural distinctions of class and class fraction, Pierre Bourdieu (1984) has argued – quite correctly – that matters of taste are as much about such expressions of rejection and revulsion as they are to do with positive enjoyment. A sense of disgust towards certain objects or practices tells us a good deal about the social subject who feels it (my final chapter contains a fuller assessment of Bourdieu's theory of consumption – including remarks on his failure to deal adequately with gender difference). It is therefore essential that the 'two worlds' of TV are considered in opposition to each other, because the women in Hobson's study classify themselves by what they don't like as well as by what they do.

However – as I tried to make plain at the end of Chapter 2 – distinction isn't simply a question of difference. Some people's tastes carry greater social 'value' or legitimacy than others', and what Hobson calls the feminine world has traditionally been denigrated by cultural commentators for whom it is alien territory. Few genres can have been subject to the kind of ridicule which soap opera regularly receives from the critics (see Brunsdon, 1984, who reports several instances of this in the British press). By comparison, news and current affairs has a far higher level of respectability – and its viewers tend to be treated as citizens in pursuit of information rather than 'telly addicts' looking for the next fix. Inevitably, these social judgements had a profound impact on the way Hobson's housewives perceived their personal choices and preferences. She noted that 'although their own world is seen as more interesting and relevant to them, it is also seen as secondary in rank to the . . . "masculine" world' (Hobson, 1980:111). For example, they seemed to accept that male partners have an automatic right to watch news programmes.

I continue with the theme of gendered tastes in the following section – focussing on further attempts by feminist media theorists and audience ethnographers to 'rescue' the genres of soap opera or romantic fiction from outright critical dismissal. Hobson's paper on daily media usage by women working in the home created a crucial space in which it was possible to address sympathetically the salience of cultural forms for feminine readers. The work I will be reviewing here is also indicative of a gradual, yet quite general, shift in media and cultural studies during the 1980s – an increasing commitment to taking 'the popular' more seriously. Many academics became unhappy about straightforwardly writing off mass entertainment as the ideology of the dominant in society, and started to search for signs of contestation or resistance in 'vulgar' forms and pleasures (Bennett, 1986, draws on Gramsci's notion of 'hegemony' in an influential statement of the position). It may be that the pendulum has now swung too far in this direction – I have in mind John Fiske's recent writings on TV and popular culture – but the initial intellectual and political motivations for such a shift were nevertheless commendable.

Gender, Genre and Reading Context

Annette Kuhn (1984) suggests that if we are to come to terms with the formations of pleasure clustered around 'women's genres', it is necessary for us to examine both the text's inscribed reader/spectator and the 'social audience' which receives the text. These two categories will be familiar because they resemble those developed in the CCCS Media Group's critique of screen theory, where there was an insistence on the separation of implied and actual readers for the purposes of analysis. The first is a subject position which is put on offer, inviting identification – while the second is a situated group of consumers who have previously been produced in relation to a set of other discourses and interpretative resources. Having established their division, though, a model of genre and taste must be able to account for the dialogical interaction of 'readers in the text' with specific social audiences. In Kuhn's opinion, Charlotte Brunsdon's 'Notes on Soap Opera' (1981) – already cited briefly in the preceding chapter – had made some of the most promising advances along this line of inquiry. Even if Brunsdon's formulations were speculative, with no foundation in empirical research, her essay presented an extremely useful theoretical framework within which to conceptualize popular TV fiction.

To appreciate soaps, the social reader has to possess a number of extra-textual competences. Without these, the genre's identifications and narrative pleasures cannot be experienced. Brunsdon (1981:36) gave three examples – a basic understanding of generic rules or conventions, knowledge of a particular serial's characters and history, combined with an ability and willingness to engage emotionally in the moral codes of personal conduct. The last of the three is perhaps the most important, and it is a skill which women in our society are on the whole more likely to have at their disposal than men. This is not to invoke any essentialist idea of 'natural' female attributes, but to recognize that under present political arrangements it is women who are usually placed in relation to the realm of what Brunsdon (1981:34) calls 'emotionally significant personal interaction'. She is adamant that the identification is socially constructed – that it is the product of unevenly distributed types of cultural capital (indeed, I would want to add that there is nothing essentially feminine about soap as a textual form). It would be perfectly possible, in other historical circumstances, for a biological male to occupy the same imaginative world. In practice, as a consequence of current masculine discourses and subjectivities, men rarely do.

Reciprocally, the genre of soap opera – in present social conditions – 'textually implies a feminine viewer' (Brunsdon, 1981:37). The narrative structure of the continuous serial is multi-layered and open ended. It is made up of short non-linear segments and refuses final closure, a plurality of story lines with no end in sight (see Geraghty, 1981, for an excellent discussion of serial narration). A criticism frequently levelled at soap operas, and especially at the British and Australian varieties, is that nothing seems to happen in them. In contrast to the fast-moving action of an adventure film this is evidently the case, but to denigrate *Coronation Street* or *Neighbours* for that reason is to profoundly misunderstand the workings of these fictions. Narrative progression is not achieved by direct linear flow towards a dramatic climax. Instead, there is 'an endless unsettling . . . and resettling of acceptable modes of behaviour within the sphere of personal relationships' (Brunsdon, 1981:35). Soap proceeds chiefly through dialogue – talk between characters on screen and between audience members in everyday life who are constantly invited to speculate on outcomes or to pass judgement on moral and emotional dilemmas (will he leave her? should she have the baby? etc.). The sort of talk involved here – so central to the continuous serial and the pleasures of its viewers – is commonly known as 'gossip'. As the sociolinguist, Deborah Jones (1980:197), remarks : 'Gossip is a staple of women's lives, and the study of gossip is the study of women's concerns and values, a key to the female subculture.' We might even call it a feminine 'genre' of speech.

These textual (and contextual) features of soap opera could easily be seen as serving to reproduce the subordinate social position of women. An obvious political critique of the continuous serial is the allegation that its pleasures help to bolster patriarchal relations of power by confirming that a woman's place is in the world of family life, romance and interpersonal intrigue. While there is undoubtedly a lot of truth in this argument, it is well worth noting Terry Lovell's challenging thesis that soaps can actually subvert the values of a male-dominated society. In her paper on the ideological operations of *Coronation Street*, the longest-running serial on British television, Lovell (1981:50) writes :

> the conventions of the genre are such that the normal order of things . . . is precisely that of broken marriages, temporary liaisons, availability for 'lasting' romantic love which in fact never lasts. This order, the reverse of the patriarchal norm, is in a sense interrupted by the marriages and 'happy family' interludes, rather than vice-versa.

She contends, too, that a programme like *Coronation Street* needs a number of strong, middle-aged female characters if it is to function successfully – and 'to retain their dramatic interest, these women must remain independent' (Lovell, 1981:50). Encouraging us to depart from a simplistic assessment of soap opera as the opium of masses of women, she tries to show how there are potentially oppositional elements in this sort of TV entertainment. Her theoretical reference point is the Gramscian conception of 'common sense' – popular consciousness as a complex and politically contradictory mishmash of ideological beliefs and reflections on lived experience (for a useful introduction to Gramsci's thought, see Bennett *et al.*, 1981b). Lovell (1981:49) insists that 'because popular culture does not belong to . . . feminism and revolution, it is not captured for reaction, patriarchy and domination either . . . it is situated ambivalently and in contradictory ways, in relation to both'. If some recent critics like Meaghan Morris (1990) have condemned such formulations (rather too hastily, in my opinion) for their 'banality', it is important to remember the advantages that Gramscian perspectives in cultural studies had over the Althusserian or Lacanian approaches fashionable during the 1970s.

Brunsdon's essay did not go so far as Lovell's in claiming that the continuous serial can be 'progressive', but she nevertheless sought to foreground the skilled nature of viewers' decodings and the discriminating character of their tastes. What Brunsdon and Lovell share, of course, is a conviction that soaps are worthy of serious and sustained academic attention. The first ethnographic study in Britain to devote this kind of attention to the genre and its 'reading public' was carried out, once again, by Hobson (1982). Following her work on housewives and the mass media, she went on to investigate the production and consumption contexts of a TV serial called *Crossroads* – chosen for analysis because it had been singled out as a favourite show by many of the women interviewed in that earlier research. Hobson's book, *'Crossroads': The Drama of a Soap Opera*, was only partly concerned with audience interpretations – she has much to say about the institutional conditions of programme making as well – although I will be dealing here with her relevant comments on viewing practices and pleasures. As with Hobson's previous ethnographic inquiry, the research involved recording conversations with consumers in the household setting. She visited the homes of several women who were regular viewers of the programme – sitting with them as they watched and using the episode they had just seen as a way of opening up discussion. By positioning herself as a fellow fan of the serial, Hobson managed to gain the confidence of interviewees. They were able to talk in a relatively open way to another woman about their experiences and enjoyments (the gender of the interviewer was obviously a crucial factor in these interactions).

Crossroads – a soap opera that revolved around the lives of staff working in a motel – was broadcast by commercial TV early on weekday evenings (for several years, it would actually have clashed with part of the BBC's *Nationwide*). This was a particularly busy period in the daily routines of many of the women who discussed the serial with Hobson. They frequently found themselves caught between the responsibility of providing food for their families and the desire to watch a favourite programme. The difficulty was compounded by a shift in the scheduling slot from 6.30 to 6.05 as Hobson was conducting her study. She was therefore presented with an excellent opportunity to discover how these viewers created space in the hectic tea-time period to follow the soap narrative. Describing one of the domestic scenes she encountered, Hobson (1982:112) wrote : 'the woman with whom I had gone to watch the programme was serving the evening meal, feeding her five- and three-year-old daughters and attempting to watch . . . on a black and white television situated on top of the freezer opposite the kitchen table'.

The fact that serial story lines are carried primarily by talk rather than at the visual level helps viewers in a situation like this to keep track of developments. Hobson pointed out that some women had evolved ingenious methods of 'half watching' – listening to the dialogue even while their backs were turned to the screen. The segmented construction of the narrative and the recurrence of information vital to the plot are further textual features which aid the distracted domestic consumer. Indeed, on occasion, broadcasters will deliberately produce fragmented forms for times of the day when they know audiences are likely to be caught up in other household activities. One can think, for example, of breakfast TV and its characteristic use of segmentation and repetition (Ellis, 1982, proposes that these are the two main properties of narration in broadcasting). To a certain extent, then, TV aesthetics are determined by the context of consumption – and Hobson called on media theorists also to acknowledge the medium's place as 'part of the everyday life of viewers'. She was critical of approaches which seek to isolate the text from the conditions of its reception, emphasizing that 'watching television . . . is not a separate activity undertaken in perfect quiet . . . in a darkened room . . . as in academic studies' (Hobson, 1982:110). TV is, to borrow Ellis's words, 'a profoundly domestic phenomenon' (Ellis, 1982:113). It was in the setting of home and family that the women in Hobson's research had to arrange their viewing of *Crossroads*, incorporating enjoyment of the programme into the regular duties of home management.

An additional aspect of these women's consumption of soap opera – one which had already been touched on in Hobson's 'Housewives and the Mass Media' paper – was the low status or value that their pleasures have in the wider 'cultural economy'. The knowledges they possessed as fans of the genre – the cultural competences admired by Brunsdon – were worth little outside the fictional space of the serial and the everyday world of its followers. This was especially true for fans of *Crossroads*, probably the most devalued of all British soaps until its eventual removal from the schedules in the mid–1980s. Understandably, viewers who spoke to Hobson were either apologetic or defensive about watching the programme. Some seemed to accept, with reluctance, the dismissive judgements made by TV critics and by husbands, yet others were perfectly well aware of the rich stock of feminine skills at their disposal. Compare, for instance, the following three extracts from the interview transcripts:

I mean they're terrible actors, I know that, and I just see through that, you know. I just, now and then I think, 'Oh God, that's silly', you know, but it's not the acting I'm interested in, it's what's going on. I suppose I'm nosey. (quoted in Hobson, 1982:117)

I like family stories and things like that . . . I mean Jill had her ups and downs, didn't she, and so did Meg . . . I mean that can happen in real life, can't it? To me, it's a real family story. (Hobson, 1982:122)

men are not supposed to show their emotions and feelings and so if they watch 'Crossroads' and something comes on like Glenda and Kath talking, then they think it's just stupid and unrealistic because they are not brought up to accept emotional situations. . . . They don't like it 'cause it's sometimes sentimental . . . I don't know any men who watch it. (Hobson, 1982:109)

Here, the first speaker almost excuses herself for liking a serial that is treated in such a derogatory fashion by non-fans. Significantly, she picks up on a criticism commonly directed at soap opera – the often misplaced allegation of 'bad acting' – and she goes on to undermine her own pleasures by claiming to be 'nosey' (a category of behaviour which has negative cultural connotations). The second quote comes from Hobson's discussion with an elderly woman who is, by contrast, unashamed of her enjoyment in the programme and enthusiastic about what she sees as its realistic qualities. When these words are juxtaposed with the final comments referenced above, divergences between masculine and feminine readings become evident. The last speaker knows very well that *Crossroads* is only 'true to life' in the realm of sentimentality, emotion and gossip. For men who lack the abilities required to access this sphere of intimate talk and feeling – or who are unable to admit they have the necessary skills – soaps can appear 'stupid' and 'unrealistic'.

Remarks of this sort raise a series of important issues concerning our understanding of realism. How can the same text be true to life for one reader but not for another? Is realism simply a style of representation – the deployment of particular naturalistic codes in classic Hollywood films or TV documentaries (the sense in which several of the theorists featured in Chapter 2 use the term)? Or should we be speaking in the plural, locating different 'realisms' in the relations between specific media products and consumers? For answers to these difficult questions, and for a valuable contribution to the debates around gender and genre, I look next at Ang's *Watching 'Dallas'* (1985). There, Ang offers a 'symptomatic reading' of forty-two letters sent to her by Dutch followers of the popular American soap. The writers, almost all of whom were women, replied to an advertisement she had placed in a magazine in Holland called *Viva*. Although her research data were in the form of written responses to the text, and despite the absence of any background material on the correspondents or their contexts of consumption, Ang's analytical aims were nonetheless in keeping with the broad objectives of reception studies. She may have been severely limited by relying solely on the letters rather than on interview tapes and observational notes, but Ang produced a qualitative interpretation of audience decodings all the same – setting herself the task of explaining viewers' engagements and identifications with *Dallas*.

Many of those who responded said they found the programme to be realistic, and indicated that their enjoyment was derived in large measure from the serial's relevance to everyday experience : 'I like watching it . . . because those problems and intrigues, the big and little pleasures and troubles occur in our own lives too . . . it's really ordinary daily problems more than anything that occur in it and that you recognize . . . the characters reflect the daily life of a family, I find' (Ang, 1985:43). Bearing in mind the obvious material imbalance between the Ewings' extravagant lifestyle at Southfork and the day-to-day domestic circumstances of most TV viewers in the Netherlands, we might be surprised initially – as Ang was – to find that *Dallas* is perceived by these letter writers as 'taken from life'. For Hobson's *Crossroads* fans, at least there were strong geographical ties which bound together text and reader. Ang was therefore left with the predicament of how to account for the puzzling claims made by correspondents. Her solution was to introduce the concept of 'emotional realism'. She proposed that, in this instance, consumers were expressing a recognition of 'the real' at a connotative level – as opposed to the level of denotation. They empathized with characters and situations in what is basically a family tragedy. Existing theories of realist representation were, according to Ang, inadequate for the task of explaining the associative meanings produced by her watchers of *Dallas*. It was an emotional resonance which made the fiction real and pleasurable for them.

As melodrama, *Dallas* embodies what Ang calls the 'tragic structure of feeling'. I mentioned earlier that British and Australian serials have sometimes been ridiculed for their absence of dramatic action, but critics of American soap operas usually accuse them of the reverse – of overplaying sensational incident (the idea that 'too much happens' – see Glaessner, 1990, on this contradiction). It is true that in the life of the Ewing family there is a literally unbelievable stream of major events and crises. The purpose of such exaggerated plot lines, though, is to heighten emotional tension. To try to dismiss the programme as 'overdone' is to miss the point completely. It actually strives to stir the passions with its continual round of remakable incidents. Whether or not audiences are duly stirred depends, of course, on the cultural dispositions that are brought to the text by its readers:

> the tragic structure of feeling, which is inscribed in the meaning-structure of 'Dallas', will not automatically and obviously agree with the meanings viewers apply to 'Dallas'. That will only happen if they are sensitive to it. In other words, the tragic structure of feeling suggested by 'Dallas' will only make sense if one can and will project oneself onto, i.e. recognize, a 'melodramatic imagination'. Viewers must therefore have a certain . . . orientation to understand and evaluate 'Dallas' in a melodramatic way. (Ang, 1985:79)

This 'melodramatic imagination' is, in Ang's opinion, a predominantly feminine recognition. She notes that it emerges out of a willingness to face 'life's torments' from a certain psychological standpoint. It results in a vicarious identification with characters such as Sue Ellen or Miss Ellie – a wife driven to drink by her scheming husband and a mother who carries the worries of the whole family on her shoulders – both seen as 'really human' by several of the women who wrote letters. These soap opera heroines can hardly be held up by feminists as examples of progressive role models. To imagine yourself as Sue Ellen is to take up a position of powerlessness and self-destruction – a profoundly masochistic mode of femininity. Yet in a later piece, Ang (1990b) argues that there may be a necessary place for melodramatic identifications in a politics of social change. She speaks about her personal experience as a viewer of soaps before commenting that:

sentimental and melancholic feelings of masochism and powerlessness, which are the core of the melodramatic imagination, are an implicit recognition . . . of the fact that identity . . . takes its shape under circumstances not of one's own making . . . identification with a melodramatic character like Sue Ellen also validates those feelings by offering women some room to indulge in them, to let go as it were, in a moment of intense, self-centred abandon . . . a moment in which the complexity of the task of being a woman is fully realized. . . . No wonder melodrama is often accompanied with tears. (Ang, 1990b:86–7)

She even goes so far as to suggest that feminism as a practice has a distinctly melodramatic edge. After all, it is a struggle of transformation which is frequently marked by frustration and despair. The difference is that, where Sue Ellen was seemingly resigned to a lack of power, those involved in sexual politics continue to fight against the odds for it.

Popular programmes like *Dallas* obviously don't go out to a wholly female audience, and Ang realized that there must be pleasures in the text which are on offer to men as well. Speculating about masculine readings, she wondered whether enjoyment came more from a recognition of 'the business relations and problems, the cowboy elements, and the power and wealth represented' (Ang, 1985:118). For men, she suspects, there is not the same orientation towards the tragic structure of feeling (although, as I have stressed, we can't rule out the possibility of male viewers having the odd melodramatic moment – even if this is far less central to senses of masculine subjectivity). In a recently published survey of prime-time soaps in Britain and the US, Christine Geraghty (1991) traces the growing trend of introducing narrative features stolen from other genres into the continuous serial. To widen the appeal of their programmes, producers are bringing in a greater range of male characters – developing plot lines which are reminiscent of crime series or Westerns, and working with business or sports themes. British soaps like *Brookside* and *Eastenders*, each born in the 1980s, are examples of the process that Jane Root (1986) has tellingly referred to as 'defeminization'. However, I would want to insist that in its continued emphasis on interpersonal intrigue and its reliance on gossip for storytelling, the popular serial retains the basic ingredients of what Hobson called a 'feminine world' of TV. We should remember also that the daytime schedules are still populated with a range of soaps which conform to the traditional formula.

Before leaving Ang's *Watching 'Dallas'*, it is important to discuss a further dimension to her study – one that is not strictly relevant to my review of work on gender and genre, but which merits passing mention here. I am thinking of the implications that her research has for debates about cultural imperialism – and especially for notions of 'Americanization' (Tomlinson, 1991, is a useful general primer on the terms of debate). At the height of the show's popularity, the name 'Dallas' became a password for entry into arguments concerning the global influence of a US ideology and lifestyle (so, for instance, fears about the increasing amount of North American programmes on European TV stations have come to be expressed as the 'wall-to-wall "Dallas" ' scenario). Alongside previous exports like 'Coca Cola' or 'Levi's' jeans, this soap was regarded by some 'as yet more evidence of the threat posed by American-style commercial culture against "authentic" national cultures and identities' (Ang, 1985:2). Undoubtedly, US exporters have enjoyed economic domination of world markets in cultural goods over many years now – making massive financial gains from the sales of commodities overseas. The cultural domination thesis is harder to prove, though. When stated, it is often based on the assumption of an undifferentiated effect and is rarely explored by way of empirical research. On the evidence of Ang's modest book, we must already have considerable doubts about the straightforward penetration of 'Americanism'. The meanings her letter writers construct are determined principally by their gendered conditions of existence on another continent, rather than by any message to do with the virtues of US society.

Complementary inquiries into cross-cultural readings of *Dallas*, carried out by Elihu Katz and Tamar Liebes (1985; see also Liebes & Katz, 1990), have revealed a wide variety of critical interpretations and responses. Much of their interview work was done amongst different ethnic groups living in Israel – but they have interesting observations too on the serial's lack of success in Japan. While it would be foolish for us to jump immediately to a 'no influence' conclusion in the wake of these studies, we surely have to reassess the problem of media imperialism as one involving an interdiscursive encounter. Dick Hebdige (1982) – in his essay 'Towards a Cartography of Taste 1935–1962' – shows how American styles and goods were regularly appropriated by sections of the British working class as symbols of opposition to traditional cultural values and aesthetic judgements. He talks about particular forms of product design ('streamlining') or popular music (jazz, rock 'n' roll) functioning as polysemic texts on their insertion into the British national context. They were simultaneously objects of pleasure for their consumers and objects of revulsion for those middle-class commentators who saw them as 'vulgar'. Clearly, then, the issues are politically complex and the meanings of imported commodities are relatively autonomous from their position in an international economic transaction.

The final example of ethnographic research on 'feminine audiences' to be discussed in this section is Janice Radway's work on the household consumption of romantic fiction (Radway, 1987). An academic based in the US, Radway has a curious intellectual background in American studies and popular literary criticism. Her introduction to the London edition of *Reading the Romance* explains how – operating out of that tradition – she was able to raise questions about women's reading which were similar to those being explored by British writers in the field of cultural studies. At the time she was conducting her empirical investigation of romance readers, Radway was unaware of the kind of feminist scholarship practised by Brunsdon, Hobson and others like Angela McRobbie at the Birmingham CCCS. Themes that pass through their writings – of everyday life, domestic labour and gendered cultural competences (what Radway would have termed 'variable literacies') – intersect her work as well. The fact that she was external to mainstream mass communications research made it possible for her to think outside the limits of the behavioural paradigm. Consequently, amongst media and cultural theorists in the UK, Radway's book has received enthusiastic critical acclaim as a US export!

Still, there are some significant differences between *Reading the Romance* and material covered in the preceding pages. These are chiefly to do with the structure and function of romantic fiction in relation to the continuous serial. Where soaps are never-ending stories which are pleasurable precisely because they can articulate the emotional reality of viewers' daily experiences, readers of the romantic novel go in search of narrative resolution and a complete release from their domestic circumstances. The appeal that reading appears to hold for Radway's consumers is located in the potential it has to 'transport' them, albeit temporarily, away from their day-to-day routines – and into an imagined world of fantasy. That she is dealing with literary fictions rather than TV programmes is another relevant variation. Books usually require a type of attention which television as a medium does not always demand, and this has implications for the meaning of acts of consumption. It is a self-evident distinction to draw – yet the comparison forces us to qualify our use of the all-encompassing phrase 'texts and readers'. As I have maintained throughout my overview so far, there can be no single, generalized model of text–reader relations which applies equally and adequately across all audio-visual and print media. A social semiotics of reception must remain sensitive to the specificities of medium, genre and mode of engagement.

Radway's book gives a detailed account of involvements with a 'community' of women readers in the Midwestern town she calls Smithton. Her point of access to this loosely constituted group was a contact named Dot, who worked in the town store that specialized in selling romantic fiction. Dot introduced Radway to regular customers, enabling her to talk at length with the women about their pleasures and preferences – and what they told her actually served to widen the study's analytical focus. Having set out originally to investigate consumers' interpretations of the literature, she realized during the course of the research that it would be crucial to consider 'the meaning of romance reading as a social event in a familial context' (Radway, 1987:7). In other words, for the Smithton group, the very act of reading the romance was as significant as the sense they made of the narrative. It provided them with an opportunity to mark out a time and space of their own in a day which, as wives and mothers, they devoted largely to the care of others.

Rosalind Coward (1984:199) has written of fantasy as 'the "other place" of the mind . . . like a secret room or garden, to be visited in a spare moment'. She says that women 'talk of looking forward to the moment of escape when they can enter the rich and creative world of their own minds, hidden from the rest of the world' – and it is exactly this sort of imaginative excursion which is warmly anticipated by the Smithton readers. As Dot herself explained: 'when I am reading . . . my body is in the room but the rest of me is not' (quoted in Radway, 1987:87). To the frequent irritation and annoyance of husbands, the women would employ books to erect a 'do not disturb' sign. They treated themselves to relaxation by cutting off mentally from the domestic surroundings. Reading silently often entails blocking out an immediate social setting and – to borrow Radway's words – 'what reading takes them away from is the psychologically demanding and emotionally draining task of attending to the physical and affective needs of their families' (Radway, 1987:91–2). These circumstances forced the researcher to critically unpack the idea of 'escapism', which has traditionally been used as a derogatory term. Her contention was that, when contextualized within the women's everyday experiences of home and family, the will to be transported elsewhere through the medium of fantasy literature is perfectly understandable. The books facilitate an escape in two interrelated senses of the word, both of which were expressed by interviewees:

> On the one hand, they used the term literally to describe the act of denying the present, which they believe they accomplish each time they begin to read a book and are drawn into its story. On the other hand, they used the word in a more figurative fashion to give substance to the somewhat vague but nonetheless intense sense of relief they experience by identifying with a heroine whose life does not resemble their own in certain crucial respects. (Radway, 1987:90)

This second usage is, of course, important in establishing why the women seek escape via the genre of romance and not through other types of literature. They see in the heroine a character who (although she suffers an initial humiliation or rejection by the male object of her desire) is finally united with a man who shows himself to be capable of caring. Within the narrative logic of romantic fiction, the hero's coldness is eventually melted so that he is then in a position to demonstrate tenderness towards the heroine (see Radway, 1987:150). Radway's readers actively associate with someone in the fantasy who is, in the end, nurtured – for in their own daily lives they are destined only to nurture others. Pleasure here is compensatory. Unlike the open-ended narration of TV soaps – where enjoyment is based mainly on gossip and speculation about future plot developments – romances are 'feminine fictions' that depend on rather predictable closures. The resolutions in question are ones that simultaneously free the Smithton women from their domestic conditions, yet confine them to the discourses of heterosexual romance which put them there in the first place.

Amongst the best-known advocates of ethnography as a method for cultural inquiry is Paul Willis – who has spoken about the scope that fieldwork gives us for being surprised by what we find, 'of reaching knowledge not prefigured in one's starting paradigm' (Willis, 1980:90). *Reading the Romance* bears this out, and is a study which does perhaps more than any other discussed so far to illustrate the advantages of qualitative research on media reception. The strength of Radway's approach was her willingness to be swayed by the women's own accounts of their consumption practices. Naturally, she moved beyond those accounts to try to offer a theoretical explanation and political assessment of them – but as she admits in the passage reproduced below, the words of Dot's customers moved her in a previously unforeseen direction:

> it was the women readers' construction of the act of romance reading as a 'declaration of independence' that surprised me into the realization that the

> meaning of their media use was multiply determined . . . and that to get at its complexity it would be helpful to distinguish analytically between the significance of the event of reading and the meaning of the text. (Radway, 1987:7)

Textual analysis alone, or even a narrowly conceived investigation of decodings, could not have anticipated the division Radway identifies. Commenting on her work, the social theorist John Thompson (1990:312) has stressed that if we 'focus on the activity of reading as distinct from the texts which are read, we can see that reading romances is, to some extent, a way of resisting or protesting against a situation which the Smithton women experience as unfulfilling'. Radway's findings alert us again to the potentially contradictory dynamics of popular media reception – which can be at once resistant and compliant, neither neatly coincident with a dominant ideology nor simply a terrain of spontaneous opposition (the politics of 'the popular' is a theme I will return to in due course).

In drawing this part of the chapter to a close, I ought to make note of a key omission – not just from my own discussion, but from the development of audience ethnography more generally. While there is now a wealth of valuable material on feminine genres and on the contexts of women's media consumption, there is still very little work in reception studies which has given sustained critical attention to masculine reading pleasures and competences. Maria Black and Rosalind Coward (1990) have highlighted the difficulties of getting men to recognize that they are 'gendered' at all – arguing that men tend to think of themselves primarily as 'people' and to designate woman as 'the sex'. Similarly, Lidia Curti (1988:155) has pointed out that : 'when most male critics . . . venture into matters of gender they automatically mean female. The "male stuff" still has a right to be considered neutral.' Curti's remarks clearly challenge researchers to address the gendered constitution of masculine tastes and, with the current growth of critical interest in masculinities (for instance, Hearn & Morgan, 1990), future years should witness the emergence of new inquiries into 'men's genres'. Recent ethnographers of family TV consumption do touch on masculine preferences and styles of viewing (as we will see next when we look at Morley's *Family Television*) – although their observations need following through with a detailed analysis of discursive forms and subjectivities. Existing examples which hint at ways forward are Derek Longhurst's essay (1989) on masculine discourses in science fiction, and David Jackson's autobiographical reflections (1990) on, amongst other things, the role played by boys' adventure comics in helping to articulate his gender identity. However, these two pieces do not rely on an empirical investigation of audience groupings – and they tend to lack the rich insights offered by feminist work on soap opera or romance.

The Power Relations of Family Viewing

I now want to pick up some of the threads from my earlier commentary on Lull's work, and to consider at greater length the dynamic activities of TV reception in domestic settings. In the main, my discussion here will revolve around Morley (1986) and his efforts to understand family viewing as a situated 'social event'. The study was based on conversational interviews with members of eighteen south London households (all drawn from roughly the same class and ethnic background – white working class/lower middle class – and all nuclear family units). It shared with Lull's investigations an emphasis on the 'relational' aspects of watching TV, on the relationships that viewers in the home have to the medium and to each other. As I have already suggested, he is more acutely aware than Lull of sitting-room 'politics', seeing the familial context first and foremost as an arena of power. For Morley, practices of media consumption were to be read as signs of a cultural struggle between men and women in the domestic environment (we could say between parents and children too – see Simpson, 1987). No doubt TV also facilitates moments of genuine harmony – but it is conflicts and inequalities that are central to *Family Television*, as they must be to any critical anthropology of everyday life.

Apart from Lull's inquiries into the social uses of TV, there were further projects and perspectives that Morley acknowledged as influential in shaping his research. One of these influences came from a rather unexpected source – the family psychology of Irene Goodman and others, who had become interested in studying viewing behaviour as a way to explore the operations of the family as a system (Morley, 1986:22–30). In the past, what went on around the dining-room table had often been the focus of attention for such psychologists. Questions would be asked about who prepares and serves the food, which rules govern manners during the meal, or what topics of conversation are permitted while household members are eating. Goodman was proposing that TV consumption can, in turn, tell us as much about domestic processes. Somebody else whose writings Morley drew on and admired was the German academic, Hermann Bausinger. Describing certain features of a weekend's media-related activity in the lives of a family called the Meiers, Bausinger (1984) attempted to analyse their interpersonal dynamics within what he termed the 'specific semantics of the everyday'. So, in an incident on the Saturday evening, Herr Meier tells his wife she's looking tired: 'She is surprised that he cares, but she goes up to bed. He fetches a beer from the kitchen. Unfortunately, his wife comes back to get a drink. Suddenly the penny drops. "My God! The sports programme. That's why you sent me to bed!" ' (Bausinger, 1984:348). Subtle negotiations of this kind – taking place between a husband and a wife around the TV set – only make sense if we contextualize them in the broader daily circumstances of their embedding.

Two researchers who collaborated with Bausinger, Jan-Uwe Rogge and Klaus Jensen (1988), have presented a wealth of additional material gathered over a five year period in ethnographic projects at the University of Tübingen. Their interpretation of the data is strongly informed by a particular analytical technique in family therapy known as 'systems theory':

> By 'family system' we mean that all events and all activities (including those having to do with television and other media) have a systematic character. . . . For example, the father who reads the newspaper at the breakfast table ignores other members of

the family; the mother who prohibits television for the children is boycotted in this by the father; the sports programme causes the family to postpone their evening meal together; during the ensuing discord, the television is on in the background to enforce silence or to make the stillness easier to bear. (Rogge & Jensen, 1988:86)

This type of psychological 'systems' perspective undoubtedly helps to shed light on the relational practices of domestic life. There is a danger, though, because family therapy – rather like Lull's uses typology – has tended to take insufficient account of the power relations between household members which, as I have persistently stated, are so important for critical reception ethnographies (a useful feminist critique of the systems approach to families can be found in Perelberg & Miller, 1990). It is a perspective which often rests on the naive assumption that men and women are equal in the system to begin with.

Morley found that this was emphatically not the case in his eighteen London households. Chiefly as a result of the different positions they occupied within divisions of labour, the men and women in the *Family Television* study actually had very different feelings about the homes they lived in. The meanings of domestic space for husbands and wives varied considerably. For him, it was fundamentally a site of leisure – defined in opposition to an external place of work. For her – even if she had paid employment elsewhere – it was a space in which she was rarely ever 'off duty'. These women were still responsible for housework while situated in the domestic context. As sociologist of leisure, Rosemary Deem (1986:80), has written: 'The home for most women, employed or not, is a workplace in a way that is true for few men. . . . Workplaces do not convert easily into places for leisure. Especially for women who are at home all day, undone domestic chores and other aspects of housework are omnipresent.' (Think back here to the mother in Hobson's ethnography who had to fit in watching *Crossroads* as she fed her two young children.)

The disparity in their 'relative freedoms' to partake in domestic entertainment led to a gap between masculine and feminine styles of viewing – with many of the women participating in a form of distracted consumption. Although the men interviewed by Morley expressed a preference for watching quietly and attentively, the wives' viewing habits usually involved the 'performance of at least one other domestic activity (ironing, etc.) at the same time' (Morley, 1986:150). Sitting in front of the TV, on its own, was felt by several of the women to be unproductive – 'I knit because I think I'm wasting my time just watching. . . . You think, "Oh my God, I should have done this or that". . . . There's always something else . . . I can watch anything while I'm doing the ironing' (quotes from Morley, 1986:151). Engaging with TV in a concentrated gaze, then, was something that husbands seemed far better placed to do. They were without the particular sense of responsibility to others that was constantly experienced by their wives.

Only at times when the rest of the family were absent did women have an opportunity to indulge in the 'guilty pleasures' of a solo viewing, taking a complete break from household duties. Morley (1986:160) cited the case of one female viewer who 'particularly enjoys watching early morning television at the weekends . . . as these are the only occasions when her husband and sons "sleep in", these are, by the same token, the only occasions when she can watch television attentively, without keeping half an eye on the needs of others'. Such stolen moments of relaxation come closest to the escapist practices of Radway's romance readers – but because TV is more frequently consumed *en famille*, occasions like the one described here are the exception rather than the rule. Nevertheless, if we are to develop a working model of situated TV use, it is important for us not to lose sight of instances like this. As a fellow British audience ethnographer, Ann Gray (1987:51) has said, the domestic context 'is not singular and unchanging, but plural and open to different permutations'. Indeed, Gray's own research on video recorders in the home (to which I return in Chapter 4) revealed a situation where women who lived close to each other had clubbed together to hire films they watched communally whilst children were out at school. They were able to resist the isolation of housework – and some of the guilt associated with what Morley termed a 'solo' viewing – by constructing a collective 'women only' event for themselves:

> The idea of viewing together during the day for this particular network of women living on the same street came when one of them found herself continually returning the video tapes which her husband had hired the night before. She discovered that there were films which she would like to watch but which her husband never hired. . .
> The major impetus for a viewing group like this is that films which women enjoy watching are rarely, if ever, hired by their male partners for viewing together because they consider such films to be 'trivial' and 'silly', and women are laughed at for enjoying them. (Gray, 1987:48–50)

Inevitably, this brings us back to issues of gender and genre – but also, and crucially, it takes us forward to questions concerning power and control over viewing choices. Whether it is a decision on what video to hire, or simply on which channel to watch, some household members have more choice than others. In *Family Television*, there are strong echoes of Hobson's findings on the 'two worlds' of TV. Morley confirmed that men have, or at least claim to have, a greater interest in news, current affairs and documentaries than in the fictional output preferred by wives and daughters. Husbands typically dismissed feminine genres for exactly the reasons women enjoy them ('it's a fantasy world . . . no, I can't get on with that'). However, it is the ability which the men in his study have to impose their preferences on the rest of the family that stands out most clearly. Morley referred to the remote control device – or 'zapper' – as 'the symbolic possession of the father . . . used almost exclusively by him . . . a highly visible symbol of condensed power relations (the descendant of the medieval mace perhaps?)'. These interview extracts demonstrate women's frustrations with masculine dominance of the gadget:

> It is aggravating, because I can be watching something and all of a sudden he turns it over to get the football result . . .

> I don't get much chance, because he sits there with the automatic control beside him and that's it . . . I get annoyed because I can be watching a programme and he's

flicking channels to see if a programme on the other side is finished, so he can record something . . . I just say, 'For goodness' sake, leave it alone'. I don't get the chance to use the control. I don't get near it . . .

The control's always next to dad's chair. It doesn't come away when dad's here. It stays right there. (Morley, 1986:149)

Actually, there are some quite striking parallels between these remarks and accounts given by women in a recent British ethnography of domestic food consumption (Charles & Kerr, 1988). If family psychologists like Goodman have switched their attention from meal-time rituals to TV viewing practices, so media theorists might equally turn to food preparation and dietary preferences for another access point to household dynamics and power relations. Sociologists Nickie Charles and Marion Kerr found that while the women they interviewed were responsible for cooking, the content of meals was usually determined by the husband's choice. The wives' tastes were less conservative – they were willing to try out new flavours and foreign dishes – but the men's demands to eat so-called 'proper meals' limited what could be served up:

My husband is very traditional-minded about food, he doesn't like anything Chinese or foreign, he doesn't like anything with herbs in it . . . so I tend to stick to the same thing most weeks – I rarely buy anything just for myself . . . I'd like to eat all sorts of food, foreign foods, but I don't bother . . . it's too expensive to buy just for myself so I forgo it. (in Charles & Kerr, 1988:70)

If I cook something that's got a whiff of herbs in it he'll put his knife and fork down and say, 'I'm sorry but I'm not eating it' . . . He usually waits until my parents come and I've prepared something a bit out of the ordinary, and he'll leave it. I'm not happy but there again I'll not make a scene. I'm not one for rowing – I'll go off and have a little weep to myself . . .

I cook what I know he will like . . . I mean I won't try things knowing he won't like them. Things like pasta, I know he won't eat that, so I don't cook it. (Charles & Kerr, 1988:72)

Gendered relationships to the different technologies involved – a remote control device and a kitchen cooker – are obviously not the same. Men dominate use of the former but delegate responsibility for operating the latter to women. Still, the dynamic revealed above in each set of quotes is a common one. Where there is a clash of tastes, it is masculine preferences which prevail. Charles and Kerr (1988:71) did find, though, that some wives would make a point of eating what they wished when husbands and children were out in the daytime. For example: 'I have a passion for spaghetti and butter, that kind of thing, which nobody else in the family likes, so occasionally I do that sort of thing when I'm on my own . . . For me . . . a treat is anything which I like and nobody else in the family likes.' Paraphrasing Morley, perhaps we could call this the guilty pleasures of a solo serving? What such comparisons open up, of course, is a further important issue to do with the boundaries of media reception studies. I think we have to ask to what extent Morley's book is really about television at all. In many ways, his work is focussed on processes of domestic interaction and on patterns of household leisure/labour. TV certainly provides him with a starting point for studying those processes, but isn't it just one of several ways in? My own answer (and it is reflected in the last two chapters of the book) is that we should welcome a blurring, or overlapping, between research on audiences and wider studies of cultural consumption, technology and everyday life. Only this blurring can give us a proper insight into the embedded character of reception practices.

So *Family Television* is a signpost for further advances and research agendas – as well as an empirical realization of the developments in Morley's approach since he wrote *The 'Nationwide' Audience*. Like the earlier book, however, it is marked by certain limitations and absences. One of the doubts that Morley (1986:174) expresses in his 'Afterword' is a concern over whether 'there is a tendency in the interviews to slide back towards a parallel analysis of "gendered individuals" rather than a fully-fledged analysis of the dynamics of the family unit'. Having committed himself to an investigation of social power relations within household 'systems', he worried that the research method had failed to grasp the complexity of relational processes in the domestic sphere. For instance, it proved extremely difficult to sustain lengthy conversational interviews involving both children and parents. In practice, younger children were only spoken with briefly towards the end of a visit – and this resulted in the generational dimensions of TV viewing being underexplored.

The other, possibly more important, limitation was the way in which his sample for the study precluded any real comparison between various types of households from a range of social backgrounds. Elsewhere, Morley (1988) defends the decision he made to focus on 'traditional' nuclear families by arguing that the stereotype still retains a strong ideological resonance – even though a minority of people in Britain actually live in circumstances which correspond to it. Richard Paterson (1980) has pointed out, too, that the stereotype is firmly imprinted on the minds of those who arrange the broadcasting schedules. My purpose in raising this as an issue, then, is not simply to criticize the author for an oversight (he is perfectly well aware of the absences) but to highlight gaps in the research literature requiring attention. Given the narrow class, ethnic and geographical locations of the homes in Morley's sample, we need to find out – amongst other things – if gendered uses and interpretations of TV are organized differently outside of the main social groups and family forms represented by his research. In the final chapter of *Family Television*, the notes on 'programme type preference' contain a particularly interesting passage on a household where the wife (a mature student at the local college) possesses more legitimate stocks of cultural capital than her husband (a council flat caretaker). Here the pattern of tastes is almost reversed, with the woman watching current affairs and documentary programmes such as *Newsnight*, *Question Time*, *World in Action* and *Horizon*. She criticizes her partner for not being interested in these texts, and goes on to denigrate popular serials like *Crossroads*, *Eastenders*, *Dallas* and *Dynasty*. What this exceptional case suggests is that feminine tastes can be constituted differently depending on the articulations of gender with educational achievement or class position. Morley (1986:53) himself admits: 'I would be amazed if . . . the gender differentiation within the families in my sample . . . was repeated among highly educated professional families'. Presumably there could also be a significant variation in viewing styles and power negotiations between the nuclear unit and the one-parent home, or between white households and British Asian or Afro-Caribbean families, or across the boundaries of national culture (see Lull, 1988). *Family Television* gives us a vital foothold from which we can explore the diversity of domestic contexts – but there is a good deal of ethnographic fieldwork that remains to be done.

On Children Watching Television

If the practices of younger viewers were something of a blindspot for Morley, the last few years have seen a notable growth in qualitative research on children's interpretations and uses of the medium. By no means all of these new studies address the everyday settings of home and family – often there is a narrower concern with decodings of specific programmes – yet together they offer a potential challenge to established ways of thinking about 'the child viewer'. In the present section, I look at several recent examples of reception analysis in this area. Before reviewing those projects, though, I want to begin my discussion by reflecting for a moment on the more established, traditional perspectives – considering why it is that the 'children and television' couplet has so consistently served as a source of public fears and anxieties. To understand the debate, it is necessary to appreciate its terms and origins.

It seems to me that we ought to start with 'childhood' itself because, as the historian Philippe Ariès (1979) has shown, this is a socially constructed category rather than a pre-given and universally recognized life stage. In contemporary Western cultures, our notions of childhood have led us to treat young people predominantly as 'innocents' who are in need of adult protection and supervision (Jackson, 1982). On the whole, children are seen as passive victims of the influences around them – absorbing what they watch and hear without the capacity for active discrimination. Combine that construction with the generally low cultural status of popular television in our society and the reasons for anxiety become evident. Moreover, TV's position in the private domain (precisely the place where younger family members are supposed to be shielded from the outside world) frequently results in insecurities about the sounds and images being transmitted. David Oswell (1991), in his fascinating work on the early formation of institutional discourses around the child viewer, examines the fears of psychologists and doctors from the 1950s – that children might be subject to delinquent behaviour or a disrupted education, and that watching too much TV could cause bad eyesight or even a displaced jaw ('malocclusion'). These kinds of ideas regarding the negative impact of the medium on innocent minds and bodies have characterized investigations of children's TV consumption ever since. Amongst the latest condemnations of broadcasting for its harmful effects on the young is a piece which is tellingly entitled *The Disappearance of Childhood* (Postman, 1982).

On the opening page of her book, *The Lively Audience*, Australian media critic Patricia Palmer (1986:1) writes:

> Research on television and children cannot take a neutral stance. It enters into a public arena where the lines of debate have already been drawn and the verdict against television seems already to have been delivered – television is 'bad' for children and the more TV they watch, the worse it is.

These are the circumstances in which Palmer and a number of other reception analysts (I talk below about Hodge & Tripp, 1986; Buckingham, 1987, 1990) have sought to make an intervention and to shift the current lines of debate. In keeping with the aims and intentions of audience ethnography, they have concentrated on children's active engagements with TV and tried to dispel the myth of the 'square-eyed' juvenile – endeavouring to comprehend programmes and viewing practices from the child's own perspective. Their conclusions have profound implications for our approach to childhood, even though the actual category remains intact in their studies, and there are also important educational issues raised in relation to the concept of 'literacy'.

Within her broadly ethnographic framework, Palmer (1986, 1988) carried out a three-stage project employing multiple strategies of inquiry. She began by recording individual conversational interviews in primary schools with a total of sixty-four children. Discussions were initiated by asking deliberately open-ended questions – 'Do you watch television?', 'What do you watch?' – and the direction of conversations was guided primarily by interviewees. In addition, the child was encouraged to draw a picture of him- or herself watching TV. At the second stage, a small team of researchers between them visited twenty-three homes for spells of part-icipant observation. These observers spent several hours of viewing time in the company of children and returned to the households on three separate occasions. Palmer assumes, as Lull did, that this mode of participation in daily domestic life enables a more 'naturalistic' account to be compiled. She is aware, however, that research relations in the field are 'symbolic interactions' of a sort – rather like encounters between the media and their audiences (Palmer, 1986:12). The final part of the study consisted of a larger, questionnaire-based survey involving nearly 500 school pupils. If the multiple choice survey seems out of keeping with the qualitative stages of the project, Palmer stresses that material for the third phase was shaped by the earlier conversations and observations. Questionnaires even incorporated versions of the initial drawings – showing diverse activities in front of the TV set. Each of the three elements of her project was conducted with a different sample group of children, but all phases drew on a mixture of eight-to-nine and eleven-to-twelve-year-old boys and girls from varied class locations in the Sydney area.

'The first task of this research,' says Palmer (1986:28), 'was to gain a systematic understanding of children's ways of defining television . . . their own experience of television viewing' – and it was abundantly clear from the outset that talking with them about TV evoked positive feelings of excitement and pleasure. When asked what they watched, the immediate response was to list a string of favourite programmes. She reports that none of the original replies included any comments on content that was disliked or experiences that were unpleasant. In sketches made for the researcher, the children represented themselves with smiles on their faces and occasionally pictured scenes from a particular show on the screen (drawings are undoubtedly an inventive method of entering the lived cultures of young viewers, although we probably need to know a little more about the conventions of that genre before we can properly 'read' the images produced – in what other circumstances are smiling faces drawn?). The survey material provided interesting evidence of a discrepancy between children's definitions and the perceptions that adults have of their TV consumption. While nearly 60 per cent of youngsters taking part agreed with the statement that 'TV is great', only 14 per cent of those thought that was their mother's opinion and still less believed it was a feeling shared by teachers (see Palmer, 1988:143).

Observations in the domestic setting focussed on children's skilful manipulation of the space around the TV to create a viewing situation which suited their purposes. Part of the pleasure involved in watching preferred programmes was the production of a 'cosy intimacy' – sitting or lying close to the screen, accompanied by familiar objects like cushions, blankets, beanbags or household pets (Palmer, 1986:51–7). Whereas parents often worried about them being too close to the TV, and sometimes tried to make rules preventing it, the proximity of children to the set was bound up with their intimate involvement in and enjoyment of a favourite fiction. Once again, there is a difference in the meanings of the viewing activity for adult and for child. Palmer (1988:150) has pointed out that this form of rapt attention – which can be seen by adults as evidence of 'passive gazing' or a 'dream-like trance' – would in fact be rewarded with praise if it was associated with classroom teaching instead of TV reception.

In any case, it wasn't the only type of engagement with the medium identified in her research. She comments on the use of programmes as resources for game playing – both in the home and at school. So two eight-year-olds invent an imaginary news bulletin which they then read on to a cassette recorder in the bedroom (Palmer, 1988:148), and a group of eleven-year-old girls act out scenes from a soap opera in the playground – casting their teacher in the role of 'a real baddie' (Palmer, 1986:111; see Fiske, 1987:69, for his remarks on the re-enacted drama). Also, when questions were posed in the survey about the range of routine practices that would be performed while the set was switched on, replies included 'jump and dance', 'do homework', 'play with toys' and 'eat a snack' (Palmer, 1986:63). Working-class children especially had developed ways of incorporating TV into other tasks. They watched for longer hours than their middle-class counterparts, whose parents could afford to send them to various leisure and recreational activities outside the household – but they generally found more things to do in the presence of television.

Palmer succeeds in demonstrating her key point – that children are active in negotiating their everyday relationships with TV – and by asking how they 'define the situation' for themselves, she starts to counter some long-held views about broadcasting's damaging influence on young people. Unfortunately, in her understandable hurry to oppose these established 'effects' perspectives, she runs the risk of ignoring any ideological force that the medium's sounds and images might have in defining the social world for children. This is not just a difficulty for Palmer, of course. Much of the work featured in the current chapter has turned its direct attention away from problems of textual power, which must not be allowed to slip from the agenda altogether. A further consequence of her emphasis on the child's own experiences and perceptions is that she fails to deal as fully as she could with inter-generational ties and tensions over TV use in the home. As I said earlier, Palmer does touch on parental attitudes to broadcasting – but given the otherwise rich material gathered by her participant observers, we should really have learned more about domestic conventions and conflicts. How does watching television fit in with rules governing bedtime? What frictions can arise if there is a clash of tastes or priorities between parent and child? When does an adult intervene in an attempt to shape interpretations of a programme?

The only existing book which takes such issues on board is a collection of short essays edited by Philip Simpson, *Parents Talking Television* (1987). Contributions are, as the title indicates, written chiefly from the adult's point of view – and the parents doing the talking are almost all media professionals or academics. Even so, these autobiographical accounts serve to illuminate TV's hazardous place in household relations with children. Here are three extracts, each applying to one of the queries I raised at the end of the previous paragraph:

> The main conflict between us and Jessie used to be the 'just five more minutes' plea that was regularly made when bedtime arrived. Tired of arguments we now set rigid bedtimes – 8.30pm on school nights and 9.0pm at weekends. Since television schedules do not always fit in with those times, particularly the 8.30 time, any variation is agreed in advance. Needless to say, Jessie never wants to go to bed earlier than those set times, and she invariably insists on watching to the very last credit of the last allowed programme – and then trying to catch a glimpse of what follows. (Boston, 1987:43)

> In the scramble for the paper every morning as it drops on to the hall floor, when Anna or Ben manage to get it, they turn immediately to the television section, and subsequently plan their evening programme within minutes of getting out of

bed. Sometimes their plans clash with each other's – and ours – and this has led in the past to quite bitter arguments. At their most intense these arguments . . . are amongst the worst rows we've had with the children . . . the compromise position usually reached has been that the person who picked the second shortest straw gets the black and white portable television in their bedroom. (Worpole, 1987:87–8)

Both children went through a period when they were captivated by the lechery and leering of Benny Hill. I do not think that they were drawing on the masturbatory or voyeuristic fantasies which were on offer for the adult male viewer. There was a . . . delight at forms of pantomime, and they were less interested in his endless ballads crammed with double entendres. Nevertheless, we did fall on them and made our views about Benny Hill clearly known. This resulted in Dan laughing gleefully at the antics on the screen, whilst blurting out in rapid fire succession, 'I know it's sexist. I know it's sexist. Just let me see this bit.' (Ferguson, 1987: 57–8)

Stories of this sort confirm what Lull, Morley and Bausinger have been telling us – that TV consumption is as much an interaction between family members as it is between texts and readers. Television is an object around which patterns of domestic authority and resistance are regularly played out. Its role in the realization and temporary resolution of conflicts across a generational divide is clearly illustrated in the instances cited above. However, these writings on power struggles in the private sphere can never completely replace research which attends closely to viewers' readings of a particular text. In many ways, the projects I refer to next have concerns with 'decoding' that match them up rather better with work covered in Chapter 2. I include them here, though, because they add weight to Palmer's fundamental argument about the child making creative use of TV. As we might expect, they are stronger on issues of representation and critical response – and weaker than Palmer when it comes to situating children's viewing in its usual household context (neither of the main studies discussed below has explored the home environment).

Bob Hodge and David Tripp (1986), in another Australian study, showed the first five minutes of a twenty-minute cartoon to groups of schoolchildren who were drawn from the same age brackets as those in Palmer's sample. The cartoon that they screened (*Fangface*) was unfamiliar to its young viewers – yet the children were able to speculate on the narrative outcome with an impressive degree of accuracy. And even where guesses proved wrong, the justifications offered were perfectly plausible. By forging intertextual links with fictions that were familiar to them, like *Scooby Doo* or *The Incredible Hulk*, group members could generate endings to a story that hadn't been seen before. The researchers argue that this is possible because a 'transformational model' is being employed : 'A new programme is read by them as a transformation of a number of abstract types. . . . Children's grasp of the rules of a programme type is generative – that is, they can project new and correct versions' (Hodge & Tripp, 1986:60).

As well as predicting plot developments and demonstrating their

knowledge of TV 'grammar', the children were adept at locating basic
ideological oppositions that underpinned the narrative. They quickly
separated 'good' from 'bad' characters, and were well aware of the textual
signifiers which constructed such distinctions (voice, face, colour, etc.). One
boy, Chris – to the amusement of his whole group – went on to distinguish
between 'goodies' and what he chose to call 'goody-goodies', although
Hodge and Tripp point out that the values inscribed in the text are not
necessarily shared by all its viewers. The laughter prompted by the boy's
comments appeared to indicate 'a simultaneous recognition and resistance
of the ideological rules of the cartoon universe' (Hodge & Tripp, 1986:54).
Indeed, the following material from the transcripts supports this case:

> *Interviewer*: Why would you like to be The Heap? He was a baddie.
> *Alan*: Oh, I like being The Hulk (children laugh).
> *Interviewer*: What would you do, if you woke up one day and you were The
> Heap, and you had to go off to school, what would you do when you got
> there? . . .
> *Kara*: [*looks at Alan*] Scare the teacher.
> *Alan*: Yeah, scare the teacher out of her wits and then muck around in the
> classroom.

Alan – who makes an intertextual slip by referring to 'The Hulk' –
recognizes exactly how the cartoon character in question has been classified
within the oppositions of the text, but resists the ideological construction he
is offered by openly identifying himself with the 'baddie'. The imagined
association between TV fiction and classroom context, in which this boy
fantasizes about terrifying his teacher, has similarities with the playground
re-enactment of a soap opera by the girls in Palmer's ethnography. Of
course, it was their teacher whom they cast as 'a real baddie'. In both cases,
however, television provides a resource for expressing frustrations with the
experience of school.

Drawing conclusions from the research, Hodge and Tripp (1986:214)
suggest that children are highly 'literate' when it comes to understanding the
representational codes of TV – and call on educationalists and parents to
'take this generally despised area of children's lives . . . more seriously and
with greater respect'. They propose that, rather than shunning the medium,
schools should give television studies a central place on the curriculum (the
argument for media education has also been put by others – Masterman,
1985; and Lusted, 1991, are the best examples). The willingness shown by
Hodge and Tripp to contest traditional definitions of literacy, and their
reappraisal of children's engagements with popular media forms, connects
their work with some of that being done in the UK at London University's
Institute of Education. For instance, Gemma Moss's analysis (1989) of
schoolgirls' creative writing has revealed the inventive ways in which
romance and photo-love narratives can be appropriated and, to an extent,
subverted. These genres, usually dismissed by teachers as 'clichéd', made it
possible for the teenage authors to articulate the contradictory feelings they
have about initial romantic encounters with the opposite sex. David

Buckingham, too, in *Public Secrets* (1987) – and in his ongoing project at the Institute on 'The Development of Television Literacy' – has focussed on young people's active decodings of popular TV drama.

Public Secrets is a book which set out to investigate the success of what was then a new BBC serial, *Eastenders*. It addressed institutional setting, representational form and audience consumption – and, partly because Buckingham saw the text as having 'cult status' at the time amongst schoolchildren in London, he chose to carry out the interviews for his reception study with viewers in that age group (ranging from seven up to eighteen years old). His decision to look at *Eastenders* from the viewpoint of children was interesting for a further reason. The BBC had come under attack from a well known moral welfare campaigner in Britain, Mary Whitehouse, who accused the programme of undermining family values and threatening the innocence of its younger audience. Story lines that incorporated marital conflict or domestic violence, a single mother working as a stripper to earn extra money, and the constant use of 'bad language' were disturbing for Whitehouse – particularly since the serial was being screened before the scheduler's nine o'clock evening watershed (Buckingham, 1987:146–8). A similar panic over the programme's supposedly damaging effects had surrounded the suicide attempt made by Angie, then a leading character in the fiction. Tabloid newspapers carried reports of 'copycat' suicides after the episode was broadcast. In Buckingham's discussions, though, children as young as ten were moved by the drama and yet retained a critical distance which even enabled some to ridicule what they watched. Here the topic of conversation is the moment when Angie's husband, Den, finds her close to death from an overdose: 'She was like a dummy! . . . And he said "Speak to me! Speak to me!" [*laughter*] . . . . He was really crying. . . . You felt really sorry for him' (Buckingham, 1987:166).

For these fans, and for several who spoke in the interviews, there was a continual shifting:

> back and forth between two positions – at certain points, they appear to be judging the programme and the characters from outside the fictional world, while at others they seem to accept the reality of that world, and make their judgements, as it were, from inside it . . . they clearly enjoyed playing the game of make-believe . . . well aware that it was only a game . . . the pleasures gained through this willing suspension of disbelief were, if anything, enriched by the pleasures gained from questioning and, in many instances, ridiculing the artifice. (Buckingham, 1987:172–80)

This important dimension of the *Public Secrets* study adds a new twist to the concepts of mediated/transparent reading and emotional realism raised in my earlier notes on Corner and Richardson (1986), and Ang (1985). Buckingham's research actually uncovers a playful switch from one type of involvement to another by the same viewers. The fact that such a skill is found in audience members so young also serves to strengthen the general arguments of Palmer and of Hodge and Tripp. In his later work on television literacy (see Buckingham, 1990), the interchange between critical distance and passionate absorption is again evident in transcriptions of children's talk. However, something else which is evident in his recent writings is a deepening sense of methodological doubt regarding the conduct of reception ethnographies. A piece entitled 'What are Words Worth?' (1991) sees Buckingham openly admitting to uncertainties about reading the readings children make of TV. He suggests that in our admirable efforts to let audiences 'speak for themselves', there is the danger of simply accepting what is said at face value – neglecting the social relations of research itself and, therefore, the cultural conditions in which respondent talk is produced. So, when schoolchildren tell a university academic how they interpret TV, in what ways are their words shaped by the situation of telling? His proposal is now for 'a more cautious and self-reflexive approach to interpreting audience data' (Buckingham, 1991:229) – and it leads us usefully into the chapter's final section.

Ethnography and the Politics of Research

At this point, before moving on to address a further set of developments in audience studies, we need to pause and reflect for a while on the actual practices of ethnographic research. I've spent a good deal of time here considering the politics of media consumption – discussing social patterns of taste or power relations in the private sphere – but what about the politics of ethnography, and the power relations that exist between researchers and their subjects? If we are truly committed to a 'critical' perspective, then it is important for us to turn the same critical light back on ourselves, examining the interpersonal dynamics of fieldwork and the production of academic knowledges. Clifford Geertz (1973:9) once admitted that 'what we call our data are really our own constructions of other people's constructions of what they and their compatriots are up to'. He was quite prepared to recognize the role of ethnographers as active interpreters – arguing that the analysis of culture is 'not an experimental science in search of law but an interpretive one in search of meaning' (Geertz, 1973:5). My concern over the next few pages is with the processes of investigation and translation through which those meanings are sought and re-presented. Although I am primarily interested in how such processes apply to the study of media reception, I will also be looking at the ways in which qualitative researchers in other areas have begun to theorize their own activities.

There is – according to George Marcus and Michael Fischer (1986) – a general 'crisis of representation' emerging at present in the human sciences. Across a range of disciplines and perspectives, we can see evidence of doubts and uncertainties over how social reality might adequately be described. A growing number of academics find themselves rethinking the written forms they employ to convey the experiences of others, and the relationships they have with human subjects who are the objects of their knowledge. For the ethnographer – who is trying to provide richly detailed ('thick') descriptions of cultural life – the current crisis is particularly poignant. It demands that, as well as reading the various 'texts' of culture, we pay attention to the construction of ethnographic texts. And, as I have suggested above, it demands that we are conscious of the political dynamics which operate 'in the field'. In this vein, Paul Atkinson (1990) examines the stylistic conventions that have been used by sociologists to produce authentic and authoritative accounts of everyday practices or settings. Meanwhile, Deborah Cameron and others (1992) criticize the traditionally unequal relations between researcher and researched in empirical studies of language, putting forward an alternative 'empowering' approach. Ten years earlier, McRobbie had begun to raise similar issues for the women's movement in her article, 'The Politics of Feminist Research' (1982). She was keen to stress the 'partiality' of ethnographic writings, encouraging us to understand representations as interpretations rather than pure mirror images. McRobbie (1982:52) insisted there on a reflexive consideration of the positions and subjectivities of participant observers, so as to 'locate our own autobiographies and . . . experience inside the questions we might want to ask'. Perhaps the liveliest debate, though, is taking place within American cultural anthropology – where discussion has centred around an important book called *Writing Culture* (Clifford & Marcus, 1986).

In his introduction to this edited collection of papers, James Clifford traces out two key themes. Firstly, there is the problem of poetics, of anthropological 'authorship' (in addition, see Geertz, 1988; Van Maanen, 1988). Clifford's basic argument is that anthropologists have spent too little time analysing the social activity of writing, so central to their professional careers. He sees the realist form of expression which they routinely draw on as a style that establishes objectivity, authority and transparency of representation – a hierarchical arrangement of discourses which serves, in Clifford's view (1986:13–15), to suppress the actual dialogical relations of field research : 'The subjectivity of the author is separated from the objective referent of the text. . . . Polyvocality was restrained and orchestrated in traditional ethnographies by giving to one voice a pervasive authorial function and to others the role of sources, "informants", to be quoted or paraphrased.' Here and elsewhere (Clifford, 1983), he advocates experimental writing strategies that subvert the established tradition of ethnographic realism. Reviewing some already existing examples of 'polyphonic' or 'dialogical' texts, Clifford points a way forward towards different, supposedly more progressive, ways of telling.

Secondly – and inextricably caught up for Clifford with the making of texts – there is the problem of power and inequality. Anthropology's historical formation as an academic discipline was part and parcel of 'the colonial encounter' (see Asad, 1973) between white Europeans or Americans in the West and non-white peoples of the East or New World – cultures that had often been conquered militarily, exploited economically, and which field researchers were now attempting to 'know' scientifically. In a controversial move, Clifford (1986:6) refers to the ethnographies they wrote not as objective and value-free science but as committed and incomplete fictions, partial truths:

> Ethnographic writings can properly be called fictions in the sense of 'something made or fashioned', the principal burden of the word's Latin root, 'fingere'. But it is important to preserve the meaning not merely of making, but of making up, of inventing things not actually real. ('Fingere', in some of its uses, implied a degree of falsehood.)

The influence of Edward Said's work on 'Orientalist discourse' (Said, 1978) is clearly present in Clifford's quote. Said proposed that the object which we, in the West, call the Orient is actually a 'European invention' or fiction – the product of an imaginative geography. There are, of course, real living cultures to be found in what Europe designated as 'the East' (Said himself had left one of these) – but he was principally interested in how their exotic 'otherness' has been discursively constituted by Western explorers, novelists, historians, anthropologists, and so on. Not surprisingly, this fictional construct serves to justify the West's positional superiority: 'The relationship between Occident and Orient is a relationship of power, of domination . . . Orientalism, therefore, is not an airy European fantasy, but a created body of theory and practice in which . . . there has been a considerable material investment' (Said, 1978:5–6). In keeping with Said's critique, Clifford talks of the necessity for a 'specification of discourses' in ethnography. Anthropologists should be willing, he says, to specify who is writing, about whom, from what relative position, and in what material circumstances. Hence his desire for ethnographic texts which – rather like Bertolt Brecht's plays – foreground the machinery of representation and declare themselves openly as constructed fictions.

My feelings about Clifford's argument are mixed. He is right to raise the whole issue of power and positionality – to treat knowledge as a social production, and to regard the traditional research situation as an unequal interaction – but I believe he is wrong to place quite so much emphasis on the formal, literary qualities of anthropological writing. I would suggest that his critique of realism in ethnography suffers from many of the same problems as *Screen*'s anti-realist film theory, which was dealt with in Chapter 2. Indeed, there are some surprising similarities between the case advanced by Clifford and the account of realism in the cinema offered by Colin MacCabe (1974). For example, Clifford and MacCabe each concentrate on what they refer to as the text's 'hierarchy of discourses' – with each theorist recommending strategies of disruption or distanciation to replace the realist illusion. In addition, they both show remarkably little faith in the active critical capacities of readers. Just as the spectators in a cinema hall are perfectly well aware that they are watching a projected fiction, so the academic audiences for an ethnographic text are presumably capable of recognizing its status as a constructed representation. Anthropologists have always contested each other's interpretations and assertions, and they have been able to do so without the help of textual innovations or experiments.

Researchers of media audiences are, as Ang (1989:114) points out, 'generally . . . silent about these issues'. In the enthusiastic adoption of ethnography as a method for investigating reception practices, few have yet stopped to consider the kinds of question posed by Clifford and others in cultural anthropology. Ang (1989) is, in fact, one of only a small number to have done so. Referencing the *Writing Culture* collection as a point of departure, she attempts to go back and 're-read' two of the landmark studies from qualitative audience research in the 1980s – Morley's books, *The 'Nationwide' Audience* and *Family Television* (see my earlier notes on these key texts for a reminder of their contents). The assessment that Ang makes of his work is directly related to the two central themes elaborated in Clifford's introductory essay. She begins by describing the characteristic form of Morley's writings :

> both books are written in a markedly conventional style of academic social science, structured according to a narrative line which starts out with their contextualisation within related research trends, followed by a methodological exposition and a description of the findings, and rounded off with a chapter containing an interpretation of the results and some more general conclusions . .
> Morley's voice is exclusively that of the earnest researcher; the writer's I, almost completely eliminated from the surface of the text, is apparently a disembodied subject solely driven by a disinterested wish to contribute to 'scientific progress'. (Ang, 1989:106–7)

Ang (1989:110) then proceeds to look critically at the conduct and reporting of his conversations with the *Family Television* viewers:

> Due to his academistic posture Morley has not deemed it necessary to reflect upon his own position as a researcher. We do not get to know how he found and got on with his interviewees, nor are we informed about the way in which the interviews themselves took place . . . how did the specific power relationship pervading the interview situation affect not only the families, but also the researcher himself?

I have already indicated my mixed reaction to Clifford's arguments – and my response here to Ang is also divided. She correctly identifies a failure on Morley's part to discuss, in sufficient detail, the dynamics of power in domestic interview situations. As a stranger in the living room, his presence would surely have been a significant factor in how the conversations were organized and what people were prepared to tell him. It is, after all, highly unusual for working-class families to have a middle-class researcher sitting on the sofa asking them about TV! However, the criticism of Morley's presentational style seems to me to be somewhat wide of the mark. While it's certainly true that 'the writer's I' is largely absent (we learn next to nothing about the author's subjectivity), *Family Television* does contain a long section in which transcript material from the conversations is set out in a relatively 'open-ended' way. Morley even invites readers of the mono-graph to dispute and develop his own interpretation. 'I can only hope,' he writes in conclusion, 'that others will . . . be able to re-analyse the data supplied in the central section of family interviews' (Morley, 1986:175). Is this really the same authoritative, confident voice of science which Ang hears in the text?

Walkerdine (1986) and Gray (1988) are two researchers whose recent writings on media audiences would meet more fully with Ang's approval. Their texts have a strongly self-reflexive – and occasionally autobiographical – edge to them. So, in Gray's work on women and video technology in the household setting (see my following chapter), the call is for 'a method which recognizes the subjectivity of the researcher as well as the subjectivity of the researched' (Gray, 1988:10). Remembering her first experiences in the field, she confesses to an initial disappointment and sense of frustration when interviewees talked at length about their life histories: 'I felt that we were getting away from the topic, that it was nothing to do with their use of the VCR . . . not the stuff from which significant research is made' (Gray, 1988:12). On listening to the interview tapes, though, she realized this 'storytelling' was a way for the women to take back some control over the conversations they were involved in – refusing to respond straightforwardly to questions – and it provided Gray with a contextualizing narrative within which to situate their video viewing practices (from a rather different perspective, Mishler, 1986, has also proposed that interviewee language can be understood as narrative).

'Video Replay', Walkerdine's intriguing essay, opens with a story told from the researcher's point of view:

> I am seated in the living room of a council house in the centre of a large English city. I am there to make an audio-recording as part of a study of six year old girls and their education. While I am there, the family watches a film, *Rocky II*, on the video. I sit, in my armchair, watching them watching television. How to make sense of this situation? (Walkerdine, 1986:167)

Breaking with traditional conceptions of ethnographic observation which have tended to stress its naturalistic potential – its minimal impact on the settings under scrutiny – Walkerdine emphasizes the intrusive character of her work with a family known as 'the Coles'. An immediate indication of how they saw her arrival in their home was Mr Cole's shouted announcement to his young daughter, 'Joanne, here's your psychiatrist!' (Walkerdine, 1986:175). The fact that she was a radical social psychologist at an institute of education, and not in psychiatry at all, is immaterial. Walkerdine's presence is clearly read by them as a mode of surveillance. Indeed, as she reflects on the situation described above, Walkerdine herself comes to make sense of it as a sort of voyeuristic monitoring. 'Much has been written about the activity of watching films in terms of scopophilia,' she notes – 'but . . . what about this activity of research . . . Might we not call this the most perverse voyeurism?' (Walkerdine, 1986:167).

According to her argument, academic observers are driven by a 'will to truth' which involves constantly subjecting others – in this case, domestic TV viewers – to their powerful gaze. In doing so, they constitute those others as objects of knowledge and social regulation (the link with Said, via Foucault's theory of discourse, is once again evident). As far back as the Mass Observation movement in 1930s Britain (see Harrisson & Madge, 1939/1986), anthropology 'at home' has been marked by a middle-class surveillance of working-class cultural practices. Whether that voyeurism results in an exoticization of the lives of 'ordinary folk', or in expressions of bourgeois horror and distaste, there is a systematic pattern to these relations of power and vision. Walkerdine, a middle-class academic, therefore reacts predictably when she is first faced with the sight of the Coles, a working-class family, enthusiastically watching the last brutal round of a boxing match in *Rocky II*. The father, replaying the same scene time after time on the video, cheers the film's hero to a particularly bloody victory. She talks of feeling 'paralysed by . . . violence of the most vicious kind – bodies beaten almost to death' (Walkerdine, 1986:169). Her response at that moment, then, was to dismiss their pleasures as shameful and disgusting, and to explain Mr Cole's enjoyment as the product of a reactionary macho ideology.

It was only on returning to the privacy of her office at the university, where she watched a hired tape of *Rocky II* in full for the purposes of analysis, that Walkerdine began to read the film – and the Coles' reaction to it – in a dramatically different way:

> I recognized something that took me far beyond the pseudo-sophistication of condemning its macho sexism . . . The film brought me up against such memories of pain and struggle and class that it made me cry. . . . No longer did I stand outside the pleasures of engagement with the film. I too wanted Rocky to win. Indeed, I was Rocky – struggling, fighting, crying to get out . . . Rocky's struggle to become bourgeois is what reminded me of the pain of my own. (Walkerdine, 1986:169)

To explain this shift in her response from revulsion to identification, we have to understand more about three things – the narrative construction of *Rocky II*, the class-specific version of masculinity which Mr Cole inhabits, and the contradictions and breaks in Walkerdine's own subjectivity.

If Sylvester Stallone portrays a fighter in this film fiction, then the character he plays is 'fighting' in more senses than one. Rocky is, of course, in the boxing game – earning a living with his fists – but he also fights on behalf of his wife and child, struggling to improve their social position. In fact, he would prefer to find work in a middle-class profession (Rocky tries unsuccessfully to get office or acting jobs), but is eventually forced to return to the ring. So within the narrative, use of the body not the mind appears to be the only 'way out' for Rocky. Walkerdine (1986:180) suggests that Mr Cole, too, 'sees himself as a "fighter" – against the system and for his children'. Like the working-class 'lads' and their fathers in Willis's classic study, *Learning to Labour* (1977), he invests more importance in physical strength and practical know-how than in theory or intellectual ability. For Mr Cole, then, fighting symbolizes 'a way of gaining power, of celebrating or turning into a celebration that which is constituent of oppression' (Walkerdine, 1986:182).

This later reading of Walkerdine's actually has all the ingredients of a good ethnography. She makes a genuine effort to see things 'from the point of view' of her subjects, paying careful attention to the interdiscursive ties that bind Mr Cole into the film fantasy. Crucial to her reconsideration of the Coles' viewing pleasures is the detour she takes into autobiography. As in a number of other recent essays (see Walkerdine, 1990), she explores her own contradictory location as a working-class child who – through mental labour – 'escaped' to the middle-class environment of higher education. While Walkerdine recognizes she can no longer be 'like them' (the Coles clearly treat her as an intrusive monitor), there is nevertheless an identification with their experiences. Memories of being a young girl growing up in the suburbs of Derby, a town in northern England, enabled her to connect with the family's situation – and especially with that of the daughter, Joanne (for further discussion, see Walkerdine, 1986:183–8). At the same time, though, these memories were precisely the source of anxieties she had over issues of surveillance and power: 'I . . . wanted to examine my multiple positioning as both middle class academic and working class child, to use my own fantasies in exploring how the participants perceived me and how they understood their experience' (Walkerdine, 1986:191).

The autobiographical turn which Walkerdine advocates is, in some ways, a perfectly laudable one. Feminist theorists like Frigga Haug have employed 'memory-work' techniques to good effect – using personal experiences and recollections as a resource to help them understand processes of social subjectification (Haug, 1987; also Crawford *et al.*, 1992). These projects serve to remind us of the feminist slogan, 'The personal is political' – and Walkerdine, following McRobbie and Clifford, calls implicitly for a political ethnographic practice in which analysts specify the subjective locations from where their interpretations are produced. In other ways, however, her insistence on the researcher's self-disclosure might prove to be rather impractical. The suggestion that we talk about ourselves whenever we talk of others – if carried through by all audience ethnographers – would make for very tedious reading. Quite simply, the life histories of academics are insufficiently interesting to merit such close and constant scrutiny.

A related, but far more pressing, issue raised by Walkerdine's piece is the whole question of social identifications and differences between media researchers and the non-academic audience members they study. She was initially distanced from, even horrified by, the Coles' enjoyment of *Rocky II*, yet found herself identifying with them afterwards. Other feminist writers whose work on soap opera was discussed earlier in this chapter – Hobson (1982) and Ang (1985) – chose to go further by presenting themselves openly as 'fans' from the start, attempting to ally themselves with women consumers of the genre they were analysing. Although the alliance can never be complete – Hobson and Ang have stocks of educational capital which set them apart from regular fans – their strategy does still offer a striking alternative to the traditionally neutral and 'objective' stance of social scientists. Of course, the problem they then face is in maintaining enough distance from those *Crossroads* or *Dallas* viewers to develop any kind of criticism of the programmes and their pleasures. There is a tendency, within both of these studies, towards a populist acceptance or celebration of 'the melodramatic imagination'. It would probably be fair to say that, in practice, different situations and projects demand different approaches to the researcher/researched relationship. Depending on the contexts under investigation and the positions occupied by the investigator, varying degrees of cultural proximity or empathy are possible and desirable. Over the coming years, I believe that the continuing task for reception ethnographers will be to examine sympathetically the 'meaning systems' of others – whilst retaining a crucial space for ideological evaluation and critique.

4
Media, Technology and Domestic Life

Roger Silverstone (1990:189) has spoken about 'the double and inter-dependent character of the meaningfulness of the mass media' – arguing that we need to address, on the one hand, responses to particular texts or genres brought to us by the media and, on the other, the significance of media technologies themselves in our daily lives. 'There is meaning in the texts of both hardware and software,' he writes. This distinction, which can be seen as a reworking of older ideas to do with 'medium' and 'message', helps to explain a broad shift in emphasis between the contents of my previous two chapters and the material I turn to next. We have examined, in some detail, decodings and pleasures that are generated by audiences when they interact with different forms of media output – but I now want to focus more on consumers' interpretations of technology-as-text. Of course, it would be quite impossible (and undesirable) to try to separate message from medium completely because, as Silverstone insists, they are interdependent elements. Just as David Morley's *Family Television* study looked at programme-type preference alongside use of the remote control gadget, so several researchers whose work I will be discussing here have things to say about both 'software' and 'hardware'. Nevertheless, my rationale for bringing certain pieces of ethno-graphic research together in the present chapter is that they all concentrate primarily on the second of these elements – how various media technologies get used and made sense of in everyday cultures of consumption.

A theme carried over into this chapter from the last is the concern with domestic contexts of reception – with social relations and dynamics of power in the home. Investigating the place of media technologies in household life inevitably involves raising questions about the differential uses and inter-pretations of technology-as-text across divisions of gender and generation within families, or across class and neighbourhood divides. At the same time, though, it is also necessary for us to ask about the ways in which that technology serves to 'mediate' between private and public worlds – connecting domestic spaces with spheres of information and entertainment that stretch well beyond the confines of family and locality. Communication technologies have, I will argue, played an important part in the symbolic construction of 'home' – whilst simultaneously providing household members with an opportunity to 'travel' elsewhere, and to imagine themselves as members of wider cultural communities at a national or transnational level. My own qualitative research on early radio and everyday life or, more recently, on satellite TV consumption (see below) has attempted to deal with these contradictory aspects of contemporary media culture. Throughout this work I have found Raymond Williams's notes on 'mobile privatization' to be valuable in conceptualizing the position of broadcasting technologies within modern society (see Moores, in press b), and his *Television : Technology and Cultural Form* (1974) is therefore the starting point for my discussion here.

Understanding the Technology/Society Relationship

Before proceeding to talk in specific terms about the characteristic features of TV as a medium of communication, Williams chose to begin his book with a more general account of, and intervention into, debates concerning the relationship between technologies and social formations. He was particularly keen to counter the received wisdom which is commonly expressed in statements such as 'television has altered our world': 'people often speak of . . . a new society, a new phase of history, being created – "brought about" – by this or that new technology . . . the steam engine, the automobile, the atomic bomb' (Williams, 1974:9). Williams calls this influential, yet largely unexamined, view of things 'technological determinism'. It first presumes technologies to be autonomous, almost accidental inventions – the outcome of an isolated scientific and technical process – and then assumes them to have direct effects on social life. In addition, he outlines a second, less determinist but still problematic, strand of thought which sees technologies as 'symptoms' rather than the immediate causes of social change – by-products of a historical transformation that is otherwise determined.

Both these explanatory frameworks are flawed, according to Williams, because they abstract 'technology' from 'society':

> In 'technological determinism', research and development have been assumed as self-generating. The new technologies are invented as it were in an independent sphere, and then create new societies or new human conditions. The view of 'symptomatic technology', similarly, assumes that research and development are self-generating, but in a more marginal way. What is discovered in the margin is then taken up and used. . . . Each view can then be seen to depend on the isolation of technology. It is either a self-acting force which creates new ways of life, or it is a self-acting force which provides materials for new ways of life. These positions are so deeply established, in modern social thought, that it is very difficult to think beyond them. (Williams, 1974:13–14)

His aim in the opening chapter of *Television* was, precisely, to think beyond these currently dominant explanations. Williams endeavours to write an alternative history of broadcasting technologies and their social deployment, and the framework he sets out there is comparable with what some critical sociologists have since termed the 'social shaping of technology' thesis (see MacKenzie & Wajcman, 1985b).

This approach refuses to treat technology and society as separable elements. Instead, it returns a measure of broad social intention to the technological development process – understanding innovations 'as being looked for . . . with certain purposes and practices already in mind' (Williams, 1974:14). Contrary to popular images of the brilliant scientist or inventor who works alone on an individual project, the 'social shaping' thesis asserts that 'invention is not a matter of a sudden flash of inspiration from which a new device emerges "ready made" ' (MacKenzie & Wajcman, 1985a:10). Innovations are institutionally sought after – in response to existing cultural imperatives – and their development is usually funded by large agencies which have a direct stake in the invention. More often than not, new technologies are developed by the modification and combination of already existing ones, or by the application of older techniques to different circumstances. The process is a gradual evolution as opposed to a dramatic revolution. So, for instance, Williams would want to get away from the simplistic idea that TV was 'invented' at a particular moment in time by a person named John Logie Baird. Television is, he contends, dependent upon a whole series of earlier advances in electronics, telegraphy, photography, motion pictures and radio – several of which were initially developed with the needs of commercial or military organizations in mind.

Williams also suggests that broadcasting's applied social usage (for the centralized transmission of news and entertainment to dispersed domestic audiences) met some of the crucial cultural requirements of modernity – articulating 'two apparently paradoxical yet deeply connected tendencies' in urban industrial society. The technology 'served an at once mobile and home-centred way of living: a form of "mobile privatization" ' (Williams, 1974:26). TV, then, was both a sought-after consequence of and an effective facilitator for this historically specific mode of lived experience – a condition in which 'significantly higher investment in the privatized home' is coupled with the opening of 'greater . . . social and physical distances between these homes and the decisive political and productive centres of the society' (Williams, 1974:29). Elsewhere, in a lecture he gave several years later, the connotations of his key phrase from *Television* were quite clearly spelled out:

> I can't find an ordinary term for it . . . which is why I have to call it, in one of the ugliest phrases I know, 'mobile privatization'. . . . It is private. It involves . . . a good deal of evident consumption. Much of it is centred on the home itself, the dwelling-place. . . . At the same time, it is not a retreating privatization, of a deprived kind, because what it especially confers is an unexampled mobility. . . . It is not living in a cut-off way, not in a shell that is stuck. It is a shell which you can take with you, which you can fly with to places that previous generations could never imagine visiting. (Williams, 1989:171)

TV, and radio before it, has been bound up in the contradictions of modern social existence which Williams describes here – in the dialectics of home and travel, of privacy and mobility. They are domestic artefacts – part of a range of 'consumer durables' first arriving with the electrification of household spaces in the inter-war period (Forty, 1986) – that helped to create what Simon Frith (1983) has called 'the pleasures of the hearth'. The scheduled 'flow' of their output (see Williams, 1974:78–118) is designed to fit the day-to-day routines of viewers and listeners. And yet they do far more than bring symbolic 'warmth' and a sequenced stream of information into the familial sphere. Broadcasting could be considered a technology of transportation, too, because it enables private household units to make imaginative 'journeys' to distant places and events in the public realm. In fact, Williams (1974:26) hinted at an interesting parallel between the television set and the automobile by listing them together as machines of the same historical 'complex of developments'. Both technologies emerged in the twentieth century – functioning to privatize the family group whilst, in the same instance, transporting it (either literally or metaphorically) outside the four walls of the home. When he says above that the shell of domesticity can be flown abroad, 'to places that previous generations could never imagine visiting', Williams also points to recent advances in air travel and to an enormous growth in the tourism industry (see Urry, 1990). The present-day package holiday is, without doubt, an important feature of this mobile privatization, and it is no mere coincidence that TV publicizes possible destinations through a popular genre of holiday programmes. Tourism and television are both key institutions in contemporary 'travelling cultures' (Clifford, 1992).

In *The Consequences of Modernity*, sociologist Anthony Giddens (1990) has provided us with an important account of the spatial and temporal dimensions of modern culture. Although his book makes only passing reference to the medium of TV, we might borrow productively from Giddens's theory to expand on the concept of mobile privatization which Williams outlined in *Television*. Giddens proposes that, in the transition from traditional to modern societies, there was a fundamental restructuring of time–space relations. Whereas social activity was once centred around localized face-to-face interactions – dominated by 'presence' and a strong sense of 'place' – it is now frequently organized in terms of relationships with 'absent' others which may extend over vast geographical areas. Space and place no longer necessarily overlap in conditions of modernity – and technologies of communication or transportation have contributed significantly to this process, previously characterized by Giddens (1984:114) as a 'time–space convergence'. What used to seem unbridgeable physical distances are rapidly traversed by telephone, television, car or aeroplane. Furthermore, he goes on to argue that 'place becomes increasingly "phantasmagoric": that is to say, locales are thoroughly penetrated by . . . social influences quite distant from them' (Giddens, 1990:19).

Even though Giddens writes surprisingly little on broadcasting in *The Consequences of Modernity*, the links between his own analysis and Williams's are evident – and those links can be made clearer still by looking at work done by the American communications scholar, Joshua Meyrowitz (1985). I find myself disagreeing with many of the specific conclusions which Meyrowitz reaches in his study of media and social behaviour – for example, that television has been a largely progressive force in reshaping traditional relations between men and women, or between adults and children – but I would accept his more general proposition, which is that the electronic transmission of information and entertainment has dramatically altered the 'situational geography' of social life. Rather like Giddens, he stresses how interactions in the modern era are not always dependent on the co-presence of participants. They aren't limited to a distinct physical setting or locale: 'messages seep through walls and leap across vast distances' (Meyrowitz, 1985:117). Similarly, in common with Williams, he observes: 'The . . . home is now a less bounded . . . environment because of family members' access and accessibility to other places and other people through radio, television and telephone' (Meyrowitz, 1985:vii). In my opinion, his observations on the relative 'permeability' of the household's boundaries must inevitably lead us to ask questions about which public spaces the private users of communication technologies choose to 'visit'. What different destinations and senses of belonging, which territories of transmission (Rath, 1985), are available? Who decides to travel where, with whom, and why? When investigating the mobility of media consumers, then, we ought to concern ourselves centrally with the interdiscursive constitution of various 'imagined communities' (Anderson, 1983). Later in this chapter, I will be returning to these crucial conceptual issues to do with broadcasting's 'image spaces' and the formation of collective identities (addressing them with reference to particular empirical instances of audience activity).

For the moment, however, I want to pursue my examination of the technology/society relationship a little further. In an essay which offers a sympathetic yet searching critique of Williams's ground-breaking ideas, and of more recent advances in the social shaping of technology thesis, Hughie Mackay and Gareth Gillespie (1992) have argued that this body of work tends to concentrate too exclusively on the invention, design and development of technologies. It contests technological determinism on its own ground, so to speak, and therefore fails to take issues of appropriation and signification seriously enough. Williams does, of course, raise many of the right questions about TV, technology and cultural consumption in his seminal discussion of the medium's privatizing and mobilizing tendencies – although he has virtually nothing to say about how television gets interpreted or appropriated in different ways by actual social subjects located within domestic contexts. His analysis neglects the varied 'readings' of the technology 'text' made by household members in the course of their everyday lives. He is certainly interested in spatial divisions that industrial capitalism brought into being – its creation of a familial sphere which was separated from the public world of paid work – but he remains silent on the power relations that might exist between husband and wife, or parent and child, inside the private spaces created. Williams had not recognized the importance of what, in the wake of contemporary feminism, was named 'the politics of domestic life'.

Judy Wajcman (1991), who helped to pioneer the 'social shaping' approach during the 1980s, recently touched on gendered patterns of household consumption in a review of feminist contributions to the study of technology – briefly referencing research done by Gray (1987), and by Morley (1986), on cultural power and domestic leisure (see Wajcman, 1991:90). According to Mackay and Gillespie, it is in precisely this sort of direction (towards developments in media and cultural studies) that the social shaping thesis should now be looking if it is to broaden its scope and take on board the dynamic appropriation of technologies by socially situated consumers. They indicate some of the most fruitful ways in which these matters of active use and meaning construction have been tackled in contemporary cultural theory, and suggest that an adaptation of Stuart Hall's encoding/decoding model would enable those working in the sociology of technology to conceptualize processes of signification more satisfactorily. Indeed, Leslie Haddon (1991) has put pretty much the same case as Mackay and Gillespie. He employs Richard Johnson's 'circuit' diagram of culture (see Johnson, 1986:284) as a framework for understanding the meanings of information technologies – with its four stages of 'production', 'texts', 'readings' and 'lived cultures' (I come back to Haddon's analysis of the micro-computer in another section of this chapter).

Actually, the concrete example which Johnson originally took to illustrate this circuit diagram was itself a piece of technological hardware – an example that Williams, with his interest in the automobile, would no doubt have appreciated. 'We can,' Johnson (1986:285) says rather playfully, 'whizz a Mini-Metro car around the circuit':

> This is a . . . standard later twentieth century product of capitalist business. Like most products in our society it takes the form of a material commodity. It was also endowed with an especially rich set of meanings : it was the car to save the British car industry by beating rivals from the market . . . In one television advertisement, a band of Metros pursued a gang of foreign imports up to (and apparently over) the white cliffs of Dover, whence they fled by landing craft. The Metro was a nationalist hero in an epic of the Dunkirk evacuation, played backwards! . . . 'ordinary readers' made their own sense of the thing. But, of course, there were no 'ordinary readers', only groups of extra-ordinary ones transforming the Metro-text in different ways. Beyond these readings, the car found places in the practical activity and common sense of some consumers : a way of getting to work or taking the kids to school or expressing a kind of zippy independence.

If Johnson sounds a little vague here about the readings and practical activities of consumers – not having attempted an ethnography or a social history of Metro drivers and 'decoders' – the model still remains a fruitful one. He emphasizes the 'multi-accentuality' of artefacts as cultural signs. More detailed empirical work on transport technologies and consumption practices, carried out by two of Johnson's former students at the CCCS, helps to substantiate his point (see Willis, 1982, on subcultural meanings of the motorbike, and Hebdige, 1988, on uses of the Italian scooter cycle). In the coming pages, I review several recent ethnographies and histories which could also be said to have broadly adopted this perspective – all focussing on domestic media objects, and all serving to extend the social shaping of technology approach in ways that Mackay and Gillespie (1992) recommend.

Early Radio and the Formation of a 'Family Audience'

The first of those studies is, in fact, some historical research of my own on early radio's entry and gradual incorporation into household life during the inter-war period (see also Moores, 1985, 1988). This was a small-scale oral history project that entailed the recording of conversational interviews with a group of elderly people who were living close to the centre of a northern English town. With the assistance of a community worker in the area, I gained access to 'day clubs' for the elderly and visited several of the men and women I met there at their homes. My purpose was to draw on the many recollections which they had of broadcasting's initial arrival in everyday life – and, through an analysis of these memories, to piece together a cultural history of early radio 'from the listener's point of view'. Like Paul Thompson (1978), I believed that alternative accounts of the past needed to be written from below (giving histories back to ordinary people 'in their own words'). In retrospect, my approach to popular memory and to the oral data appears a touch naive (for instance, compare Moores, 1986, with the more 'social constructionist' perspectives offered by the Birmingham Popular Memory Group, 1982). However, I think that the project did succeed in opening up certain possibilities for a new, audience-oriented history of broadcasting. It made numerous connections, too, with the emerging body of ethnographic research on contemporary media reception which is the subject of my present book.

A valuable task for any historical investigation to perform is the 'de-naturalization' of our current, taken-for-granted cultural arrangements – showing things that we now take as 'given' in the process of their formation – and in this study, I wanted to begin to understand how broadcasting's relationship with the home had evolved historically. Audience ethnographers in the 1980s and 1990s are concerned to chart the intricate 'embedding' of communication technologies in the daily routines of domestic life and the micro-geography of the household – but how, to borrow a phrase from Lesley Johnson (1981:167), was early radio originally involved in 'capturing time and space in the home' during the 1920s and 1930s? My oral history research attempted to explore that process, between broadcasting's insertion into the private sphere as an 'unruly guest' and its establishment years later, symbolically at least, as a 'good companion' to family members. In addition, though, it's necessary to situate the formations of domestic media consumption within a wider history of social spaces and social divisions of time, because the pre-existing spatial and temporal conditions which radio entered into helped to shape its applied cultural form from the outset.

Williams (1974:20), remember, explains that there was – in the very broadest terms – 'an operative relationship between a new kind of expanded, mobile and complex society and the development of . . . modern communications technology'. The social need to overcome barriers of physical distance, especially in commerce and in military or government administration, led to a quite deliberate search for new, more rapid means of transmitting messages from one place to another. Similarly, the wishes created by an increasingly domesticated yet 'outward looking' style of daily living – the desire for a sense of home and security, but also for contact with the public world beyond – served to define broadcasting as a technology of mobile privatization. Radio consolidated and accentuated an ongoing historical process which (following

Donzelot, 1980) we might call 'the withdrawal to interior space' – and, in ways that I will specify in due course, the medium gave listeners access to a common calendar of quotidian rituals and great public occasions. Its contents, schedules and modes of address invited household consumers to 'imagine themselves' as part of a constructed national community.

If broadcasting was to 'capture' a place in the times and spaces of everyday life – to win an accepted and taken-for-granted position in domestic cultures – then this victory was less than immediate. At the point of its arrival in the living room during the 1920s, far from being a focus of family unity (the fireside companion), radio is remembered by my interviewees as the cause of some considerable disturbance to day-to-day routines. Broadcasting's entry into the home appears to have been marked by quite deep social divisions between household members. In the first phase, audiences for radio tended to reflect the technological novelty of the medium. Consumers concerned themselves above all with the means of reception as opposed to programme contents – and the interview material indicates that it was mainly young men, caught up in the play of experimentation, who were listening to broadcast transmissions. There are several recollections of male relatives or neighbours involved in constructing their own radio receivers at home:

> Uncle Bill made our first set from a kit. Oh, he had diagrams and goodness-knows-what.... He used to get the components and piece them together. Uncle Bill was a bit of a one for hobbies.

> *Question*: Your brother was interested in making radios from kits?
> *Answer*: Oh yes, he loved anything like that. He started building these wireless sets and he had to send away for the blueprints ... I've known him to be working on a wireless for hours and hours – he'd be telling me to clear off when I went to see how he was getting on.

> As I remember, it was the young inquisitive fellas who took it up first. They'd all be messing around with these bits and pieces – just like the kids round 'ere are today with their cars – always pulling the guts out of the engine and shoving other bits back. And just like they run round for an engine part these days, so they always used to be on the look-out for extra little things to improve the radio sets. It was what they'd call today a 'craze', d'you get my drift?

> The other day, I was watching a programme about ... Alexander Bell – and it made me think of our old wireless set. It reminded me of when my father used to be experimenting with these radios, trying to hear a voice come through. Our first set was made from a kit ... most people had the kits.

These do-it-yourself sets were popular early receivers, and articles devoted to the construction and operation of such gadgets appeared in a number of specialist periodicals. To some extent, this preference for kits was a consequence of their relatively low cost. A home-built radio receiver could be bought at a vastly cheaper price than the ready-manufactured sets. Even so, an elementary wireless kit (purchased for around £3 in 1923) was still an expensive commodity for working-class listeners, forcing many enthusiasts to acquire parts separately – and to assemble the wireless over a period of time. One woman, for example, recalls saving money to buy the components for her husband : 'When it was his birthday, or when Christmas came, I used to give him parts for his wireless, d'you see. I'd put fourpence away every week to save up and get him the bits he was after.'

In practice, the technical limitations of radio sets made good reception a rare event : 'All you could hear was the sea, you know, like the sound of waves – but oh, there'd be such a hullabaloo if you could hear one voice, just one voice.' As historian Mark Pegg (1983:40) points out, this was 'a time when the technical problems of listening were of paramount importance, whilst programme policy or content were secondary considerations'. Indeed, he notes that three-quarters of listeners' letters sent to the BBC in the 1920s were concerned with the difficulties of getting a clear signal. Only a small minority of letter writers commented on the quality of programming. Williams (1974:25) adds usefully to Pegg's remarks by proposing that radio was a system of communication initially 'devised for transmission and reception as abstract processes, with little or no definition of preceding content . . . the means of communication preceded their content'. Broadcasting's discourses, then, were very much in a formative stage. Early radio programmes often referred self-reflexively to their own mode of production. For example, up until 1926, technical language had a strong presence in BBC entertainment – and characters appeared on air with names like 'Atmos P. Herics' or 'Oscar the Oscillator'!

So when broadcasting entered the private sphere, it did so in the shape of a 'miraculous toy' – a novel piece of electronic gadgetry that husbands, fathers, brothers and uncles could playfully experiment with. However, early radio sets and their accessories were miracles which provided an obtrusive new addition to the home's furnishings and fittings. Paddy Scannell and David Cardiff (1991:356) observe that, at the birth of broadcasting, the 'receiving equipment looked more like something out of contemporary science fiction than a simple household object'. To pick up a signal successfully, several of the original domestic receivers required a long aerial extension which had to be stretched to an outside mast. The following memories help us to visualize just how unsightly this arrangement must have been. One speaker recalls that 'all down the backs, there'd be poles. . . . They'd use clothes props and brooms and things like that – nail'em together. As long as it was high up, you'd get a better sound.' A second interviewee says : 'Oh, it was something out of the ordinary in them days, having this box in the living room . . . there was a square piece of wood and on it was all these wires.' 'You had,' she continues, 'to have a big pole at the bottom of the yard with a wire coming right in . . . all along the living room wall.'

Another sort of set, which was battery-powered by heavy wet celled accumulators, constituted a double hazard – to the furniture it rested on, and to the family member who took the batteries to be recharged (usually at the local bicycle shop) :

> I remember once when a battery leaked. It was on the dresser and it leaked all over the carpet and left a big white patch. My mother was furious.

> We used to have the radio on the sideboard in the living room – my mother used

to be going mad . . . in case it took the polish off the sideboard. My mother didn't like it on there. She was always polishing and that . . . I don't think she was as interested in the radio as my dad.

I remember when I used to take those batteries to be recharged. I was only a young girl. I used to take this glass-looking battery to the cycle shop. My mother used to tell me to keep it away from my clothes because there was acid in them, and I used to walk up the street very gingerly with it.

You had to be careful how you carried'em. If you dropped one, you'd run like hell.

Corrosive acid, coupled with the ungainly mechanical appearance of the original wireless sets, meant that the radio's location in some household spaces remained uncertain. Here, for instance, is a description which illustrates precisely this transitional stage in broadcasting's domestic history : 'We used to put it away in either the cupboard or the pantry when we weren't using it. We only brought it out when we wanted it on. It wasn't like television – stood in the corner – it was brought out.'

Also, it is important to bear in mind that most people's initial experience of listening to the wireless was not as part of a collective household group. At first, because many of the sets lacked loudspeakers to amplify incoming messages, broadcasts were usually heard over headphones. The apparatus therefore prescribed individual reception – and its single listener typically seems to have been male. In fact, on occasion, wives, girlfriends and daughters could be actively excluded or silenced by radio. The following examples from my interview data demonstrate women's evident frustration with the gadget:

Only one of us could listen-in and that was my husband. The rest of us were sat like mummies. We used to row over it when we were courting. I used to say, 'I'm not coming down to your house just to sit around like a stupid fool'. He always had these earphones on, messing with the wire, trying to get different stations. He'd be saying, 'I've got another one', but of course we could never hear it - you could never get those earphones off his head.

I had to sit with my arms folded while he was fiddling with his crystal. If you even moved, he'd be going 'shush, shush', you know. You couldn't even go and peel potatoes, because he used to say he could hear the sound of the droppings in the sink above what was coming through the headphones.

Question: Did the set have headphones?
Answer: Oh yes, only one person could listen at a time.
Question: Who had first choice?
Answer: My father, of course. I remember he used to listen to the news with the earphones on. I don't think we ever heard the news – my father always got the earphones. Well, he was in charge, you see. What he said went.

My father, he was a bit short tempered, and he'd be saying 'Would you bloody well shut up' – threatening us if we opened our mouths. Oh God, we daren't move when my father had that wireless on. None of us dared move a muscle.

There are some comparisons which we might start to make at this point – between such accounts of radio in domestic life during the 1920s, and the findings of recent qualitative research on contemporary patterns of television consumption. I would suggest that these stories concerning power and control over the use of wireless headphones have a lot in common with the way in which Morley's families talked about the role of remote control devices in present-day household cultures. In both instances, a newly arrived piece of technological hardware becomes a symbolic site of (principally gendered) frictions within the family context. So if modern channel zappers can be seen to function as a twentieth-century descendant of the 'medieval mace' (Morley, 1986:148), perhaps the earphones were like a kind of crown – also symbolizing power and authority for the men who took possession of them. Further connections with ethnographic work on, for example, the entry of video recorders into the home or the dynamics of satellite TV consumption will emerge in later sections of this current chapter.

At any rate, it is clear from the oral history interviews that radio signified something quite different for men and women. For him, the wireless was a 'craze', a miraculous toy – yet she perceived it as an ugly box and an imposed silence. The (masculine) pleasures of reception were grounded in the technical apparatus itself. In a very real sense, then, women were largely absent from the listening public. But their social relationship to the wireless was about to go through a transformation which would reposition them much closer to the centre of broadcasting's modes of address – and this transformation proved pivotal to radio's capturing of time and space in the household. Three interrelated shifts began to take place during the 1930s in the period leading up to the Second World War. First, the technological and aesthetic form of the receiving apparatus changed dramatically, turning it into a fashionable piece of living-room furniture. Secondly, there was the formation of radio discourses that symbolically constructed their audience as 'the family', and which sought to interpellate mothers as monitors of domestic life. Finally, broadcasters increasingly ordered programmes into 'routinized' schedules that revolved around the imagined daily activities of the house-wife.

By 1932, reports Pegg (1983:39), sets run off mains electricity were already being sold in greater numbers than the early kit-built contraptions or the battery-powered wirelesses. Although by no means all homes at that time would have been connected to an electricity supply, radio manufacturers increasingly encouraged household consumers to get 'mains minded' (Scannell & Cardiff, 1991:362). The pre-manufactured mains set, which remained expensive at five or six guineas for even the cheapest of models, was nevertheless dropping in price – and this newer wireless equipment made its entry into the private sphere at a moment when many homes were becoming more modern, comfortable spaces to occupy. A crucial advance in the technical apparatus was the ability these machines had to separate one incoming signal from another and to amplify sound through a small loudspeaker. So basic problems with interference on reception decreased as a result of improved tuning, whilst listeners were no longer reliant on headphones to hear the broadcasts. The days of the boffin, experimenting with set construction and operation, were coming to an end. Programme content was fast gaining in importance for audiences – over and above the actual means of communication or the pleasures of technical 'tinkering'.

Even before this moment of change, there is evidence to suggest that at least some consumers had started to modify their kit-built gadgets for 'family listening' of a primitive sort. Consider these two amusing – but rather touching – narratives which were told to me by male interviewees:

> I'd put the earphones on, and then anything my wife wanted to listen to, I'd turn one earphone outwards and she used to lean her head against mine – put her ear to it. Then we both used to listen together.

> There was a basin my brother would put on the living room table, and then he'd get the earphones. There'd be my other brothers and my sister crowding round this basin and listening to the sound coming out.
> *Question*: Sorry, I'm still not clear – what exactly was this basin doing?
> *Answer*: Well, my brother used to put the earphones in the basin and the sound was amplified by it. I can vividly remember the family crowding round and listening with their ears all close up to this basin on the table. The sound must only have been very faint, but it meant that more than one person could listen at a time.

Soon after, though, such bodily contortions could be avoided. An amplification system was built into the set, enabling household groups to sit back and concentrate on the broadcast information or entertainment. Wireless design also went through a rapid change in this period, and radio gradually became a far less obtrusive 'part of the furniture' – blending in with the fixtures and fittings of the living room. Pegg (1983:56) tells us how manufacturers 'decided to give designers their head . . . exploiting the flexibility of . . . materials like Bakelite, a whole new vista was revealed. Murphy employed a furniture designer . . . whilst Ecko employed architects.' In advertisements, Murphy claimed their sets possessed 'a quiet dignified style in harmony with any furniture'. Pye, meanwhile, were proudly announcing in their publicity material that 'the survival of the experimental era in the outward appearance of radio belongs to a chapter . . . closed by the introduction of the Pye "Cambridge Radio" '. 'Realistic entertainment and artistic beauty,' they boasted, 'have long since overshadowed the miracle of radio in the minds of listeners.' A BBC *Radio Times* magazine editorial, dating from January 1931, heralded the transformation by stating that 'the novelty of 1922 has become . . . day-to-day routine' – and two years later the well known broadcasting critic, Filson Young, described the medium as 'that inexhaustible familiar'. The wireless phenomenon was passing from the miraculous to the taken-for-granted.

Its changing cultural status and domestic significance are well demonstrated in this particular memory, where a mains set is purchased by a man as a special present for his spouse back in the late 1930s: 'I can remember it now – a black Ebonite affair. That cost me four guineas. I carried it all the way home for her from the wireless shop.' In the following accounts, too, a slightly younger married couple give detailed descriptions of the position occupied by the object in their parents' households shortly before the war. Here, the accepted place of radio in the micro-geography of the home is clearly recalled:

> *Husband*: There was the fireplace, and next to the fireplace was my father's chair, and behind that there was a bit of a recess near the chimney breast. Aye, that's right – on the other side, there was a cupboard next to the window, and near to this cupboard was another recess, and in that recess there was a shelf with glassware and ornaments on – you know, pots and china and that. Well, just underneath, there was a ledge for the wireless to go on.
>
> *Wife*: Now, I remember our living room was different to yours. We had a cupboard next to the window, and where we used to keep the coal, that was next to it. Then there was a door next to the coalplace which led to the hallway, and right opposite there was the door leading to the kitchen. We had a trolley in the corner next to that door, and the wireless was on top of there . . .
>
> *Husband*: You see, the wireless was just part of the furniture.
>
> *Wife*: Well, it was a fixture, wasn't it?

Social surveys carried out at the end of the 1930s, such as Seebohm Rowntree's *Poverty and Progress* study which he conducted in York – or a report written for the BBC by Hilda Jennings and Winnifred Gill, *Broadcasting in Everyday Life*, based on data they gathered in a working-class neighbourhood of Bristol – argued that radio had significantly increased the attractiveness of the household as a dwelling place and as a site of leisure. Both these surveys draw a rather exaggerated comparison between a previous time when, in the words of Jennings and Gill, 'the street and public house offered the main scope for recreation', and a new situation in which the cultural activities of working people were rapidly 'retreating' into the private sphere. From their middle-class viewpoint, this retreat to interior space was seen as a move in the right direction. What Rowntree refers to as the 'cosy companionship' of broadcasting in the home is contrasted with a far more threatening image of 'the unruly mob' that has long haunted the bourgeois imagination.

Judging from the following remarks made by two of the women who were interviewed in my study, this same contrast was finding expression in elements of the popular imagination as well. One of them talked enthusiastically about her enjoyment of dance band music – but when asked whether she used to go out dancing much, the woman replied: 'Oh no, you see my father wouldn't let me . . . he thought these dance halls were dens of iniquity, so there would've been trouble if I'd ever gone there.' However, she continues, 'I used to listen to jazz on the radio at home. My father wouldn't let me go to dance halls, but if it was on the radio at home, well that was different.' Another says of her father: 'He liked us under his nose . . . we were encouraged to stay in. . . . A lot of people were quite content to sit in – in fact, my father had beer in at the weekend rather than going to the pub.' Of course, while these speakers remember 'listening-in' to radio within the private confines of the family domain, many of their contemporaries in the 1930s would indeed have been out at the dance hall or pub – and I certainly don't mean to suggest that there was any overnight disappearance of public working-class culture. Still, the stories they tell – together with the accounts given by Rowntree, Jennings and Gill – do indicate a shifting relationship between the private and public settings of social life, and they also identify broadcasting as a crucial part of the shift.

We should keep reminding ourselves, though, that the process was always double-edged. By the end of the inter-war decades, the technology of radio may have increased the home's attractiveness – but the social and spatial arrangement of households served, in turn, to constrain and regulate the ways in which broadcasting could be utilized by its listeners. (In a passing reference to my historical work, Morley & Silverstone, 1990:37–8, put this case much better than I did in the original reports of the research.) The sorts of house where my interviewees were living in the 1920s and 1930s are typical of the working-class terraced homes built extensively by speculative firms from the close of the nineteenth century (Matrix Collective, 1984:68). A front room, or parlour, was usually reserved for Sundays and special occasions – while the living room at the rear would either double as, or be directly connected to, a back kitchen. These were spaces in which meals were cooked and eaten, and where families might often spend time together in the evenings. The internal geography of the home, then, provided certain frameworks for household practices (see Foucault, 1980:148–9). It sought to prescribe a model of domesticity – to establish an identity and morality for the family group.

Radio's evolving discourses came to be targeted at the social space of this 'family audience' – either at household groups as a whole or, in particular scheduled slots, at selected members of them. Its modes of address were formed within the same prescribed model of domestic relations, and they attempted to reinforce that emerging set of identities and moralities. Broadcasting considered itself 'one of the family' – with the task of supplying the kind of cosy companionship which Rowntree spoke of in his survey. The role was perhaps best symbolized by a classic programme like *Children's Hour*, where radio aunts and uncles kept the youngsters amused while Mum prepared the evening meal. Wireless presenters could play the part of extended kin – helping out with childcare at a busy time of the day. More generally, the 1930s saw the evolution of what are now very familiar early evening entertainment formats. Quiz shows, serials and variety performances were essential elements in constructing the shared pleasures of the hearth (see Frith, 1983).

Indeed, the image of the fireside was commonplace in broadcasting literature of the period. A special winter issue of *Radio Times* in 1935 declared: 'To close the door behind you, with the curtains drawn against the rain, and the fire glowing in the hearth – that is one of the real pleasures of life.' 'And it is when you are settled by your own fireside,' continued the copy, 'that you most appreciate the entertainment that broadcasting can bring.' Scannell and Cardiff (1982:168) note how the home was seen here as 'an enclave, a retreat burrowed deeply away from the pressures of urban living'. We have a striking expression of what the French philosopher, Gaston Bachelard (1969:211), has called 'the dialectics of outside and inside'. The hearth and the wireless set were represented together as a focus of interior space and family pleasure. To some extent, of course, what the *Radio Times* quote offers us is a rather idealized representation of household harmony – and actual living rooms might predictably have been less cosy and more conflict-ridden places – yet this image is, in its own terms, still a remarkable move away from radio's earlier significance as a 'toy for the boys'.

Previously excluded from the audience, housewives and mothers were in many ways central to broadcasting's new hailing of 'the family'. Daytime radio features addressed the woman as monitor of the private sphere, issuing her with information on child-care techniques or advice on home management. In their 1939 report, Jennings and Gill spoke about the everyday reception of these discourses:

> Doctors' talks on Friday mornings were said to be helpful practically, especially by mothers of small children, many of whom . . . have become more open minded and ready to seek advice as a result of the teaching of Mothercraft in the infant welfare centres. Some women said they found talks on laundry work and other branches of household management useful. . . . Their whole attitude to housekeeping and motherhood is undergoing modification in the direction of increased knowledge, control and dignity.

Health of family members was equated by such programmes with the general 'health' of the nation. The welfare of individual bodies and that of the whole 'social body' were quite explicitly connected. So, for example, the *Listener* in September 1931 stated: 'Our bad food habits are responsible for impairing our national capacity for work and output. . . . The loss of the nation's time through sickness disablement in industry now averages no less than a fortnight per head per year.' A pamphlet for mothers, *Choosing the Right Food*, was published by the BBC – in which doctors advised on the planning of a well balanced diet from basic foodstuffs. The Minister of Health delivered a radio talk entitled 'Motherhood and a Fitter Nation', encouraging women to forge closer links between the family and the doctor, clinic and hospital – whilst in 1934, a series of lectures was transmitted on 'Strong Bones and Good Muscles', 'Teeth and their Troubles', and 'Colds, Tonsils and Adenoids'.

One possible (Foucauldian) interpretation of this 'explosion of discourse' around the management of domestic life is that broadcasting was caught up in an ongoing and complex reorientation of the operations of power in society. 'Government through the family' (Donzelot, 1980:92), exercised from within, replaced a straightforward government of families, from above – with the mother being singled out as the main point of support in efforts to re-form the household. She became the state's delegate, responsible for the physical and moral welfare of husband and children. In venturing such an explanation of the situation, I am well aware of potential confusions that may arise from any proposal that housewives were 'invested with power' in the process. I should stress that the woman's empowerment was always limited to specific areas of social activity – and, furthermore, it certainly wasn't in her material or political interests to be positioned in the monitorial role (for a broader critical assessment of Donzelot's thesis, consult Barrett & McIntosh, 1982).

Up to now, I have focussed almost exclusively on radio's capturing of space in the home, and on the ways in which broadcasters addressed audiences located within this spatial structure – but it was only with the allied 'capture' of temporal routines that the technology finally completed its integration into day-to-day life. Back in the experimental era of broadcasting, there had been a deliberate effort to avoid continuity and regularity of programming. Periods of silence were left in the gaps between individual programmes, and the same feature might well return at a different moment each week. The purpose of these disruptions was, no doubt, to encourage selective and attentive reception – rather than allow listeners to slip into regular patterns of daily background use. However, with the basic information on listening habits being gathered by the BBC's audience research unit – and with the increasing success of competitors like Radio Luxembourg in delivering popular forms of output at times that consumers could rely on – there was a gradual move during the 1930s towards more predictable methods of scheduling which 'chimed in' with everyday domestic rituals. Radio began to weave itself skilfully into the repetitive rhythms of quotidian culture.

It was the imagined daily routine of the mother that provided a basis for the broadcasters' programming plans. Her supposed round of household activities was used as a general guide to the changing shape of audiences throughout the day, as schedulers tried to take account of who would be listening at what particular times. This interviewee recalls precisely how the resulting schedules came to intertwine with mundane practices of housework and child-rearing, with the man's work and leisure time, with the youngsters' school and bedtimes, and with the whole family's mealtime and early evening relaxation:

> I remember *Housewives' Choice* for women who were at home in the morning. It started about nine o'clock, and housewives used to write off and ask for a record. Oh, and *Listen with Mother* at lunchtime, for women with young children at home. There was a children's programme on late afternoon for when the older ones came in from school. And then there was the news on at the same time every night – I always used to listen to that when I came in from work, during the evening meal. Then later, there'd be music or shows or stories – maybe a quiz – and I used to have favourite programmes on different nights of the week. I remember there used to be a programme called *Monday Night at Seven* . . . of course, with everyone being in early evening, they used to put things on that kids could listen to as well . . . something for all the family.

Johnson (1981) argues that pre-war Australian broadcasting promoted itself as the housewife's constant companion – and in Britain, the BBC were to adopt similar scheduling strategies (Hobson's ethnographic research on 'Housewives and the Mass Media', which I reviewed in Chapter 3, shows that these strategies are still very much with us). It is also necessary, though, to highlight instances where women did not – or were unable to – accept the 'friendly' offer of company. For example, consider this speaker's recollection: '[*Question*] Did you listen at home during the day? [*Answer*] I never had time. There were too many jobs to do, what with baking and washing and all that.' In the case cited here, part of the problem seems to have been the set's positioning: 'the radio was in the parlour, whereas I'd be in the back most of the time'. Locating the wireless in the front room of the house, then, appeared to indicate a 'Sunday best' attitude to radio – as opposed to the more usual placing and use of the technology as an accompaniment to routine tasks in the rear living room.

A crucial point in the schedules was the transition from daytime broadcasting to peak-time evening listening – the moment of the family meal. On this delicate matter, Pegg (1983:143) refers to the words of another social survey from the late 1930s entitled *The People's Food*, which remarked that 'the hour of the tea-time meal is even more important to wireless broadcasters than breakfast and lunch'. The authors of the report warned: 'a programme of special interest to housewives will not secure its maximum listening public if it clashes with the preparation of tea or the washing up'. Evening entertainment slowly started to fall into regular nightly and weekly patterns – so, by 1937, there were already forty fixed slots in BBC output between 6.00 and 10.30 p.m. (Scannell & Cardiff, 1982:181) – but it was only in the late 1940s that scheduling became fully established. In fact, of the programmes listed above by my respondent, all except *Monday Night at Seven* date from the Second World War or after. There is evidently a compression of 'linear time' in his account, with the rhythms of 'reversible' or 'cyclical time' having left a much stronger trace in the memory.

To appreciate radio's growing concern with temporal segmentation and repetition, we need to understand something about the pre-existing arrangements into which wireless schedules fitted. Just as broadcasting was inserted into a historically specific organization of space, so it entered particular social divisions of time. Edward Thompson's classic essay, 'Time, Work-Discipline and Industrial Capitalism' (1967), proposes that the temporal structuring of everyday life in modern society has its historical roots in the regulation of a large industrial labour force. His research charts a 'general diffusion of clocks and watches . . . occurring at the exact moment when the industrial revolution demanded a greater synchronisation of labour' (Thompson, 1967:69). Similarly, Giddens (1981:133) wonders whether 'it is the clock rather than the steam engine that should be regarded as the epitome of capitalist industrialism'. He discusses how 'the "working day", calculated by worker and employer alike in terms of commodified time, became central to the worker's experience' (Giddens, 1981:137). Equally significant, of course, was the separation of home from workplace, and the social construction of so-called 'free time' outside the factory – with the emergence of new temporal markers such as 'the weekend' – periods which were of special interest to broadcasters and schedulers.

Radio helped to bring precise temporal measurement into the private sphere. It was engaged in what could best be described as a 'domestication' of standard national time. There were clocks in many households long before the wireless arrived – but only with broadcasting did synchronized, nationwide time get relayed directly and simultaneously into millions of living rooms. So the 1930s radio critic, Young, pointed out that: 'The broadcasting of time, which is one of the most commonplace and regular features of the daily programme, is also, rightly considered, one of the strangest of the new things that the harnessing of the ether has brought us' – and, as a national temporal symbol, 'Big Ben' was celebrated in this poem from the *Radio Times*: 'Time for the time signal – speak, "Big Ben" / Boom out the time to children and men / Over Great Britain's listening isles / Send your voice ringing for miles upon miles.' It is difficult to gauge just how compliant listeners were to these imposed temporal structures, although one remarkable character does appear in the interview transcripts:

> My father, everybody used to keep time by him. If they saw him walking down the street to work in a morning, they knew it was a certain time – to the minute. He was never late, and never early either. He wound his clocks up at the same time every night . . . he used to listen to the radio for the time checks . . . he'd get home from work, and each and every night he'd put the news on – regular as anything.

Perhaps this sort of routinized, ritual behaviour can be compared with what Benedict Anderson (1983) terms the 'extraordinary mass ceremony' of reading a national newspaper each morning. 'It is performed in silent privacy,' writes Anderson (1983:39), 'yet each communicant is well aware that the ceremony he performs is being replicated simultaneously by thousands (or millions) of others of whose existence he is confident, yet of whose identity he has not the slightest notion.' Opening the pages of the newspaper – and, we might add, switching on the news bulletin at the same time every evening to hear the chimes of Big Ben – are ritual practices which enable us to imagine ourselves as part of a social collectivity that shares in the same anonymous, simultaneous activity.

The imagined community made available by early BBC radio was predominantly that of 'the nation'. It sought to constitute a sense of collective identity by creating an annual broadcast calendar of great national events and public occasions alongside the little 'ceremonial' rituals of everyday consumption. Cardiff and Scannell (1987:159–60) note: 'Special anniversary programmes marked the great religious festivals, Christmas and Easter . . . days of solemn remembrance and national pride such as Armistice Day or Empire Day . . . included in the same round were sporting occasions, the FA Cup Final and the Boat Race.' Also, of course, broadcasting in Britain has consistently attempted to forge closer ties between the monarchy and the people – providing coverage of coronations, jubilees and royal weddings, as well as instituting annual events of its own such as the monarch's Christmas Day speech to the Commonwealth. An informal style of talk was adopted by the king, who sent the best wishes of his family to the assembled listeners at home, symbolically binding together a united 'national family'. However, as I suggested back in my introductory chapter, social historians like Cardiff and Scannell are in danger of implicitly assuming audiences to have identified unproblematically with these forms of address – and whilst all of my respondents had listened to most of the programmes mentioned here, by no means all were willing to recognize themselves straightforwardly as patriotic subjects. For example, there are memories of some families irreverently poking fun at the king's voice. Another interesting instance is a story about young men in the town going around on the morning of the Boat Race with Oxford or Cambridge rosettes pinned to their jackets. On the face of it, this account would seem to indicate popular acceptance of a university rowing match in London as part of a shared national calendar – whereas, in fact, their enthusiasm was chiefly to do with opportunities that the race afforded for betting. We therefore need to see collective identities as the product of public/ private articulations which are not always forged successfully. Qualitative audience research can aid us in examining those interdiscursive processes (see the final part of Chapter 4 for further discussion of this point).

Televisions, Videos, Computers and Telephones

Alongside my work on early radio's place in the private sphere, I would like to consider several other examples of recent media research that has focussed its attention on communication technologies in the home – investigations which share very similar concerns with patterns of entry and incorporation, or with everyday use and meaning construction. The most extensive study in this area is Silverstone's 'Household Uses of Information and Communication Technologies' (HICT) project – the initial phase of which he directed at Brunel University, before taking the continuing project to the University of Sussex – and his work with collaborators on the HICT research will be the subject of the following section. In advance of that discussion, though, I look at a range of smaller studies carried out either in Britain, the USA or Australia – histories of domestic TV reception offered by Tim O'Sullivan (1991) and Lynn Spigel (1992a), Ann Gray's ethnography of VCR consumption practices (Gray, 1987, 1992), as well as important investigations into the cultural significance of the home computer (e.g. Haddon, 1991, 1992; Murdock, *et al.*, 1992) or the telephone (e.g. Moyal, 1989; Rakow, 1992).

O'Sullivan (1991:159) argues, quite correctly, that 'an adequate history of British television . . . must engage with the ways in which . . . one of the most decisive cultural technologies of the post-war period entered . . . the British "home", and with how television viewing cultures became established'. He notes that whilst there has been a good deal of interest over the last few years in studying the social relations and contexts of contemporary TV consumption (as evidenced by my previous chapter), there are still no available historical accounts which address the initial experiences of domestic viewing – asking what it felt like to have the novelty of television in your home during the 1950s and early 1960s. O'Sullivan believed, as I did, that an oral history method could help to reconstruct the formation of audiences for modern broadcasting – and he recorded twenty-one interviews organized through family and friendship networks, almost all with middle-class married couples aged sixty and over, seeking to chart 'memories of the place of the medium in their lives during this time' (O'Sullivan, 1991:159). Unlike me, and to his credit, he also started to recognize the socially shaped, 'sentimentalised and fragmented' character of memory. Indeed, O'Sullivan (1991:163) actually suggests that media institutions themselves play an important role in this construction: 'For many, memories of early TV have in part been refashioned by broadcasting and popular culture's nostalgia for the relatively recent past.' The full implications of his realization for the analysis of life history accounts are difficult to gauge (and O'Sullivan's essay never really pursues the point in any detail), but it would seem to direct us once again towards a more reflexive reading of interview talk as social discourse or narrative.

Two key themes are taken up in his report of the research. Firstly, he is concerned to raise questions to do with the original acquisition of the technology, its significance for family members as an object of domestic consumption – and, crucially, its evaluation and management within different household cultures, depending on the varied cultural dispositions or forms of 'habitus' that are operating in the home (a term which O'Sullivan borrows from Bourdieu – see Chapter 5). Predictably, perhaps, it appears that the decision to buy a television receiver was usually taken by husbands. No doubt this can be explained by their control over large items of household expenditure, but it is related, in addition, to the connections between masculinity and gadgetry which we saw in my work on early radio. O'Sullivan (1991:164) describes how the men he interviewed 'tended to refer to the technicalities of fitting the aerial and the subsequent tuning-in of the set which accompanied installation'. In a direct parallel with the words of women I had spoken to, one of his female respondents remarked: 'It was really his television, he turned it on, fiddled with it and turned it off' (quoted in O'Sullivan, 1991:166). She clearly experienced precisely the same sorts of frustrations with 'boys and their toys'. At the same time, though, acquisition of a TV set and aerial in the 1950s often symbolized status and modernity for families that owned them. 'The act of getting . . . television,' writes O'Sullivan (ibid.), 'seems to be remembered above all as a sign of progress, a visible sign of joining, or at least not being left out of, "the new".'

However, once TV had arrived and assumed its place in people's homes, O'Sullivan (1991:173) proposes that the technology and its programme services were responded to in varying ways as a result of 'distinctive sub-systems of cultural classification, disposition and difference . . . the basic means by which what television offered was subject to different types of appropriation, regulation, involvement and judgement'. This level of the analysis is, on his own admission, challenging yet incomplete (see O'Sullivan, 1991:172). It serves to introduce divisions of social class and class fraction into the interpretative framework, alongside issues of gender. For example, he charts very different sets of responses to BBC and early ITV (independent television) output. The former would sometimes be seen as overly formal: 'it was really rather elitist and snobby . . . "high brow" and very "plummy" . . . we used to laugh at it sometimes – the airs and graces'. In contrast, others regarded the latter as 'popular vulgarity' – and in one extreme case, children were forbidden to watch ITV by their mother: 'I just thought it was a dreadful waste of time and I didn't like it . . . there was too much cheap entertainment and not enough education. I didn't want the boys to get used to watching it so I used to ban it' (O'Sullivan, 1991:173–4). The author is right to stress the importance of these viewer interpretations, and to ponder their wider relationship to 'popular' and 'legitimate' taste cultures – but, ultimately, his data is too limited to articulate channel preferences with patterns of cultural capital, and with educational, occupational or family background. We learn from a footnote only that his interviewees were 'in terms of social destination, middle class professional householders', information which is of little use to us in theorizing the distinctions expressed by respondents.

A second main theme in O'Sullivan's historical study, familiar from my own investigation of radio, is the place of early television in domestic time and space. He examines the routinization of daily and weekly viewing, noting how particular slots on particular nights came to be treated 'as the property of certain family members, "their programmes", and in some cases this is remembered as a cause of . . . arguments between husbands and wives or parents and children' (O'Sullivan, 1991:171). But before the technology established itself as part of day-to-day routines, there was a fair amount of uncertainty at the outset about exactly where to situate this new household object. O'Sullivan reports that, with TV's installation, there were 'various rearrangements of domestic lay-out' – as well as disagreements 'about which was the most appropriate room in the house for television'. Interviewees told him of the awkwardness and disruption that had frequently accompanied TV reception back in the 1950s.

In Spigel's book, *Make Room For TV* (1992a), and in a series of papers, articles and essays she has written over recent years (e.g. see Spigel, 1986, 1989, 1992b), we have a similar attempt to understand the arrival of television in American homes during the post-war period. Her analytical intentions closely match those of researchers like O'Sullivan and myself in the UK, although her approach does not involve the recording of oral history interviews. Instead, she draws on documentary evidence from that time – concentrating chiefly on women's home magazines published between 1948 and 1955 (such as *Better Homes and Gardens*, *American Home*, *House Beautiful* and *Ladies' Home Journal*), but looking also at advertisements, TV programmes and films. So if she displays a media ethnographer's concern with the contextual dynamics of consumption, her method is, nevertheless, a type of textual analysis. As Spigel (1992a:8–9) openly acknowledges, 'these popular representations of television do not directly reflect the public's response to the new medium', yet they do 'begin to reveal a general set of discursive rules that were formed for thinking about television'. I would suggest that any future histories of broadcasting in everyday life might fruitfully combine oral sources with the kind of detailed readings of historical documents which are offered by Spigel. This research procedure could enable us, as the social science methodology books put it, to 'triangulate' our findings – and, more significantly from a cultural studies standpoint, it might highlight areas of overlap or contradiction between publicly circulated discourses and privately enacted reception practices.

Spigel (1986), in the words of the title she used for an early paper based on her research, sees US television's entry into the private sphere as a moment of 'ambiguity' and 'hesitation'. The uncertainties voiced by O'Sullivan's respondents are repeated in the magazine texts she analysed:

popular discourses were replete with hesitation . . . television was spoken of in the context of a profound spatial problematic. The magazines spoke in seemingly endless ways about the management of household spaces and the family's relationship to those spaces *vis à vis* the coming of television. In what rooms should the television set be placed? Where should child, mother and father view television? How could the housewife prepare dinner while watching her favourite programme on the living room console? . . . the television set threatened to disrupt the efficient functioning of the household. (Spigel, 1986:3–4)

The ambiguity of this technology in the domestic arena was, most import-antly, a consequence of its relationship to pre-existing patterns of household work and leisure within American suburban culture – and, in particular, it was figured in terms of the concrete problems of women's productive labour in the home. Spigel (1989) develops that line of argument in a later article on what she calls the domestic economy of TV viewing. Her account there begins with a description of a gadget, first marketed in 1952, which appears to us in retrospect as rather an odd historical fluke – the 'TV-stove'. Advertisements for the machine show that there were two adjacent windows for the housewife to watch simultaneously (one reveals a chicken roasting in the oven, while the other is a television screen). However strange the idea of a TV-stove may seem now, Spigel (1989:337) notes how the invention serves as 'a reminder of the . . . social, economic and ideological conditions that made this contraption possible'. It attempts to find a technological solution to the potential 'problem' of housewives' labour being disrupted by television entertainment, and the solution here involves a minor social and spatial readjustment – in which the kitchen's functions are extended. Of course, some women could well have appreciated these opportunities to view and cook at the same time, but the major anxieties that lie behind such an invention are undoubtedly those of the men being cooked for.

Meanwhile, the siting of a main set in living rooms or dining rooms was presented by women's magazines as the cause of slightly different concerns. The work and home management responsibilities of housewives again emerge as a central issue, although this time it is in relation to the mess which men's leisure can create – or to fears about the threat that TV may pose to family interactions. For instance, *House Beautiful* warned of occasions when 'the men move in for boxing, wrestling, basketball, hockey. They get excited. Ashes on the floor. Pretzel crumbs. Beer stains' (Spigel, 1989:345). A proposed remedy was for the woman to relocate the set in special 'dens' or recreational spaces, away from her best carpets and furniture. Spigel (1992a:66) talks, too, about the way in which popular periodicals of that era 'presented exaggerated versions of family division, often suggesting that television would . . . sever family ties, particularly at the dinner table'. A good example is the cartoon she discusses, from *Better Homes and Gardens*, illustrating parents seated at the dining-room table as their children remain 'glued' to the TV in the lounge.

Roughly thirty years after the widespread introduction of television into households on either side of the Atlantic, there was a further dramatic development in domestic entertainment technology – the video cassette recorder. In Britain, by the mid–1980s, it is reported that well over a third of homes had already installed a VCR, and some 97 per cent of film-watching was now done outside the cinema through broadcast TV or video film hire (see Tomlinson, 1990:60–1, who points to the growth of VCR culture as 'an index of the increasing grip of the privatized context in which leisure is now consumed'). Critical ethnographic research into VCR use is essential if we are to go beyond these statistics to understand both what the technology meant for its private consumers and how it fitted into the dynamics of their daily lives. Not surprisingly, the most promising work in this field has been done within the tradition of British cultural studies. Marie Gillespie's short essay, 'Technology and Tradition' (1989), starts to address the position and social significance of video viewing inside a South Asian community in London. Despite the empirical and theoretical limitations of her piece – which is an early report on a project she is still concluding – Gillespie does highlight extremely valuable areas of inquiry around themes of ethnicity and generation (one of her central concerns is with the ways that first and second generation Indian immigrants relate differently to the imported 'Bombay films' which they watch). A rather more complete study of VCR reception is Gray's book, *Video Playtime* (1992). Gray chose instead to pursue the kind of questions about gender, labour, leisure and power that had been opened up by Morley's *Family Television* (1986) and which are aired above by Spigel.

Her data comes from lengthy conversations with thirty women in Yorkshire – all of whom lived in households that possessed a video machine during the mid–1980s (for basic biographical information, see Gray, 1992:36–41). These interviewees were contacted either through a tape hire outlet or else by way of personal introductions and 'snowball' sampling, producing a group which included women with varied class positionings. As I indicated towards the end of Chapter 3, when discussing Gray's recollections of actually doing the interviews, her respondents were not content merely to talk about VCRs. They would frequently want to relate details of their life experiences, providing the researcher with an unexpected but useful picture of the contextual circumstances in which video is made sense of. Far from being superfluous, as she had originally feared, this material, Gray realized, was necessary if the technology was to be analysed as a socially situated object. So *Video Playtime* contains a wealth of data on these women's everyday lives, and particularly on work patterns and the organization of their occasional periods of 'spare time' – outside as well as inside the family home.

In an effort to make explicit the implicit – largely unconscious – gendered meanings of different domestic tasks, objects and spaces, Gray invited the women she spoke with to code activities and technologies around the house on a scale from pink to blue (an investigative strategy which Gray adapts from Cockburn's work on gender and technical know-how – see, for example, notes on 'the kitchen and the tool shed' in Cockburn, 1985):

> This produces almost uniformly pink irons and blue electric drills, with many interesting mixtures along the spectrum. The washing machine . . . is most usually pink on the outside, but the motor is almost always blue . . . my research has shown that we must break down the VCR into its different modes in our colour-coding.

The 'record', 'rewind' and 'play' modes are usually lilac, but the timer switch is nearly always blue, with the women having to depend on their male partners or their children to set the timer for them. The blueness of the timer is exceeded only by the deep indigo of the remote control . . . which in all cases is held by the man. (Gray, 1987:42)

Responses to the questions that Gray (1992:166–7) posed about the technicalities of operating a video machine reveal a deep sense of inadequacy or self-deprecation on the part of some women in her study. She quotes several instances of this:

I don't even know how to work the thing properly . . . I mean I'll try if I'm desperate, I'll press every button and I'll eventually get on what I want, but I'm certainly not . . . I'm not machine minded really. (Kay)

He does the recording for me. The first video we had I could do it myself, it was just very basic, but as we progressed it got very complicated and I still to this day can't work out the timer, it's just a joke – I'm not very good at that sort of thing. (Susan)

Well I still have to think about the video. Mainly my own fault because I haven't bothered to do it enough and bothered to look in the instruction book . . . the timing bit I haven't bothered with . . . there's always somebody here to do it and, then again, it's just pure laziness and apathy. (Sheila)

Oh no, I haven't got a clue, no. If there's anything I want recording I ask one of the boys to do it for me. This is sheer laziness, I must admit, because I don't read the instructions. (Edna)

Certain things do need to be stressed when we consider these interview extracts. First of all, just as Charlotte Brunsdon (1981) was keen to insist that the competences required to engage with classic soap opera texts were culturally constructed as feminine – not biologically pre-given – so Gray is careful to explain the lack of competence which is evident here in relation to particular social contexts and subject positions. VCRs, like melodramatic fictions, are not inherently masculine or feminine – but they acquire gendered meanings as a consequence of their cultural 'circulation'. Technologies, genres and knowledges can, in specific historical and social circumstances, become what Gray refers to as 'colour coded' (indeed, I might add that blue and pink only signify masculinity and femininity within given cultural conventions – the colours themselves have an arbitrary connection to gender distinctions). Secondly, it is worth making a further link with my earlier commentary on feminist studies of audiences for soaps, this time back to Dorothy Hobson's *Crossroads* (1982). Hobson remarked on how regular viewers of the programme often told her about their pleasures in an apologetic fashion, and Gray's interviewees appear similarly embarrassed about their inability to operate the video controls. Such low levels of self-esteem are caught up with the relative gendered values given to various practices in the 'cultural economy'. In the end, then, we find ourselves returning to matters of social inequality.

Thirdly, though, there may be subtle shades of resistance in the refusal of these women to learn how to use a gadget like the VCR timer switch. As Gray

(1986:6) states elsewhere, they 'routinely operate extremely sophisticated pieces of domestic technology – consider the complex nature of most modern sewing machines'. On occasion, there is a conscious 'calculated ignorance' when it comes to video recorders. This is clearly expressed by Edna, who was asked whether she wanted to find out about working the timer in future: 'I'm not going to try, no. Once I learned how to put a plug on, now there's nobody else puts a plug on in this house but me . . . so [*laughs*] there's method in my madness, oh yes.' Another woman, Audrey, also says that: 'I really don't want to be taught how to do it, really deep down . . . because if so it will be my job to deal with it . . . that's the truth' (both quoted in Gray, 1992:168). Each has recognized a 'latent servicing element' in the technical know-how, and resisted it because of their already busy household routines. In conclusion to her chapter on technology in the private sphere, Gray (1992:187) asserts (a little too boldly?) that 'gender is the key determinant in the use of and expertise in specific pieces of domestic equipment' – suggesting that the pattern she identifies cuts across divisions of education and class in her sample.

Running in parallel with the 'video revolution' of the 1980s, there was a rapid boom in the home computer market – and qualitative research on computer use has also pointed to gender as a key variable, amongst others, in the dispositions users display towards new information technologies. A good example of this work is Sherry Turkle's fascinating observational study, conducted in educational rather than household settings, which explored the reasons for 'computational reticence' shown by a group of US female college students (see especially Turkle, 1988). In the case of these young women, she was not faced with a straightforward inability to operate the machine – they were quite capable of doing so – but with an openly declared reluctance to enter the predominantly masculine culture of 'computer virtuosos', where the object is taken as a partner in an intimate relationship. For many of their male counterparts, however, mastery of technology became a way of exerting perfect control in a world of safe things, free from the complexities and ambiguities of close human ties. As one of those 'hackers' tells Turkle (1988:46), he has 'tried out' having girlfriends and 'got burned' in the process: 'With social interactions you have to have confidence that the rest of the world will be nice to you . . . But with computers you are in complete control . . . you have confidence in yourself and that is enough.' Although Turkle's ethnography is focussed on a non-domestic context, her study still helps us to cast light on some of the more general issues we are seeking to tackle in the present chapter. In fact, her writing can be seen as a valuable attempt to go beyond the descriptive charting of gender differences, and provide an adequate social-psychological explanation of how particular groups of women and men interpret information technology.

Haddon (1992), whilst expressing certain reservations with regard to Turkle's project, proposes that such work on educational settings is a necessary complement to 'family-based' studies of consumption – because, he asserts: 'The popularity, patterns of usage, the meaning and the gendered nature of the home computer arise in large part from processes outside the home . . . "home computing" cannot be viewed as an activity based solely in the home' (Haddon, 1992:94). His investigations, which centre on the development and cultural significance of the BBC micro-computer, are intended to situate this machine in a whole web of social institutions and practices – considering the various stages of design, production, marketing, appropriation and use, as well as its intertextual links with other technologies and images (see Haddon, 1991). The specific aspect of his broad research agenda which I touch on here is the analysis of computers as an object of boys' classroom discourse and leisure activity.

Talking with members of secondary school computer clubs (aged from eleven to sixteen), Haddon (1992:87) discovered that there was a constant competitive banter – 'a perpetual, joking rivalry over computers, where boys derided the features of the micros which belonged to their peers'. Further, equally competitive, interchanges were concerned with the relative sizes of games collections, or with who had the superior skills to achieve high scores (in connection with this point about boys' computer/video game playing, see Skirrow, 1986; Provenzo, 1991, on the masculine genres of adventure which are frequently drawn on – typically, science fiction and war scenarios). Rather more co-operative activities included the swapping and (illegal) copying of software packages, using twin-deck domestic cassette recorders, and the evaluation of new hardware products coming on to the market. Haddon (1992:93) then goes on to ask how these features of the boys' computer culture might be followed through in ethnographies of household reception:

> there are questions concerning parental support, or lack of it, in terms of the encouragement of expertise . . . especially if this hobby is deemed to be excessive or detrimental to other commitments. . . . We also have to consider . . . how computing or games-playing are viewed by parents as leisure activities. . . . A final example of the type of question we might ask from family-based studies concerns parental reactions to the copying of software . . . under what circumstances do parents see such computer copying as trivial and sanction it, and when does it raise concerns about children's perception of legality?

These sorts of issues – principally to do with relations between parents and male children in the family environment – have been pursued in interviews with computer users recorded in the English Midlands, from 1983 to 1987, by Graham Murdock, Paul Hartmann and Peggy Gray (1992).

Their task was to map out shifting meanings and 'competing definitions' of the technology over time. An initial phase in the object's social history, they suggest, entailed the targeting of 'committed hobbyists' (see Haddon, 1988) by computer manufacturers. Next came the introduction of a new generation of machines – aimed at a much wider audience, but marketed as having 'serious' educational values and applications. Acorn's BBC micro was part of this wave of developments, and the company's advertisements plainly addressed themselves to parental hopes and fears about schooling and work prospects. 'Your child's degree ceremony might seem a long way off,' read its publicity material (from Murdock *et al.*, 1992:153), 'but . . . our new micro can provide . . . constant support throughout education, eventually graduating into business and professional use . . . It should help to put a few letters after your child's name.' The researchers report, however, that many of the families interviewed could not afford a BBC micro – and opted instead for cheaper machines like a basic Commodore or Sinclair, almost seeing the acquisition of a computer to be, in itself, a beneficial act. Yet any of these technologies which parents purchased, and justified on the grounds of education, could be put to altogether different uses by their children. Notably, the mid–1980s brought a massive expansion in the sales of games packages, with the home computer largely being redefined as an entertainment system. After a while, several adults 'had given up an unequal struggle and accepted that the machine would be mainly used for games' – with the exception of a mother who, in a similar spirit to the woman in O'Sullivan's oral history who 'banned' ITV, rationed the object's use: 'We don't like to get it out too often because it's a temptation to them to give up their swotting . . . once they start playing games, it's difficult to stop . . . So I say, "Right, we'll put it away" ' (Murdock *et al.*, 1992:157–8).

A final technology I want to deal with in this section is the telephone, recently labelled 'a neglected medium' (Fielding & Hartley, 1987) in communication and media theory. Compared with the amount of material available to students on, say, television cultures, it is certainly true that telephones have received relatively little attention as a cultural phenomenon (but see De Sola Pool, 1977, for a broad assessment of their 'social impact'). The best efforts to right the current imbalance are coming from researchers interested primarily in women's 'consumption' of telecommunications services – what Australian academic, Ann Moyal (1989), terms 'the feminine culture of the telephone'. Moyal's investigations, along with a richly detailed ethnography written by Lana Rakow in the United States (*Gender on the Line*, 1992), represent precisely the kinds of direction we should now be moving in if the telephone is to claim a more central place on the cultural studies agenda. The work of these researchers connects up well with a number of the projects I review in Chapter 4 and elsewhere in the book.

Following a pilot questionnaire, in which elderly phone users were asked about the routine patterns of their calling, Moyal conducted a national study – with the aid of fifteen research assistants – involving in-depth conversational sessions with 200 women from across Australia. Her sample contained a spread of women in a diversity of social situations (for example, those at home and in the workforce; in urban or rural settings; of different ages; drawn from various ethnic groupings). The method was qualitative, 'since the object of the survey was to gather the experience, attitudes, and voices of women' (Moyal, 1989:8). For analytical purposes, she invited interviewees to distinguish between 'instrumental' calls – making appointments, seeking information or coping with emergencies – and 'intrinsic' ones, where they maintained close interpersonal contact with sometimes distant relatives or friends. Both the pilot and main surveys revealed that the women used a telephone principally for the second of these types of communication, investing great importance in the technology as a means of 'kinkeeping'. Intrinsic calls were more frequent, and of far longer duration. They helped to construct and sustain a 'psychological neighbourhood' which serves as a substitute for regular face-to-face contacts. (For an intriguing historical angle on this distinction between the instrumental and intrinsic content of telephone talk, see Fischer, 1991, who shows that the earliest phone companies actively discouraged so-called 'trivial gossip' until they discovered the economic potential of such sociability.)

Examples cited by Moyal from her interview data include numerous references to intimate exchanges between mothers and daughters. A retired resident of rural Queensland remarks: 'Each night my daughter and I talk for half an hour by phone. We discuss the routine of the day, things we want to do when we meet. It helps my life entirely . . . my daughter too. We get very depressed and lonely otherwise' (Moyal, 1989:12). In addition, there are stories of women managing to keep a network of friendships going over the telephone line – described by one suburban housewife as 'a link with colour and variety and with people one loves'. Moyal (1989:20–2) also refers to the technology's significance for women in immigrant communities, where the ability to talk with others in their native tongue – whether inside Australia or overseas – has increased confidence and offered a feeling of security in new surroundings. Even if Moyal's theoretical framework resembles, in many respects, that of the 'gratificationist' school in mass communications research, she is still able to foreground the gender politics and public policy implications of her work. The 'feminine "information flow" ', she writes, is 'as important . . . as the more . . . visible and highly rated masculine business information flow' (Moyal, 1992:67). It should be remembered, too, that her qualitative survey was partly financed by Telecom Australia, to whom she advanced policy recommendations on call charges and the desirable shape of future services (see Moyal, 1989:26–8; 1992:68–9).

Less bounded by the demands of funding agencies, Rakow (1992) adopts a self-consciously feminist academic and political stance at the outset. In its findings, *Gender on the Line* has remarkable overlaps with those reported by Moyal – considering the location for this study, halfway around the globe in an American Midwestern settlement of just under a thousand people which she dubs 'Prospect'. Rakow's research can safely be described as ethnographic, without fear of upsetting traditional anthropologists or sociologists (I refer the reader back to my opening chapter), because her book is based on an extended stay in the town during which she lived 'as a member of the community, shopping in the small grocery store, buying fresh meat at the meat market, having coffee in the cafe, picking up my mail in the morning at the post office with the rest of the community, getting my car fixed at the local garage' (Rakow, 1992:6). Over a period of weeks, her project became a topic of local conversation and she was known to residents as 'the telephone lady'. In total, she spoke at length with forty-three women in Prospect about their use of the phone service – and the second half of *Gender on the Line* presents six of these women's accounts in full.

Williams's concept of 'mobile privatization', as well as Giddens's ideas about modern forms of time–space structuration (see above), might effectively be brought to bear on the material Rakow gathers. For in a host of ways, her interviewees are addressing matters of geography, place, community and travel. When asked 'Has the telephone changed your feelings about how far away things are?', Ethel – who lives alone on a farm outside Prospect – replies:

> Oh, my goodness, yes. My friends say to me, 'Too bad your children are so far away'. Well, they are in a way; they aren't next door the way many children are to their parents, but when I can go and dial them or go and get on a plane when I need to. . . . No, if it weren't for the telephone, I would have a much different existence here. We talk every week, sometimes twice. Weekends . . . we like to talk a long time. (quoted in Rakow, 1992:103)

This speaker, argues Rakow (1992:9), 'has found the telephone an important source of emotional support . . . a link across time and space to a larger world . . . and demographically dispersed family'. However, there is an unwillingness on the author's part simply to treat such communications as a wholly satisfactory substitute for presence with others. The sense of absence is relieved to a certain degree, yet 'use of the telephone in these cases should be seen as a symptom – of isolation, loneliness, boredom or fear – rather than as a cure' (Rakow, 1992:151). She proposes that control over time and space is not equally available to everybody. Indeed, women's reliance on the technology in Prospect has a lot to do with their restricted control over location, with many finding themselves in the town because of job moves by husbands. Assuming for the moment that phone networks 'did make all points equidistant', we must remember 'the point from which these women are starting is not necessarily of their own choosing' (Rakow, 1992:62). Her insistence on underlining the material limitations that govern a 'feminine culture of the telephone' (not only geographical but financial – see Moyal, 1989, on the 'telephone poor') thus enables Rakow to understand this particular culture as a creative set of gendered practices which are always, ultimately, acted out within determinate social constraints. The theme of 'creativity versus constraint' resurfaces again on several occasions later in my text.

Consuming Technologies : The HICT Project

All the domestic media discussed in the preceding pages (TV, VCR, home computer, phone) have recently been gathered together under the umbrella of a single research project – an ongoing investigation into 'The Household Uses of Information and Communication Technologies', which is being funded by the UK's Economic and Social Research Council. The initial phase of this study was carried out by a team including Roger Silverstone, Eric Hirsch, David Morley, Andrea Dahlberg and Sonia Livingstone – who were associated, at various times in the late 1980s and early 1990s, with the Centre for Research into Innovation, Culture and Technology at Brunel University. Their joint work merits close scrutiny because of its commitment to looking comprehensively at a collection of objects in the household media environment, its efforts to elaborate an overall conceptual model for exploring the role of information and communication technologies in home life, and its concern to develop a 'methodological raft' for empirical research on domestic cultures. I am therefore devoting an entire section of my present chapter to the HICT investigation – reflecting, in turn, on issues of theory, method and ethnographic description.

In 'Families, Technologies and Consumption' (Silverstone *et al.*, 1989), a paper which reviewed several bodies of literature relevant to the research and provided an opening statement of intentions, the Brunel group makes brief mention of the household's 'moral economy'. This concept has since become a central term in writings that arise out of the HICT project, and it informs much of their analysis. 'We want this notion,' they state, 'to refer to . . . families' own way of working with the social, economic and technological opportunities which frame their world' (Silverstone *et al.*, 1989:1–2). An extended account of the concept and its applications can be found in a subsequent theoretical essay (Silverstone *et al.*, 1992:19), where the authors explain:

> To understand the household as a moral economy . . . is to understand the household as part of a transactional system, dynamically involved in . . . the production and exchange of commodities and meanings. . . . At stake is the capacity of the household or the family to create and sustain its autonomy and identity (and for individual members to do the same) as an economic, social and cultural unit. . . . In the continuous work of reproduction – and via the mesh of class position, ethnicity, geography and the rest – the household engages in a process of value creation in its various daily practices. . . . Different families will draw on different cultural resources, based on . . . beliefs . . . biography, or the culture of a network of family and friends, and as a result construct a (more or less permeable, more or less defended) bounded environment – the home . . . The moral economy of the household is . . . grounded in the creation of the 'home'.

What the lengthy passage reproduced here implies, in short, is that the uses and interpretations of media texts or technologies in domestic contexts will be negotiable – depending upon the material and discursive resources which are accessed by households and their members. Such a view, it has to be said, is nothing dramatically new (certainly not to readers of this book). However, the concept of a moral economy does serve to crystallize particular ideas about audience activity and domestic culture that were already in circulation, but which perhaps needed expressing in a more systematic fashion. A novel addition to existing approaches within cultural studies is the Brunel group's strong emphasis on the part that ICTs can play in achieving a sense of 'ontological security' in day-to-day living (a phrase taken directly from Giddens – see Silverstone, in press).

Four elements are identified by Silverstone, Hirsch and Morley (1992) as constituting the dynamics of this moral economy – processes of appropriation, objectification, incorporation and conversion. A technology gets appropriated, they argue, as it's sold and then owned or possessed by a household. That is the point at which a commodity crosses the threshold between public and private, beginning its new life as a domestic object. The next element, objectification, is a reference to practices of display in the home:

'physical artefacts, in their arrangement and display, as well as . . . in the creation of the environment for their display, provide an objectification of the values, the aesthetic and . . . cognitive universe, of those who feel comfortable or identify with them' (Silverstone *et al.*, 1992:22–3). For an artefact to be incorporated, the Brunel group suggest it has to be made active use of in the performance of a task (a slightly narrower definition of the word than the one I have been operating with in my own work) – and, lastly, 'whereas objectification and incorporation are . . . aspects of the internal structure of the household, conversion, like appropriation, defines the relationship between the household and the outside world' (Silverstone *et al.*, 1992:25). In the case of conversion, though, movement is turned back in the direction of the public sphere. It marks a 'trading in' of pleasures, meanings and competences which are cultivated in the private domain. The best example they offer of the process is that of a teenager who employs his skill at computer games, partly developed at home in the bedroom, as a 'ticket' into peer culture (clearly echoing the experiences of Haddon's young male interviewees). Whether such fine-grained distinctions are actually necessary to conceptualize the consumption of communication technologies is debatable. So, in situated empirical instances, these four categories might well collapse into each other – yet the analysis advanced by Silverstone and his colleagues tries hard to delineate moments of ownership, display, use and exchange.

Outlining the precise methods of investigation which were chosen for their research on twenty families living in the south-east of England, the Brunel team characterize that work (following Malinowski's opinions on the nature of anthropological inquiry) as listening to and engaging in a long conversation. When they say they are studying 'conversations', though, Silverstone's group mean more than words alone. The object of their research is, in a far broader sense, the 'dialogical' interactions which households have with ICTs and, through those media technologies, with a world beyond the boundaries of home. In order to understand how this social dialogue evolves, the HICT group itself evolved a raft of investigative procedures – 'a multiply triangulated set of research inputs' (Silverstone *et al.*, 1991:216) for the purpose of reporting and interpreting the usually unrecorded private existence of family and domestic technology.

To start with, in a fifth of their twenty households, participant observation was the chief method employed. Whilst it supplied valuable in-depth material on daily events in these homes over a fortnight or so – undoubtedly more detailed than that assembled in any previous audience ethnography – it was still not considered a sufficient source of data when taken in isolation. The researchers saw an immediate need for forms of investigation which could supplement the observational strategy – making it possible for them to draw better comparisons between families being studied, and to gain greater knowledge of historical and geographical context. For a further tranche of sixteen households, then, Silverstone, Hirsch and Morley added complementary methods that were used during a much longer period of up to ten months in which a total of nine visits was made to each home. This so-called 'raft' of procedures included getting family members to complete a time-use diary, and sketch out 'mental maps' illustrating the perceived spatial location and significance of various technologies, as well as diagrams of kin and friendship networks stretching outside the walls of the house. A session to discuss the family's photo album was also added.

We might even want to conclude that the material generated in this phase of the project went a little too deep! The vast amount of data collected has evidently proved difficult to sort and manage – because some years after the fieldwork was finished, the only sustained accounts which are available up to now are 'portraits' of three out of the twenty households (see Silverstone & Morley, 1990; Hirsch, 1992). These attempts at ethnographic portraiture give a good indication as to the wealth of their data. Indeed, I adopt a similar reporting technique in the following part of Chapter 4 when speaking about my present research on satellite TV consumption (and see Wallman, 1984; Pahl, 1984, for earlier examples of the same focussed writing style in modern social anthropology and sociology). Nevertheless, it is both disappointing and frustrating that much more of the HICT material has not so far been written up for publication – given the fact that this remains the most extensive and comprehensive qualitative survey of its kind yet to be carried out.

Hirsch's case study of the Simon family (Hirsch, 1992:213–21) offers us a taste of the ethnographer's 'banquet' which must be lying in an archive at Brunel. It serves to highlight the key aspects of a household's distinctive moral economy, and to focus attention on the different types of boundary that we may construct around our homes. The Simon parents are a relatively well off middle-class couple in their forties who have five children aged from eight to sixteen. Charles, the father, works as an inventor – developing new applications of microchip technology – while Natalie, his wife, is a primary school teacher. They live in a three-storey property in north London, but spend a lot of time during the school holidays at their Cornwall cottage where a sailing boat is kept. As Hirsch (1992:213) notes, the family 'has the cultural and economic resources to extend its domestic life beyond the city, into the country', so that it 'oscillates between an urban life of intensely hard work and wide-ranging social relationships and a rural . . . cut-off life where social relationships are at a minimum' (Hirsch, 1992:221). These separate spaces of existence are, according to Charles and Natalie, mutually reinforcing. In London, the door is always metaphorically open. Their city residence has a constant stream of visitors or guests passing throught it and, by way of two telephone lines and an answering machine, the Simons declare that they are 'available . . . twenty-four hours per day'. By contrast, in rural Cornwall, the cottage is inaccessible by road – and the family are more inaccessible still when away on the boat.

The London home is filled with an assortment of communication and information technologies which are distributed within the house's internal geography. For instance, the husband has two IBM computers in his office on the first floor (he occasionally allows the children to play with graphics software on the PCs). A small music room with a mixture of electronic and acoustic instruments is nearby, and up on the second level the youngsters have their own radios and cassette recorders situated in bedrooms. From the kitchen downstairs, Mrs Simon utilizes an intercom system to call the family down for meals or to wake them in the morning. Meanwhile, in the ground floor sitting-room area, the TV and CD player have recently been joined by a video recorder – the installation of which was hotly disputed. Hirsch (1992:219–20) explains how the lengthy debate that they had over its appropriation and incorporation indicates 'a particular axis of values which are intrinsic to the moral economy of the Simon family'. He reports:

> television . . . was downgraded as a passive and inappropriate form . . . to spend much time on. Charles and Natalie place a high value on active doing rather than passivity. The word 'activity' was frequently used by the Simons. . . . Their relationships with objects and others, and those of their children, are informed by this and related values. This sentiment was exemplified early on in our visits. When talking about whether or not they had a video, Charles said they made a conscious decision not to. . . . It is interesting, then, that in the six months that separated the start of our fieldwork from its completion a video made its way into the Simon home. (Hirsch, 1992:218–19)

Purchasing the VCR equipment was eventually justified by these parents for a couple of reasons – both of which were related to their specific outlook on leisure pursuits and the upbringing of children. Mr Simon plans to buy them a video camera, so that 'they would be "making" . . . not just sitting there watching *Neighbours*'. Natalie also wished to record the minor TV performances which two of the youngsters had made (acting parts gained through membership of a local theatre company). In this respect, of course, the Simons are no ordinary family – and there are obviously questions for Hirsch to answer concerning the 'representativeness' of such a case study (consult his concluding statement). He succeeds, however, in demonstrating some of the wider processes of domestic consumption identified by the Brunel group as they occur in a single household.

    After taking up a chair at Sussex University, Silverstone continues to direct the HICT investigation in its secondary phase. His collaborator on the next stage of the project is Haddon – whose writings on micro-computers will be familiar from my commentary. The task of field research they have just begun is to comprehend the implications of new 'teleworking' practices for the organization of domestic cultures, and for divisions between private and public spheres (see Haddon & Silverstone, 1992). Here, very similar interests in the household's moral economy are carried through into a different order of issues which are to do with the meanings of information technologies as home-based work objects. Once again, their study promises to deliver important insights on the subjects of time–space structuration and family dynamics.

Satellite TV as Cultural Sign

My current research (see also Moores, 1991), rather like the work I did a few years ago on early radio's arrival in the private sphere, is concerned with the place of a new media technology in everyday life. It is an investigation of satellite TV's cultural significance as an object of domestic consumption. Through an analysis of conversational interviews recorded at the homes of consumers living in a South Wales city, I am mapping out various meanings which have come to be invested in the technology at the point of its entry into specific social contexts and situations. The method of inquiry, then, can broadly be described as ethnographic – and my purpose has been to chart the conditions of satellite TV's 'multi-accentuality' within and across different household and neighbourhood cultures. This final section of Chapter 4 offers a series of reflections on the study, addressing some of the general theoretical issues that underpin the project and identifying particular themes which have emerged in the course of the fieldwork.

I begin by discussing three terms, or keywords, that help to provide a conceptual framework for the research. The first of these, 'consumption', is evidently undergoing something of a rehabilitation in media and cultural studies at present. If, in the past, it has often been placed alongside production in a binary opposition – with passive consumption as the poor relation to an active production – then a number of theorists have now begun to redress the imbalance by referring to consumption itself as 'productive'. It is a moment at which objects and texts are actively appropriated and interpreted as they come into contact with the everyday practices of social subjects. Of course, there can be dangers associated with this kind of approach. In focussing on the meanings that consumers create when they 'read' satellite TV, we should be careful not to lose sight altogether of the technology's design and marketing or the sounds and images that are broadcast. Satellite TV's significance is partly determined by its positioning within the home and residential area, but the moments of manufacture and promotion also exert considerable pressure on reception activity. So technologies are not completely open to be used and made sense of in any way one chooses. A degree of closure has already been imposed elsewhere in the cultural circuit (Johnson, 1986).

Another, related danger is the populist celebration of consumer freedoms. Despite his good political intentions, John Fiske (1989a) presents us with a model of cultural consumption which is guilty of such a mistake (see Chapter 5 for a fuller critique). Following Michel De Certeau (1984), he has emphasized the 'tactical resistances' of subordinate groups in their constant daily struggle against the power of the dominant. For Fiske, 'the popular' is a site where the weak frequently succeed in putting one over on the strong – 'poaching' on the commodities of a capitalist system, and asserting their own meanings and pleasures in the process. Although it is undoubtedly the case that culture is a contested sphere, his writings unfortunately suffer from an overly optimistic and rather romantic perception of everyday life in the postmodern world. Fiske tends to overestimate the progressive potential of consumption practices and fails to acknowledge any of the profoundly reactionary elements at play in popular culture.

Somebody else who might be accused of straightforwardly celebrating the 'symbolic creativities' of consumers is Paul Willis in *Common Culture* (1990).

However, Willis's recent book has important advantages over Fiske's. He grounds his commentary in an extensive empirical study of young people's cultural experiences, and he is keen to stress the material and social constraints that bear down on those research subjects. In the strand of British cultural studies which is represented by his continuing work (see also Willis, 1977, 1978) – and by Morley's audience inquiries too (Morley, 1980a, 1986) – detailed attention to questions of interpretation, use and context has always been accompanied by a genuine sociological concern with the patterning of culture and communication. I would want my own investigation to be considered part of this same analytical strand, because it opens up a convenient pathway between De Certeau's interest in imaginative ways of 'making do' and Pierre Bourdieu's preoccupation with the structured distinctions of consumer behaviour (Bourdieu, 1984). What we require is a theory and method that recognizes both creativity and constraint in quotidian life.

The second term in my conceptual vocabulary is 'embedding'. I employ it in an effort to stress the situated nature of consumption practices and cultural objects. Studying satellite TV's position in the day-to-day lives of social audiences necessarily involves an understanding of the technology as embedded at several, interconnected levels or instances (Silverstone, 1990:174). Primarily, there is the level of households and families – the immediate physical and human contexts of reception. This includes spatial divisions inside the home, the temporal routines of its inhabitants, and the interpersonal ties and tensions that have formed between household members. Any new commodity that arrives will inevitably become enmeshed within the existing dynamics of power in the domestic realm. It therefore has to be analysed in conjunction with the range of artefacts and activities that are already in place. Once again, though, potential problems arise when the notion of embedding is taken up in ethnographies of media use, just as there were certain dangers associated with ideas about the productivity of consumption. We run the risk of assuming domestic cultures to be fixed entities into which goods are inserted and incorporated without any resulting impact on the pre-given structure. Instead, as I have found in my conversations with consumers, the family is best seen as a 'system in process'. To a limited extent, practices and dynamics may change over time, and the entry of a new technology can occasionally serve as the signal for a renegotiation of internal boundaries and relationships in the home.

Communication technologies can also be implicated in the redrawing of boundaries and relationships between the private sphere of the household and various public worlds beyond. This actually goes for 'communications' in its most general sense, and would apply just as well to a machine like the motor car as it does to the medium of television. Both these objects are in the business of transportation – albeit of slightly different sorts – and each facilitates what Giddens (1984) has called a 'time–space convergence'. They have brought individuals and families into the presence of places and events that were previously distant or unknown, enabling them to identify with dispersed yet knowable communities and to imagine themselves as embedded in regional, national and even transnational collectivities. It is worth remembering here how Williams (1974:26), in his book on television as technology and cultural form, lists broadcasting side by side with the car when discussing the tendency in twentieth–century living which he refers to as 'mobile privatization'. So, in researching the domestic consumption of satellite TV, I am interested in asking about the kinds of mobility that the object and its texts offer viewers – to what new destinations is it promising transport and who chooses to make the journey?

At an intermediate level, between the micro-context of the home and the large-scale 'imagined communities' to which the media provide access, there is the artefact's embedding in particular residential neighbourhoods and urban cultures. Few household technologies are visible from the street – they are usually hidden out of sight behind closed doors and drawn curtains – but satellite TV's dish aerial is an extremely public symbol of possession. Displayed on exterior walls or rooftops, dishes openly announce the technology's arrival. They give outsiders a fair indication of the types of sounds and images that are being consumed in private. We could pursue the comparison with automobiles a little further now, because just as the car parked at the front of the house says something about the lifestyle of its driver, so the satellite aerial is a sign to be read by neighbours and passers-by. How it is valued will depend, of course, on the person making the judgement and the geographical area in which it is sited. For onlookers, the dish can either be a focus of disgust or a matter of indifference. Similarly, for owners, it may be a source of pride or else a cause of embarrassment. The task is to match these varied decodings and dispositions to social patterns of taste in contemporary culture.

This leads us neatly on to questions of 'articulation', the last of my keywords. As Hall (1986a:53) has pointed out, the term can have a dual significance. On the one hand, it refers to the act of speaking – to the production of linguistic utterances – and on the other it implies a linking together, a connection that is forged between two separate things. For example, in his writings on the British New Right, Hall (1988) employs the word to account for a linkage of ideological elements in the political discourse of Thatcherism. I make use of the term rather differently here, whilst retaining its double-edged meaning. My own concern is with the ways in which a new media technology gets 'hitched up' to lived cultures of consumption, and thereby enables social subjects to actively 'voice' senses of identity and distinction. As satellite TV is embedded at each of the levels or instances outlined above – articulating with relations in and between the private and public spheres – it gives consumers an opportunity to articulate their subjectivities.

In these simultaneous practices of connection and expression, the technology becomes – to borrow Valentin Volosinov's remarks on the spoken word – 'a little arena for the clash and criss-crossing of differently oriented social accents' (Volosinov, 1973:41). The continual dialogue between artefact and everyday contexts is what transforms satellite TV into a multi-accentual sign and what allows it to function, quite literally, as a 'medium' for cultural forces of identification or differentiation. Hall (1986a) reminds us that articulations are always contingent and non-necessary. There is nothing inevitable, he suggests, about the coupling together of discursive elements. This applies to the embedding of media technologies as well. We cannot predict, simply from the development of a new means of broadcasting, how it will eventually come to have significance for audience groupings. It is certainly the case, as I noted earlier, that designers and advertisers play an important part in encoding the object prior to consumption. Programming policies are also formulated with specific viewing publics and market segments in mind. However, the linkages made with local settings demand detailed empirical investigation. My commitment, therefore, has been to qualitative research carried out at homes in selected neighbourhood areas where satellite dishes have recently been erected. Households in my study are distributed across three different areas of the same city (the basic idea for such a geographical segmentation is borrowed from models now being employed in commercial market research – for example, see CACI Market Analysis, 1985). By talking to family members about their newly acquired commodities, and by observing the domestic and residential environments, I believe it is possible to construct suitably 'thick' descriptions (Geertz, 1973) of situated consumer activity.

For the purposes of the present discussion, I intend to concentrate on data from one of my three neighbourhoods (a more complete account of all the households will appear in a forthcoming monograph). This particular district is made up of privately owned properties that were originally built just after the turn of the century – a collection of large bay-fronted Edwardian terraces and detached houses. Situated in it is a small park with trees and a stream, surrounded by ornate antique railings. Estate agents refer to its 'authentic' historical qualities, and while some of the road names echo those of English stately homes, others recall famous military battles overseas. Lying approximately five kilometres from the city centre, the area has a mixed population of skilled manual workers and middle-class professionals. In some ways, then, it is comparable with a community in the north-west of England that was studied by Derek Wynne (1990). He sought to contrast the lifestyles and leisure patterns of housing estate residents who had very different sorts of 'cultural capital' at their disposal – and his fieldwork highlighted the frictions between them over matters of taste. Similar clashes of interpretation and disposition in my own district give rise to certain anxieties about satellite TV which are frequently expressed in the conversational interviews.

A distinguishing feature of the neighbourhood I have chosen to analyse here is its age. Wynne's ethnography was conducted out of town on a modern estate. The households discussed below are located in a city suburb which, for various reasons outlined in the previous paragraph, has strong connotations of 'heritage'. In these circumstances, the arrival of a new communications technology – with its futuristic dish on open display – results in a curious collision of aesthetic and cultural codes (early promotional material for satellite TV made interesting use of science fiction imagery – with advertisements for the popular 'Amstrad Fidelity' system picturing the dish and receiver unit together on a cratered moonscape). Brunsdon (1991), in her review of newspaper reports on controversies over the siting of aerials, notes that tensions tend to surface when the objects are installed on old buildings considered to have architectural merit. Discourses of innovation and conservation confront each other, exerting pressure in opposite directions, and it is precisely this contradiction between senses of 'the modern' and 'the traditional' which runs through much of the following commentary. Such a conflict, I will argue, is not confined to antagonisms at the level of the residential area. It can get 'gridded', in complex and shifting ways, on to social divisions of gender or generation within domestic life – and may also help to constitute our broader feelings of collective identity.

Let me start to unpack these remarks now by looking in more detail at some of the homes in my neighbourhood (names of the families have been changed). For instance, the Gibsons – who have a 'Cambridge' dish – live in an old house which once belonged to a well known family of solicitors in the city. There is a striking divergence of tastes and competences between Mr Gibson and his nineteen-year-old son. The father takes great pleasure in the 'character' and heritage value of the building they own. He is currently restoring one of the original antique fireplaces, which he discovered hidden behind a plasterboard wall, and has plans to strip and varnish a wooden dresser in the back dining room. As we shall see, he is extremely anxious about the dish's appearance on their housefront. It was the son, Tony, who wanted a satellite receiver. Since he left school three years ago and gained his own independent source of income as a shiftworker in a bakery, Tony has chosen to buy a range of the latest media technologies. These commodities adorn his attic bedroom, described to me by Mr Gibson as 'a conglomeration of electronics'. To understand the position that satellite TV occupies in this particular family's inter-generational and time–space relations, it is necessary for us to explore the dynamic structure of identifications and distinctions which is in play.

At the top of the house, separated from the main living area by a narrow staircase and landing, is Tony's room. He is intensely proud of this space and the objects that are arranged inside, regarding it as a place into which he can retreat and as a symbol of independence from the rest of his family: 'I'm the only one who really knows how to use any of my electrical equipment. Nobody else comes in my room – I think of it as my space . . . up here, I can watch anything I want, read, sleep, think about life, listen to music.' Around the television set there is a remarkable 'entourage' (Leal, 1990:21) of technological hardware and software, as well as an array of decorative images and artefacts. Two video recorders, a hi-fi system and the satellite receiver are all stacked on shelves underneath the TV. They have been wired together, too, so that the sound comes out of four 'Dolby Surround' speakers mounted on brackets in each corner of the room. According to Mr Gibson, 'it's like a disco in there . . . if he turned the volume up any more, it'd blow the whole roof off'. Tony has moved his bed to a central point between these sources of sound, and five different remote control devices rest on top of the 'Bart Simpson' duvet cover (*The Simpsons* is an American cartoon show broadcast on Sky). On a bedside table there is a Simpsons alarm clock which wakes him in time for the shiftwork. The walls are covered with posters of sports cars, whilst neat piles of video tapes and CDs lie on the floor. His viewing preferences are for science fiction and horror – recording several films off the Sky Movies channel – and he also collects tapes about the making of films, especially those concerned with stunts and special effects.

It is possible, I believe, to read these assembled goods as signs of a struggle to fashion some limited degree of autonomy in the face of parental authority. The bakery job has not earned him enough to get a home of his own, enforcing a reliance on parents for accommodation, but he is able to save up and purchase things – items that are treasured precisely because they provide a statement of personal identity. Of course, that identity takes shape under conditions not entirely of his own choosing. He is, as the poststructuralists would say, constituted as a subject only as a consequence of being 'subject-ed' to and positioned within the symbolic order of culture. Tony inhabits a specifically masculine world of gadgets, fast cars and sci-fi fantasies (a world which he shares, incidentally, with his friends and fellow workers). However, in the spirit of current developments in audience studies, I want to insist on a more situated theory of subjectivity and discourse that recognizes a measure of human agency and understands meaning as negotiable. For this teenager in this immediate context, then, satellite TV is part of a constellation of technologies and practices which provides the cultural material to express difference and establish competence. Tellingly, his father confesses complete incompetence when it comes to operating the machinery in Tony's bedroom: 'He knows where everything is, but I don't . . . I remember glancing over at it – the electronics and wiring – and just one look was enough for me.'

Mr Gibson's interest in restoring antique furnishings and fittings has, it should be stated, grown considerably over the period since satellite TV entered their home. This heightened investment in the traditional is a direct response to his son's passion for the modern. As I argued earlier, the introduction of a technology into the family system occasionally coincides with a redrawing of domestic boundaries and relationships, and it certainly appears to be the case here. Tony makes a partial bid for independence. His father, meanwhile, defines a clearly contrasting field of knowledge and skills. The inter-generational pattern is clear – although there remains a single exception to the general rule. Mrs Gibson's taste for sixties pop music has been inherited by Tony, who started borrowing her scratched LPs when he was still at school. Those same recordings have now been bought on CD, forming a large part of his musical library. Perhaps the raiding of styles from a previous era is not so surprising – considering the contemporary trend in youth cultures which Dick Hebdige (1988) has termed 'retro-chic' – but it adds a further twist to the oppositions between 'old' and 'new' in the Gibson household.

The story of how their external dish was selected and then positioned on the front wall is a revealing account of conflict and compromise. In this instance, installing the satellite aerial was very much a public enactment of private tensions. It was also going to be a potential cause of embarrassment for Mr Gibson, given the 'tone' of the neighbourhood they live in. Realizing the technical impracticalities of siting at the rear of the house, Tony had to enter into a debate with his father over the aesthetics of display. Mr Gibson's comments on the circular Amstrad dishes – the most commonly seen aerials – are decidedly uncomplimentary. He calls them 'frying pans with handles on', and says:

> They look completely out of place on houses like this, old houses with character . . . I didn't want an unsightly thing hovering up there. If it was just a prefabricated sort of house, then sure, I wouldn't mind – but as we've got bay windows and all the stonework at the front, I wasn't going to have something that wouldn't blend in . . . wouldn't retain the character of the area.

After consulting one of the consumer guide magazines which have recently come on to the market, Tony eventually managed to convince his father of the 'Cambridge' system's unobtrusive qualities. The name itself suggests a higher-status commodity, with distant associations of education and heritage, and its aerial is a rectangular stone-coloured block rather than the usual white sphere. Even Mr Gibson admits that 'it's compact and looks neater on the side of houses . . . there's many a person'll pass and not notice you've got it' (I return to the theme of 'invisibility' later).

This tentative agreement between father and son is not quite the end of the story, though. When a workman came to fix the dish at the front, there were reception difficulties caused by a tall tree which stands across the way from their home. A snow-like effect was created on the screen, and the interference problem could only have been solved by using an extension pole stretching out a metre or so above the bay. Predictably, Mr Gibson refused to accept such a solution – 'it'd be stuck out like a lollipop' – so the aerial went up in an alcove of the bay window despite the rather poor picture quality. Thereafter, Tony had a constant visual reminder as he watched of the intriguing compromise that was struck. It took the launch of a second 'Astra' satellite, and another visit from the installation engineer to realign his dish, for the situation finally to be rectified.

My closing comment on the Gibsons – one which provides a convenient link with the next household I discuss – concerns their identifications, through television, with larger national or transnational communities. Some might protest that small-scale ethnographic research of the sort I have been doing is an inappropriate means of investigating the cultural construction of collective identities. The best existing work on this theme has taken public representations and narratives as a starting point for analysis (e.g. Formations Collective, 1984; Bhabha, 1990), rather than trying to explore the sentiments of actual social subjects in the private domain. However, a recently published book by Michael Billig – *Talking of the Royal Family* (1992) – demonstrates the relevance of conversational interviews with families for examining discourses of nationhood. Getting them to speak about the British royals, he points to powerful 'common sense' articulations of monarchy, domesticity and nationality. Talking about TV, in both its terrestrial and satellite varieties, can deliver similar insights into processes of identification. As Morley (1991:12) puts it, 'the sitting room is exactly where we need to start from if we finally want to understand the constitutive dynamics of abstractions such as "the community" or "the nation" '. Although Morley overstates the argument a little, broadcasting does connect the space of the home with electronic 'image spaces', and in the case of the Gibsons an interesting distinction is made between different territories of transmission. Tony's positive feelings about the Astra broadcasts (he tunes in to continental stations like RTL Plus or Pro 7 as well as the Sky channels and MTV Europe) are intimately related to his dismissal of established terrestrial programming as traditional and old fashioned. In fact, he labels it negatively as 'British' TV. Mr and Mrs Gibson use precisely the same label themselves, but here its value is completely reversed. They prefer to watch BBC or ITV in the living room downstairs.

For the Harveys, a family living nearby, there are further interesting connections being forged between everyday experience and the new 'spaces of identity' made available by satellite TV. Dave and Liz Harvey are in their late twenties and have three young children aged five, four and six months. They moved to the city four years ago from the Midlands region of England, where he had studied for a polytechnic degree in electronic engineering. She works as a housewife and Mr Harvey is now self-employed, having given up a salaried job to start his own small business designing and manufacturing computer robotics equipment for export. This married couple perceive the satellite technology to be offering them an expanded range of viewing choices – although Dave gets to exercise that choice more than Liz – and, significantly, he speaks about the 'larger feel' created by a type of television transmission which transcends the boundaries of narrowly British broadcasting.

Whilst the first of these perceptions is what we might reasonably expect to hear from satellite TV consumers, since the technology has been marketed as offering increased freedom of choice for its viewers, the second set of feelings is far less predictable. Mr Harvey explains that:

> When I'm watching Sky – because it's from a European satellite – and when I'm looking at some of the other continental stations that are available, I very much get the sense of being a European. A lot of the channels are an hour ahead, they're on European time. If you're just channel-hopping, which is a bit of a sport for me – buzzing round eight or nine stations to see what's going on – you do get the feeling of not being restricted in the good old British way. It's quite something when you can sit down in your own front room and watch what's on in another country.

Willis (1980:90) has written about the potential that ethnography has for 'surprising' us – for throwing up empirical data and conceptual issues not prefigured in the researcher's starting paradigm – and in this early interview, I was genuinely surprised by Dave's statement of identification. The opposition he constructs here between restriction and mobility is mapped on to another distinction in which 'Britishness' and 'Europeanness' are contrasted ('not being restricted in the good old British way'). Even if his viewing pleasures take the form of a 'touristic grazing', it remains the case that satellite TV is helping him travel to new places and to reimagine the boundaries of community. Of course, the image spaces produced by a communications technology cannot reshape national subjectivities on their own. Only when those audio-visual territories are articulated with existing situations and discourses can a fiction like Europe be 'realized' by certain groups of people.

So Mr Harvey, who manufactures hi-tech goods for the export market, already identifies strongly with a transnational business community. The fact that his parents have bought a retirement home on the continent also contributes to Dave's recognition of himself as 'a European'. Their villa is now a regular destination for family holidays abroad. Mrs Harvey, too, finds that the idea of Europe has a certain limited salience. When her younger sister – an arts student at university – came to visit with a boyfriend from France, they were able to show them French-language programmes on satellite TV. Some of these circumstances are obviously unique to the Harvey household – while others, such as the commercial and cultural significance of a single European market, have much wider currency. What we need to specify, though, are precisely those interdiscursive moments at which private lives and public worlds meet and mesh together. Any transformation of collective identities will inevitably be uneven in its development and will necessarily be grounded in quotidian practices.

The theme of 'modern versus traditional' runs just as powerfully through pursuits and disputes in the Harveys' home as it did through the Gibsons'. In this family, it is the father who is a self-confessed gadgeteer. From the time he began playing around with lightbulbs and circuits as a teenager, Dave has always been enthusiastic about electronics. He can be located within what Haddon (1988) has called 'hobbyist' culture – a predominantly masculine sphere of social activity where consumers are concerned to experiment with all the latest innovations in information and communication technology. Their house currently contains three computers (one of which he assembled himself out of IBM parts), two VCRs and two televisions, in addition to the satellite system and a compact disc player. An interest in electronic music has also resulted in plans to buy a synthesizer. Liz, however, is extremely conscious of the fact that 'people do take the mickey out of us . . . we're constantly tripping over monitors and things'. Her feelings towards these gadgets are distinctly more ambivalent than those of her husband. Indeed, she is clearly frustrated by the fact that money spent on his 'toys' is money which goes unspent on her preferred pastime of collecting antique furniture (there is a growing body of work on family resource distribution and the control of money within marriage which serves to illuminate these sorts of situations – see Brannen & Wilson, 1987; Pahl, 1989).

If the household dynamics and differences of taste appear to be organized chiefly along gendered lines, they are best highlighted by focussing on interpersonal relations across three generations – by looking first at the ties that Mr and Mrs Harvey have with their children, and then at the tensions which arise when her parents come from the Midlands to visit. Although the youngsters are denied access to certain areas of domestic space, including the front living room where satellite TV is watched, this does not mean that they are kept away from media technologies altogether. On the contrary, the older video recorder was 'given to the kids' and Dave's micro-computer from college days has now been handed down to the five-year-old, Phil. These are very good illustrations of the 'cultural biography' of objects (see Kopytoff, 1986; Silverstone *et al.*, 1992), where a technology's position and function within the home environment has shifted, and its 'career' can be traced against the changing biographies of family members. Goods and competences here are passing through a gradual process of inheritance. Mr Harvey reports proudly on his son's progress with the micro: 'he knows how to put discs in, knows what disc drives are, and can operate them . . . which is great because I'd like him to get into computing'. Understandably, Liz is less sure about the acquisition of his father's enthusiasm for electronic gadgetry. She readily acknowledges the educational advantages of a technological literacy – yet describes Phil with some regret as 'a child of the nineties'. Her own recent efforts to hand on nostalgic pleasures to the children ended in bitter disappointment. Mrs Harvey purchased a video recording of the BBC's original *Watch with Mother* broadcasts as a gift for them, only to discover that they found it slow and boring in comparison with modern American cartoon shows like, for example, *Teenage Mutant Hero Turtles*.

Meanwhile, Mrs Harvey's mother and father have taken exception to the satellite aerial which is mounted on the house exterior. It has been the source of arguments between parents and daughter when they come to stay. 'My mum thinks it's rather vulgar,' Liz explains. 'She says to me, "You really shouldn't have that thing on the front of such a lovely Edwardian home".' There could be no more emphatic statement of the innovation/conservation conflict. Comparing the perceived ugliness of an Amstrad dish with the assumed beauty of period architecture, the grandmother forms a critical judgement on the basis of certain moral and aesthetic values that privilege past over present. We have seen how this juxtaposition of traditional and modern codes is at the root of numerous frictions in the Harvey family. Liz's desire for pieces of antique furniture is opposed to Dave's fascination with electronic gadgets. Similarly, the uncertain feelings she has about Phil learning to use a micro-computer contrasts with Dave's evident pride in his son's achievements. As for the disagreement between Mrs Harvey and her parents over the dish on the front wall, she chooses temporarily to side with her husband – reluctantly identifying with 'modernity' because she is forced on to the defensive by their unfavourable comments. In these different situations, Liz has to negotiate the contradictions of her gendered and generational subject positions as they are related to particular senses of 'old' and 'new'.

Both Mr and Mrs Harvey are amused by her parents' remarks on the satellite dish, and yet there are strong indications that they too are anxious over its appearance. So Dave sees it, in part, as a symbol of technological progress – a sign of being ahead of the times – but worries about the connotations it may have for others in view of the 'character' of the neighbourhood. He admits that if they were to put their property on the market in the near future, he would seriously consider taking the aerial down – 'if it proved detrimental to the sale of the house'. Liz confesses that 'most of the people we know do actually think it's a bit vulgar'. Also, a local councillor has been distributing leaflets to residents in the district, asking for opinions on the spread of dishes. The following extract from my interview with the Harveys clearly demonstrates the anxieties they have about the positioning and visual impact of the aerial, which Dave installed himself, on the front wall:

> *Liz*: We did try to put the dish round the back, didn't we? . . . Still, I don't think it's
> as bad – as noticeable – on our house as it is on some where there's just a straight
> row of houses in a line. Then it can look awful.
>
> *Dave*: Yes. If it was out at the end of the bay, it'd be apparently obvious from all
> directions. Whereas at the moment you can actually come down the road and
> not realize it's there.

It is interesting to compare the sentiments being expressed here with the opinions that were voiced by Mr Gibson. He perceived aerials on modern 'prefabricated' buildings as less of an eyesore than those on traditional Edwardian houses. Mrs Harvey disagrees – but only because she believes bay fronts help to hide them better. What Liz and Dave share with Mr Gibson is a desire for the object to be made 'invisible'. On this point, Mr Harvey announces his intention to site their next dish in the loft. One of the specialist magazines for satellite TV consumers ran a feature recently on the possibilities of receiving a signal through acrylic glass rooftiles, and he is willing to try the idea out for himself. In fact, there are regular advertisements in these magazines for pigments that promise to stain the aerial in colours which blend neatly into any residential background – adding the tactic of camouflage to existing methods of seclusion.

Listening to the accounts given by other families in the same neighbour-hood, we can hear a whole range of 'resonances' with those processes of consumption, embedding and articulation that are at work in the Gibson and Harvey households. In my two portraits, I have opened up and explored a number of important issues. Close attention has been paid to the ways in which media technologies get stitched into the fabric of domestic cultures – and, in particular, to the ways in which social divisions of gender or generation produce differential dispositions towards a technology like satellite TV. The part played by this new medium in helping to construct senses of collective identity and transnational community was also discussed. I anticipate objections to using conversational interviews for such an inquiry, but continue to argue that field research provides us with valuable material on the interrelations of private and public in everyday life. Finally, my analysis has sought to understand the contested meanings of satellite dishes in a specific residential setting – including the feelings of pride, disgust or embarrassment evoked by these objects. Pursuing each of the thematic strands developed above, I now want to cite some further examples from the interview data in order to amplify my ethnographic reading.

For instance, there is a definite pattern of satellite technology being desired and acquired by male consumers. Only in one family, the Clarks, have I come across a situation in which the woman was responsible for the decision to purchase a dish – and in this case, it was a mother buying her thirteen-year-old son a special gift at Christmas. The boy – a keen follower of the sports coverage on Astra – always used to be out watching at a friend's house before the Clarks got a receiver just over a year ago. His mother wanted him to spend more time at home in the evenings, and saw satellite TV as a means to that end. Programmes on the Eurosport and Screensport channels have been the main attraction to male viewers from other households in the neighbourhood too. So, against their wives' wishes, Mr Morgan and Mr Lloyd bought aerials which enable them to see soccer and boxing matches that are not shown on the terrestrial stations:

> *Mr M.*: I was the one who wanted to have it. She didn't want me to have it at all. I was watching sport all the time and she didn't like it. It cost us two hundred pounds. That was the other thing she didn't like – the money it cost – but I won in the end, I always do.
>
> *Mrs L.*: He got it for the sports channels.
>
> *Mr L.*: The boxing . . . they've got a lot on there which you don't get on the ordinary television. It's on nearly every night.
>
> *Mrs L.*: I didn't want to have it. I was very much against it, but I had to get used to it.

There is also another instance of a young gadgeteer in his bedroom – echoing the experiences of Tony Gibson. Steve Price, a merchant sailor in his early twenties, still lives in an upstairs flat at the parental home for several months of the year when he is not at sea. With the money he earns, Steve has put together a high-quality hi-fi system and owns two video machines in addition to the satellite TV equipment. By contrast, and in common with Mr and Mrs Gibson, the mother and father 'never watch it . . . they're not interested – they get the ordinary channels on their set downstairs'.

This young man, much like Dave Harvey or Tony, talks about feeling 'limited' by the four stations which are available from terrestrial broadcasting services. His work in the merchant navy occasionally takes him to the USA, where he has witnessed multi-channel cable systems first hand. Steve's acquisition of satellite television on returning to the UK was an attempt to recreate that experience: 'I've watched quite a bit of TV over there, and thought "the more the merrier", you know – a wider variety – which is why I bought it.' The sign of 'America' is prominent here, rather than the idea of 'Europe', but the principles of travel and mobility (both actual and imaginary) are present again. There has, of course, been a long history of debates concerning the export of American styles to Britain (Hebdige, 1982) – with some social groups branding US culture as vulgar and others choosing to celebrate it. What we have to do, as ethnographers of media reception, is seek out those interdiscursive moments of connection I spoke about earlier in this chapter – where identifications with new image spaces are made. One such moment can be found in my interview with the Sharmas, a middle-class Asian family. For the father, Astra's 'non-Britishness' is of particular significance. Comparing the modes of address employed by announcers on BBC1 and Sky News, he comments that:

With the BBC, you always feel as though the structure of society is there – the authority. Their newsreaders speak just like schoolmasters. They're telling you, like schoolmasters telling the kids. I think Sky News has more of a North American approach. It's more relaxed. They treat you like equals and don't take the audience for a bunch of small kids.

Mr Sharma's assessment is the consequence of a broader hostility towards establishment values in white British society – and towards the BBC as an institution which, from his perspective, embodies them.

Anxiety over the public display of dishes, clearly evident in my family portraits, is widely expressed by consumers elsewhere in the neighbourhood. Mrs Clark, the woman who purchased a satellite receiver to please her son, found that she worried about the aerial's appearance when it was fitted to the front of the house: 'I wanted it to go on the back . . . they're a bit unsightly, and nobody else in the street has got one.' Similarly, Steve Price admits to second thoughts after installing a dish by himself. 'I do wonder if it looks a bit out of place,' he says, 'because the local council have painted the old railings and made the park nice – I suppose that's why.' It is the now familiar opposition between innovation and conservation which provokes his doubts, and this conflict of cultural tastes functions in the Morgans' home as well. While the husband usually gets his way in disputes over the acquisition and use of media technologies, the wife controls decisions in the domain of interior decoration. Mrs Morgan has created an antique look in the lounge with traditional ornaments and furnishings, alongside a fireplace which she had specially restored for the room. Her general opinion of satellite TV, as I have previously noted, is low – and there are concerns about how the aerial is interpreted by people living in their street. Mr Morgan, a lorry driver, refers to the views of a teacher's wife across the road: 'She thinks it lowers the tone of the area with a dish out the front . . . there's a lot of doctors and teachers round here, and I don't think they're keen on them.' As for his own perception, Mr Morgan is less anxious than most interviewees in the district. 'Why worry?' he asks. 'Life's too short, isn't it?' In fact, his expression of indifference has more in common with responses recorded in my working-class neighbourhood. There, the erection of dishes seems to be relatively unproblematic.

On a final note, I would like to stress the considerable divergences in emphasis and method between my own current work and existing academic writings on satellite broadcasting. In the main, published essays and monographs (Negrine, 1988; Collins, 1990; Critcher & McCann, 1990) have focussed on institutional and policy issues. They outline patterns of ownership, draw from the available quantitative data on audience size, and make speculative forecasts about the future take-up and economic viability of the technology. What remains totally absent from this literature is any understanding of the significance that satellite TV has for consumers in everyday social contexts. Of course, all types of research (mine included) will have their 'opportunity costs' – those lines of inquiry which are sacrificed in favour of others – and I am certainly not suggesting that the matters dealt with by these authors are unimportant. However, I am insisting on the need for an analysis which engages with the fine-grained detail of situated consumption practices. My investigation can therefore be seen as contributing to what Klaus Bruhn Jensen (1991) calls 'the qualitative turn' in mass communications research – and it forms part of an emerging tradition of work in cultural studies that is addressing the domestic uses and meanings of media technologies.

5
On Cultural Consumption

This concluding chapter proposes that we might usefully connect developments in the study of media audiences with broader debates concerning the practices and politics of cultural consumption. The tendency of the research projects discussed in Chapter 4 has been to direct our attention towards the intricate embedding of communication technologies in everyday cultures. It was suggested that, in order to understand properly the meanings of media reception, ethnographers need to contextualize audience responses in relation to a further range of social activities, artefacts and interpretations. So as well as looking at the ways in which radio and television, or videos and computers, are used and made sense of by consumers, it may also be appropriate now for us to start inquiring about the clothes that they choose to wear – or the sorts of food they eat, or about how their homes are furnished. As I've indicated on a couple of occasions earlier in the book, such a move threatens (perhaps 'promises' would be a better word) to blur the boundaries of media research, and to widen dramatically our object of study. Nevertheless, it is a shift we should welcome rather than resist – even if it results, ultimately, in the decline of a specialized field known as 'audience ethnography'.

Running through the material which is to be covered here there are a number of closely related conceptual themes and oppositions. At root, these are amongst the oldest and most important themes in social theory – arising out of a long-running debate about human agency and social structure – and they will enable us, in turn, to reflect back with greater clarity on the work done by audience researchers over recent years. In the specific context of writings on cultural consumption, I would prefer to talk of an opposition between 'creativity' and 'constraint' rather than agency versus structure – but the issues raised remain roughly the same. Some theorists, then, have stressed the capacity of consumers to actively appropriate commodities and put them to creative use in the construction of everyday cultures. Others have tended to give more weight to the structural constraints that impose themselves on consumers – the limited economic and cultural resources available to those creative agents as a consequence of their social positionings. Depending upon the complex intersections of class location with gendered, ethnic and generational subjectivities, it is argued that our access to both material and symbolic resources is inevitably constrained and patterned in certain ways. Alongside this pairing of agency/structure, or creativity/constraint, another key opposition is that between the forces of social transformation and the pressures of social reproduction (resistance versus domination). My final chapter attempts to chart a viable course through these various themes, perspectives and arguments – advancing a particular model for making sense of contemporary cultural consumption.

Bourdieu's Sociology of Taste

In *Distinction: A Social Critique of the Judgement of Taste* (1984), the French sociologist Pierre Bourdieu presents us with what is probably the most important statement to date on the patterned practices of consumer cultures. A favourable British review of his book described it as 'a searching critique of all essentialist theories of cultural appropriation' (Garnham, 1986:424) – because Bourdieu's study sets out to challenge any notion that preferences for certain cultural activities can be innate, or that the meanings of cultural objects are fixed and given. Disputing the idea that some people have naturally 'good' taste whilst other people's cultural pursuits are naturally 'vulgar' in comparison, he focusses on the socially constructed character of all preferences, interpretations and value judgements. This proposal is supported by an extensive empirical survey of French culture which, argues Bourdieu, clearly demonstrates the connections between taste, lifestyle and social position. Far from simply reflecting the differential locations of social subjects, though, he believes that patterns of consumption also play a significant part in actually reproducing those divisions and differences. His conception of culture is therefore a political one, and Bourdieu's study is designed to unveil the fierce struggles which take place between social groups in the cultural arena.

The principal method employed in that research was a large-scale questionnaire survey technique – something of a departure from the type of ethnographic work I have been advocating elsewhere in this book. An obvious advantage of Bourdieu's approach here is the ability it gives him to paint, with very broad brushstrokes, a panoramic picture of general patterns in consumer activity. He attends to the ways in which numerous practices and preferences are articulated together in distinctive styles of living, noting that 'loss of precision . . . in the analysis of particular areas . . . is offset by a gain in systematicity' (Bourdieu, 1984:506). His two main surveys were conducted in 1963 and 1967–8 – well over a decade before the original publication of *Distinction* in France at the end of the 1970s – and they were carried out at the homes of participants in Paris, Lille and a further, small provincial, town. There was a total of more than 1,200 respondents, with the survey sample being drawn from a range of occupations to provide a wide distribution across divisions of class and class fraction. Twenty-six questions were posed on topics as diverse as musical tastes, the purchase of home furnishings and preferences for different photographic images. A closed set of alternative answers was provided for many of these questions – for example, subjects were invited to choose responses which came closest to their own opinions on art. These included statements such as 'Galleries aren't my strong point', 'I love the Impressionists' and 'Abstract painting interests me as much as the classical schools'. Interestingly, this questionnaire format resembles one which is used nowadays by commercial market researchers in 'psychographic' consumer surveys (which will be discussed in the next section).

Bourdieu sought, then, to obtain a large amount of comparable data so that it could be treated statistically – and on several occasions he produces diagrams or graphs which set out the survey's findings. A good illustration of this statistical treatment is the figure entitled 'Distribution of preferences for three musical works by class fraction' (Bourdieu, 1984:17). After requesting that participants select their favourite from a short list of classical pieces, the researcher analysed the choices made – representing them in a series of histogram tables and thereby distinguishing three separate 'zones of taste'. 'Legitimate' taste was marked by a preference for Bach's 'The Well Tempered Clavier', concentrated in that fraction of the middle class which is richest in 'educational capital' (university lecturers and artists, along with some secondary school teachers). Gershwin's 'Rhapsody in Blue' was most strongly appreciated within what Bourdieu termed a 'middlebrow' culture – by junior executives, industrial and commercial employers, engineers and technicians. 'Popular' taste, meanwhile, was typified 'by the choice of works of so-called "light music" or classical music devalued by popularisation such as "The Blue Danube"' (Bourdieu, 1984:16). Strauss's well known waltz music was frequently selected by manual workers, craftsmen and commercial employees.

At another point in the survey, when questioned about the kind of meal they would prefer to serve to guests, respondents were offered a number of possible replies which varied from 'plentiful and good' or 'appetising and economical' to 'original and exotic' or 'delicate and exquisite'. Asking about food preparation and eating habits was crucial for Bourdieu, who stated on the opening page of his book: 'one cannot fully understand cultural practices unless . . . the elaborated taste for the most refined objects is reconnected with the elementary taste for the flavours of food' (Bourdieu, 1984:1). Of course, the term 'taste' may refer narrowly to our palate for different dishes – as well as denoting cultural preferences in a more general sense – and he contends that the way in which food is served and eaten by its consumers often helps to indicate the place they occupy in the social structure. Following this particular aspect of Bourdieu's thesis through, Daniel Miller (1987:153) compares working-class preferences for 'the immediacy of abundance, a plentiful table proclaiming its sustenance . . . an unfussy array of quantity wherever possible' with bourgeois tastes that are characterized at their extremes by 'nouvelle cuisine' – 'which refuses any suggestion that food might be for sustenance, a minimalist food which emphasizes the aesthetic of presentation, an austere but cultivated pleasure'.

According to Bourdieu, this plurality of culinary preferences corresponds to a much wider division between 'dominant' and 'popular' aesthetics – the former usually involving a cool detachment and a concern with the formal qualities of cultural objects, while the latter tends to be manifested in a more sensual and immediate gratification, favouring mimetic modes of visual representation. So, to cite an example offered by Graham Murdock (1989:92), if Van Gogh's most celebrated painting appears to one type of spectator merely 'as a picture of flowers' (a reproduction of which might serve to 'brighten up the room') then another sort of viewer will be able to place it 'in relation to Van Gogh's total oeuvre, to compare his subject matter and technique to other artists of the period, to say that it was Expressionist rather than Impressionist, and so on'. (See Bourdieu, 1968, for a fuller commentary on sociological factors influencing the perception of artistic works.) Bourdieu argues that such varied ways of relating to cultural objects are ultimately rooted in the material conditions of existence of different social classes. It is no accident, he suggests, that the dominant groups in society – freed from the grip of immediate necessity – develop an aesthetic of distanced contemplation and formal abstraction. However, although his account is persuasive and points us in the direction of a properly materialist theory of consumption, Bourdieu has come in for criticism from some commentators like John Frow (1987:62) – who warns against the dangers of slipping into a further kind of essentialism which posits direct links between an aesthetic logic and a common 'class experience'. Frow is particularly concerned to refute any proposal that working-class audiences are necessarily uninterested in questions of form. I confess that my own sympathies here remain broadly with Bourdieu's sociological intentions – even if there are occasional exceptions with which we can challenge his thesis (for instance, consider the spectacular formal experimentation of working-class youth subcultures in post-war Britain – and see below).

More crucial still than the positive preferences of consumers are those feelings of disgust and embarrassment which can sometimes be evoked by the tastes and practices of other groups in society. The title of Bourdieu's book, *Distinction*, refers to this profound sense of social difference and distance that we feel when confronted by cultural activities and consumer choices which offend our aesthetic sensibilities. Just as the signs in Saussure's language system have their values determined negatively within structured relations of difference, so Bourdieu (1984:56) notes that tastes 'are the practical affirmation of difference . . . when they have to be justified, they are asserted purely negatively, by the refusal of other tastes'. They are, he continues, 'perhaps first and foremost distastes . . . provoked by horror or visceral intolerance ("sick-making") of the tastes of others'. Culture, for Bourdieu, is all about processes of identification and differentiation – with identities being produced through practices of distinction. The negation he describes above is precisely that feeling which helps to 'classify the classifier'. We distinguish ourselves by the distinctions we make – between 'cultivated' and 'vulgar', 'down to earth' and 'pretentious', and so forth.

There are clearly signs of Bourdieu's early structuralist influences (see Richard Jenkins, 1992) in his theory of cultural distinction, but this is not to say that his work is simply concerned with the synchronic analysis of a symbolic system of differences. He is also aware to some extent of diachronic shifts, sensitive to rises and falls in the value of cultural goods over time – depending on the changing social contexts of consumption. In a useful discussion of Bourdieu's ideas, Mike Featherstone (1991:88) gives an example of the kinds of change that may occur: 'mass marketing . . . [of] the William Tell Overture or the introduction of a relatively inexpensive champagne in supermarkets and stores such as Marks and Spencer . . . will necessarily mean the upper groups move on to more avant-garde pieces of music or purchase a new rarer drink or drink vintage champagne'. These shifts result, then, in a headlong rush by the dominant to re-establish recognizable distinctions. When following the career of an artefact, we should understand – as Bourdieu (1984:21) did – that 'there are very few which are perfectly "univocal" '. Within the relational dynamics of the cultural domain, their meanings are negotiable. Indeed, it is quite possible for a single object or cultural form to circulate in different 'taste zones' at the same time. Think of the popularization of performances by the opera singer, Pavarotti, over recent years in Britain. After the BBC borrowed his voice for their 1990 World Cup soccer coverage – and satellite TV broadcast a live open air concert in London, complete with banners reading 'Pav is Fab' – it became possible to buy 'Pavarotti's Greatest Hits' albums in just about every high street record store. Simultaneously, though, there will be long-time admirers of the singer who continue to purchase less readily available recordings in specialist music outlets, preferring to attend expensive venues such as the English National Opera in Covent Garden rather than watch 'Pavarotti in the Park' on Sky. Social distance is thereby maintained.

This system of distinctions generally serves to sustain and reproduce relations of domination and subordination between class groupings because variations in taste and consumption are not only a matter of difference – some preferences and practices are invested with greater social value than others (for instance, they can be 'traded in' for academic qualifications in educational institutions). Bourdieu believed it was possible to talk about the existence of a cultural 'economy', and he employs the concept of 'cultural capital' to refer to the accumulation of symbolic wealth in the sphere of culture. So as well as having more financial wealth than the working-class, the middle classes seek to ensure that their cultural pursuits are given greater value too – by legitimizing their own tastes and devaluing other people's pleasures as vulgar. However, Bourdieu goes further than the general division between dominant and popular aesthetics which I have outlined above. He was also interested in what he saw as a specific struggle within the middle class between those fractions that are richest in financial terms and an intellectual stratum which chooses to accumulate the symbolic wealth of cultural capital (think back to Bourdieu's separation of 'middlebrow' and 'legitimate' taste zones in discussing musical preferences). The financial and cultural economies do operate with at least some degree of autonomy, then, and social classes may have internal fractions within them that are locked in competitive combat.

Featherstone (1991) adds an intriguing aside to the debate about sectional differences – one which will be of particular interest to readers of my book. Pursuing Bourdieu's analysis, he highlights a further site of struggle inside the intellectual strata of the bourgeoisie between 'traditional' and 'vanguard' fractions. It demonstrates the point that nobody – even intellectuals who consider themselves to be engaged in a contemplative reflection on society – is ever free from the game of culture, power and distinction. Those of us inhabiting the relatively new domain of academic activity known as 'cultural studies' could be seen to be in the business of making careers for ourselves by challenging older disciplines, and by 'consecrating' subjects such as the media and popular culture as appropriate objects of study. 'Rock music, fashion, the cinema become canonized as legitimate intellectual areas for critics,' writes Featherstone (1991:93), who notes: 'One of the subversive strategies of outsider intellectuals . . . is to seek to legitimate new fields to stand alongside and undermine the traditional restricted definitions of taste provided by . . . established intellectuals.' Of course, the catch for students of popular culture is that we don't just hand out degrees to reward an intimate knowledge of, say, punk rock or soap opera. Cultural studies ultimately keeps a respectable distance from the popular by demanding that its students apply certain theoretical and methodological frameworks to their objects of investigation (e.g. 'television with added semiotics'!).

Having established the fundamental principles and processes of distinction, it is also necessary now to examine in greater detail exactly how social subjects come to relate to their cultural environment in different ways – introducing a concept which appears across the range of Bourdieu's writings on culture. Power relations and struggles between and within class groupings are, he asserts, reproduced over generations through the transmission of distinctive types of group 'habitus'. This is his term for the durable yet transposable set of dispositions that is inculcated in the subject during the early years of socialization within the family, and which is developed, or denigrated, in later years at school (see especially Bourdieu & Passeron, 1977, for an important contribution to the sociology of education – not dissimilar to Bernstein's work in Britain). The habitus provides 'basic conceptual categories and action frames through which people think about and respond to the social world' (Murdock, 1989:93) – and yet it needs to be understood as always more than a number of cognitive capacities, being physically embodied in certain styles of walking, gesticulating or speaking. Bourdieu himself is keen to stress that the whole business of inculcation is unconscious – at least in the sense that the subject is involved in a 'forgetting' of its socially constituted character. In his *Outline of a Theory of Practice* (Bourdieu, 1977:78), he calls the habitus 'history turned into nature'. It is neither an individual nor a universal system of dispositions, but rather a mark of social position. When studying tastes and lifestyles, we must therefore attend to the formation of particular kinds of habitus which do a job of mediating between the objective conditions and cultural practices of social classes and class fractions.

As I stated in my introductory chapter, Bourdieu has probably come closer than any other contemporary theorist to elaborating a comprehensive sociological account of consumption practices. His concepts of distinction, cultural capital and habitus – and the accompanying empirical research on patterns of taste and lifestyle – provide us with invaluable material for the critical investigation of culture. There are, nevertheless, several aspects of Bourdieu's approach that we might want to interrogate further, pointing to possible problems or absences in the theory and method. The first objection – one put by Nicholas Garnham and Raymond Williams (1986), or more recently by Richard Jenkins (1992) – is that his analysis of social reproduction displays a troubling functionalist tendency. Just as Louis Althusser's essay on ideology and the state was compared by some with the structural functionalism of Talcott Parsons, so Bourdieu's name too has been associated (unfavourably) with this conservative American social scientist (see Richard Jenkins, 1992:81). What is implied here is that, despite the radical intentions of these two rather different French theorists, both ultimately develop a model of stable reproduction which is based on the internalization of norms and values – and which, for all their references to 'struggle', allows little or no room for the chance of radical social change. In other words, they explain the continued dominance of the dominant so neatly that the position of subordinate groups in society seems unlikely ever to alter. This political pessimism can be related to an added problem for Bourdieu, which he tries hard to avoid but which he has again been accused of falling into. I refer to his attempts at resolving the old agency/structure, subjective/objective tensions in social theory. Richard Jenkins (1992:82) writes: 'Given the close, reproductive, link between the subjectivities of the habitus and the objectivity of the social world it is difficult not to perceive them as bound together in a closed feedback loop, each confirming the other.' In those circumstances it is also difficult, he says, 'to imagine a place in Bourdieu's scheme of things for . . . the meaningful practices of social actors in their cultural context. One can only speculate as to how "objective structures" are . . . changed by that practice.' Constraint, then, completely outweighs creativity.

A second limitation to Bourdieu's work is his almost exclusive focus in *Distinction* on class relations, over and above other sorts of social division. As Murdock (1989:98) asks: 'Is class position necessarily always the major stratifying principle underlying cultural consumption? How important are the cross-cutting dimensions of stratification – sex, age and life-cycle stage, and ethnicity?' In earlier chapters of this book, I have been suggesting that when we study household consumption and domestic leisure, it is vital for us to look at the ways in which gender differences operate in connection with class position to help give rise to certain consumption practices and preferences. The findings of media audience researchers such as Dorothy Hobson, David Morley or Ann Gray spring to mind as obvious examples – but to take a topic of special interest to Bourdieu, we might equally consider the specificity of masculine and feminine tastes for food within the same class groupings (see Charles & Kerr, 1988).

Finally, there is the matter of whether a large-scale questionnaire survey of the sort used by Bourdieu can cope on its own with the significance of consumer activities in everyday life. There are, as I mentioned only a few pages ago, real advantages to be gained from the use of this method (enabling the researcher to map out broad cultural patterns of identity and difference) –

although Bourdieu (1984:506) himself had recognized the fact that it 'leaves out almost everything to do with the modalities of practices'. So whilst the survey presents a valuable general picture, it is less fruitful for our understanding of the complex meanings which underpin instances of consumption in specific situational contexts. For that task, a more qualitative approach is needed. Indeed, Miller (1987:154) registers his surprise that Bourdieu did not use the fieldwork techniques learnt right at the start of a long academic career as an anthropologist in North Africa (see, for example, the impressive ethnography of the Berber house, in Bourdieu, 1972): 'having worked previously as an ethnographer, Bourdieu makes no attempt to employ the ethnographic method in his work . . . [the] questionnaire can provide only explicit responses, rather than insight into actual practices'. 'Thicker' forms of description, to borrow Clifford Geertz's term, could serve to complement the survey data – and an English social researcher, Derek Wynne (1990), has taken up precisely where the French theorist left off with a fascinating detailed account of 'taste warfare' on a middle-class housing estate. Wynne develops Bourdieu's arguments about economic and cultural capital in a British setting by considering the diverse leisure activities of residents on the estate – where two separate fractions of the class choose differently how to decorate their homes, where to go on holiday or for a night out, which sports to play, and so on.

Market Segmentation in the Commercial Sphere

Outside of sociology and cultural studies, of course, there lies a whole field of commercial research which is concerned with issues of taste and consumption that are similar to those raised in Bourdieu's *Distinction*. Even though market researchers are motivated by a desire to identify potential purchasers for commodities and business services – rather than by an academic or political interest in providing accounts of cultural power and social reproduction – I want to propose that the work they do may still be of relevance to academics engaged in the analysis of consumer practices. In fact, marketing discourses can be read as signs of quite fundamental shifts in capitalist modes of production and consumption during the twentieth century. The growth of marketing as a profession parallels the movement from an era of so-called 'mass consumption' to newer, flexible and specialized, forms of production – with correspondingly more diverse and fragmented consumer subgroups. It is highly appropriate that in the jargon of recent debates on the Left of British politics, this has come to be known as a transformation from 'Fordism' to 'Post-Fordism' (see several of the contributions to Hall & Jacques, 1989), because the car industry shows clear evidence of the changes taking place. When the Ford Motor Company once said of its famous 'Model T' that buyers could have any colour they wanted so long as it was black, few foresaw the day when, counting all the multiple combinations of engine and optional accessories, one type of car would be available in over 69,000 varieties

(Loudon & Della Bitta, 1988). Car advertising campaigns are increasingly targeted at specific audiences – promoting the spacious saloon for family use, sports performance for the young executive or a stylish hatchback for the independent woman about town.

Whilst they share no common consensus on exactly how to conceptualize consumer divisions, all commercial market researchers are involved in a process known as 'segmentation'. It entails an 'overt recognition that consumers are not homogeneous' (Oliver, 1986:89). Peter Chisnall (1985:264), in his text written for business students, explains that strategies of this sort are 'a deliberate policy of maximising market demand by directing marketing efforts at significant subgroups of customers' – and in the following notes, I consider various models of market segmentation which have proved influential in the commercial sector over the last twenty years or so. I begin with those that divide consumers by socioeconomic status or geographical location, before going on to assess recent approaches which disaggregate markets into lifestyle categories with particular 'psychographic' profiles. Work on family purchasing decisions is also considered for its pertinence to the critical study of domestic cultures.

Amongst market researchers in Britain, the most widely employed classification of socioeconomic groupings is still the six category JICNARS scale. This was originally used for an investigation into the distribution of newspaper and magazine sales – now administered by the Joint Industry Committee for National Readership Surveys, which represents a range of publishing and advertising organizations. The model is basically a segmentation of the population by occupation. Group 'A' are described in the JICNARS scale as upper middle class: 'the head of the household is a successful business or professional man . . . or has considerable private means'. 'Bs' – middle class – are also 'senior people but not at the very top of their profession or business . . . quite well off, but their style of life is generally respectable rather than rich or luxurious'. The 'C1' category denotes 'white collar', lower middle-class consumers who are 'in general . . . the families of small tradespeople and non-manual workers who carry out less important administrative, supervisory or clerical jobs'. 'C2s', meanwhile, are the skilled working class in 'blue collar' jobs ('serving of an apprenticeship may be a guide to membership of this class') – and category 'D' consists of semi- or unskilled manual workers. Lastly, 'Es' are those at the lowest levels of subsistence, 'casual workers or those who, through sickness or unemployment, are dependent on social security schemes' (quoted in Chisnall, 1985:120–1).

Although the JICNARS divisions remain an important element of marketing discourse, a series of objections have now been made to the use of this classification system – reflecting doubts in the industry about whether occupational differences alone can enable an accurate 'carving up' of contemporary consumer markets. An evident shortcoming of the model is its sole reliance on the job done by 'heads of household' – assumed to be male – as an indicator of family consumption habits. It takes no account either of women's paid work or of households without a male breadwinner (in addition, it mistakenly sees 'the family' as a single, uncontradictory consuming unit – a point to which I return in due course). Another crucial problem is the failure fully to recognize generational, or life-stage, distinctions. For that particular reason, in the early 1980s, a company named Research Services developed the 'Sagacity' segmentation. Rather than relying just on occupation, the consumer categories they introduced treated demographics 'multi-variately' (see Crimp, 1985) – producing a twelve-scale framework which sought to combine data on positions within the life-cycle, along with income (allowing for the working status of spouses and levels of disposable income), and occupation too. So, for instance, the Sagacity categories incorporate stages such as 'Dependent', 'Pre-family', 'Family' or 'Late'. They indicate whether households are 'Better off' or 'Worse off', and they distinguish 'White' from 'Blue' collar.

The last decade has also witnessed the arrival of market segmentation models which differentiate between areas of housing, or else between broader geographical spaces and communities. ACORN (A Classification of Residential Neighbourhoods) is a British system that seeks to map geographically the concentrated clustering of certain types of consumers in certain residential districts. Gordon Oliver (1986:96) explains how 'advocates for this segment base would argue that where we live is intimately connected with how we live, and how we live subsumes what we consume'. The neighbourhood context might also tell us something about how a cultural object gets utilized and made sense of – hence my own interest in geographical segmentations as a starting point for ethnographic research on the household consumption of satellite TV (see Chapter 4). In promotional material for their ACORN model, CACI Market Analysis (1985) describe the way in which it applies published census statistics and classifies small enumeration districts of around 150 homes into one of eleven neighbourhood groupings. For each of these alphabetically ordered segments, specific kinds of lifestyles and cultural practices are identified. So in group 'B' here – 'modern family housing, higher incomes' – there are 'relatively weak community networks and a fairly high expenditure on consumer goods and family leisure'. For the 'better off council estates' that form group 'E', 'movement away from relatives and the close community networks of the inner city often results in a weakening of traditional social attitudes, leisure patterns and consumer preferences . . . households become more confident in their ability to use credit'. And in the 'high status non-family areas' of group 'I', residents 'tend to be frequent readers of books and journals, receptive to new ideas and products and, especially if they are single, likely to spend much of their leisure time and money on outside entertainment and on eating out'. A potential difficulty for this sort of analysis is in dealing with divided and contested areas like the one that Wynne (1990) has written about – or the neighbourhood of a South Wales city which I spoke of at length towards the end of the preceding chapter. Nevertheless, in the business world, many companies have drawn on ACORN data in deciding where to locate a new store or how to focus the distribution of mailshot advertising.

PRIZM (Potential Rating Index by Zip Market) is a close relative of

ACORN's on the other side of the Atlantic. A 'zip' number is the five-digit American postal code, and PRIZM divides a total of over 35,000 neighbourhood codes into forty 'zip market clusters' – with titles ranging from 'Pools and Patios' to 'Bohemian Mix' to 'Norma Rae-Ville'. These clusters are constituted with reference to a combination of demographic and social variables – such as housing stock, education, ethnicity and urban/rural divisions. A rather different form of geographical segmentation in operation there is Joel Garreau's 'Nine Nations of North America' chart. He encourages marketers to forget about formal political boundaries between countries and states, and in their place he constructs nine regional categories called 'The Foundry', 'Dixie', 'Breadbasket', 'Ecotopia', and so on. Each is seen to have a capital city and its own distinctive way of life (for 'capsule summaries' of the nine nations, see Loudon & Della Bitta, 1988:96–7). This is certainly an ambitious effort to map out imagined communities, although there has been a good deal of debate amongst American market researchers concerning its practical application to consumer targeting.

At this juncture, before moving on to consider the emergence of a currently fashionable method of segmentation known as psychographics, it may be appropriate to discuss just briefly a general problem with models like JICNARS, Sagacity, ACORN and PRIZM – which is the tendency they have to view the household as a taken-for-granted unit of consumption. I am not disputing the fact that the private sphere of family life is indeed a major domain in which commodities are consumed – that much will be evident from Chapter 3 and from Chapter 4 too – but what should also be clear after reading those chapters is that households are best understood as places where there are key differences in taste and consumer activity. Some market researchers have, it is true to say, done interesting work on the question of domestic dynamics by investigating processes of decision-making in families. For example, James Engel and Roger Blackwell (1982) comment on research carried out in Belgium during the 1970s on the relative influence of husbands and wives in purchasing decisions for twenty-five specified product-types (including food, furniture, clothing, car, etc.). Four sorts of decision were identified – 'husband dominant', 'wife dominant', 'syncratic' and 'autonomic'. The first two of these are fairly self-explanatory, whilst a 'syncratic' decision is one which over half of the survey respondents said they took jointly, and 'autonomic' refers to instances where less than half decided together. In principle, that survey approach seems to be quite promising. However, in practice, it is both conceptually and politically dubious. It needs to go further by asking more directly about power relations between men and women in domestic life. So who is controlling the large items of household expenditure and who looks after, say, the day-to-day shopping for foodstuffs? Even there, might the person buying and preparing the food for meals make choices on the basis of satisfying others' preferences?

Psychographics – the latest trend in market segmentation to be imported from the USA – makes a fundamental break with the socioeconomic and demographic models I have been describing up to now. It distinguishes consumers according to 'cognitive styles' (Loudon & Della Bitta, 1988), rather than by the jobs they do or the places where they live, and it involves researching into their activities, interests and opinions (AIOs). At root this is a psychological approach to cultural consumption – one that posits the determining influence of particular personality traits or 'consumer profiles' (Gunter & Furnham, 1992). Typically, such research is done by mailing questionnaires to members of a panel who are invited to respond positively or negatively to a large number of AIO statements like, for instance, 'a woman's place is in the home', 'premarital sex is immoral', 'the use of marijuana should be made legal' or 'I buy many things with a credit card' (Engel & Blackwell, 1982:187). Working with the responses given, psychographic segmentations proceed to put consumers into a variety of lifesyle categories. Although these classificatory schemes display a profoundly dangerous tendency towards psychological reductionism, their popularity within the marketing community is growing – and while my argument will be that the overall approach is seriously flawed, I nevertheless believe that psychographics may deliver a few productive insights into cultures of consumption.

'Needham Harper Worldwide' is the title of a US classification which separates out over 3,000 survey respondents into ten lifestyle groups, each given a different name to denote a certain sort of personality. Half are male – Herman the retiring homebody, Dale the devoted family man, and so forth. The other half are female, with examples here being Mildred the militant mother, or Eleanor the elegant socialite. Indexes of predicted product consumption are then linked up to the ten profiles. VALS (Values and Lifestyles) is another well known American system, employing a form of 'attitudinal cluster analysis' and thereby constructing a typology which comprises four main market components – need driven, outer directed, inner directed and integrated individuals. This ordering is derived from the notion that there exists a universal 'hierarchy of needs' in human societies. So need-driven individuals are concerned with satisfying the basic physiological requirements for nutrition and shelter. Outer-directed personalities invest most value in the possession of material goods, and inner-directed individuals are thought to have a more 'spiritual' set of concerns with self-realization. Meanwhile, those credited with an integrated personality manage to combine both material values and spiritual or social awareness. Within the four main categories is a series of subdivisions – for instance, the outer-directed segment is made up of 'Belongers', 'Emulators' and 'Achievers' (for a detailed breakdown, see Kotler & Andreasen, 1987:138–43). It is worth mentioning, incidentally, that public arts organizations outside the business sector have also begun to use the VALS research in an attempt to define their existing and target audiences.

On British shores, the 'Monitor' social value group model – devised by the Taylor Nelson agency – provides something of a parallel to VALS. Based on an annual survey of attitudes, Monitor is a 'seven cluster solution' to the problem of charting values and beliefs. Once again, each cluster has a label (e.g. 'self-explorers', 'conspicuous consumers', 'survivors'). In addition, each name is accompanied by a key phrase which is supposed to typify the outlook of a specified consumer grouping – 'I'll try it', 'Look at me' and 'My family comes first' are three of the seven. Actually, this style of drawing on brief, indicative phrases is not dissimilar to Bourdieu's writing strategy in parts of *Distinction* (for a selection of illustrations, see Bourdieu, 1984:288–90; 334–6; 391–3). He was interested in precisely what market researchers call 'attitudinal clusters' – choosing instead to use terms like disposition or habitus – but the telling difference with Bourdieu's work is his insistence on always seeking to relate cultural values and perceptions back to the socioeconomic level. If, as I suggested earlier, he has been open to accusations of sociological essentialism, that is still far preferable in my view to the kind of reductionist psychology we find in much psychographic market research. The question is surely how the VALS and Monitor classifications connect with older occupational seg-mentations – or with the geographical divisions of ACORN and PRIZM. What should concern us in studying patterns of cultural consumption is exactly how social demography and social psychology intersect.

De Certeau and the Tactics of Popular Resistance

So far, in discussing Bourdieu's sociology of taste and methods of commercial market research, we have come across an attempt to identify structural constraints on consumer practices in daily life – and a preoccupation with social patternings and segmentations. I now turn to perspectives that are focussed primarily on the active construction of everyday cultures through a creative consumption or appropriation of commodities. The following section will trace out a tradition of work in British 'subcultural' studies which has given careful consideration to the symbolic creativity of young consumers – but first I examine the influence of another French theorist whose writings on culture can be contrasted quite fruitfully with those of Bourdieu. In *The Practice of Everyday Life*, Michel De Certeau (1984:59) admires his fellow countryman for 'scrupulously examining practices and their logic' yet at the same time criticizes him for reducing them finally 'to a mystical reality, the "habitus", which is to bring them under the law of reproduction'. De Certeau's outlook is altogether more optimistic about the abilities of subordinate groups in society to evade or resist the power of the dominant, and he characterizes popular practice as an ongoing 'guerrilla warfare' being fought on the territory of an oppressor. This form of resistance does not lead to wholesale social transformation, although it is an important means of getting by or 'making do' in otherwise unfavourable circumstances.

From De Certeau's point of view, quotidian activity is seen to be 'tactical' in nature. Mundane everyday practices such as talking, reading, dwelling, walking, shopping or cooking take on a fresh significance in his writings as artful 'ways of operating': 'victories of the "weak" over the "strong" (whether the strength be that of powerful people or . . . of an imposed order), clever tricks, knowing how to get away with things, "hunter's cunning", manoeuvres

. . . joyful discoveries, poetic as well as warlike' (De Certeau, 1984:xix). He is generally interested, then, in language as enunciation rather than as structure – and compares the speakers of a language with walkers who weave their own paths through the planned streets of a city. The latter are understood to perform 'pedestrian speech acts': 'walking is to the urban system what the speech act is to language,' writes De Certeau (1984:97). Similarly, the reader of a book is compared with someone who rents an apartment – so that reading, through its skilled 'metamorphosis of the text', makes the book habitable, just as the tenant 'transforms another person's property into a space borrowed . . . by a transient' (De Certeau, 1984:xxi). These are the guerrilla tactics he refers to – or again, to lift a further metaphor from *The Practice of Everyday Life*, they are guileful practices of 'poaching'.

In all cases, though, what the author tries hard to uncover is a widespread popular resistance to the existing social order – expressed not through overt political opposition but by an often disguised trickery, making creative use of those materials which are to hand in 'the other's place'. His specific term for this aspect of disguise is 'la perruque' or, in English, 'the wig'. De Certeau (1984:25) explains that it 'may be as simple a matter as a secretary's writing a love letter on "company time" or as complex as a cabinetmaker's "borrowing" a lathe to make a piece of furniture for his living room' (see Westwood, 1984, for an ethnography of women workers in a clothing factory who engage in ruses of the same type – constructing an informal shopfloor culture of resistance). Thus the ordinary person 'succeeds in "putting one over" on the established order on its home ground' (De Certeau, 1984:26). By extension, a broad span of consumption practices outside the workplace are also thought by De Certeau to involve tricks and ruses played on the powerful – appropriating and rearticulating the products imposed by a dominant economic system.

Following the Gramscian re-evaluation of 'the popular' in cultural studies during the 1980s – and the corresponding turn to active audiences in qualitative media research – these arguments have recently begun to find their niche outside of French theory within an already developing approach to consumption and daily life. Amongst those English-speaking analysts and commentators who write with some enthusiasm about De Certeau's work are Roger Silverstone (1989) in the UK, John Frow (1991) in Australia, and Henry Jenkins (1992) from the United States – whose book about fans of the cult TV series *Star Trek* takes its title, *Textual Poachers*, from a De Certeauian concept. However, by far the best known current 'popularizer' of De Certeau in media and cultural studies is John Fiske – a British expatriate academic who has taught in Australia and now lives in America where he is a professor at the University of Wisconsin. In two companion volumes, *Understanding Popular Culture* (1989a) and *Reading the Popular* (1989b), Fiske adds the Frenchman's name to a longer list of intellectual celebrities including Roland Barthes, Stuart Hall and Mikhail Bakhtin (alias Volosinov) – applying his thesis on everyday practice to activities as diverse as the wearing of jeans, playing arcade video games or listening to Madonna records. An earlier book on television (Fiske, 1987), with its curious assertions concerning TV's 'semiotic democracy', had laid the foundations for this particular appropriation of De Certeau's ideas.

Fiske (1989a:23) proposes, rather uncontroversially in the context of previous developments within cultural analysis, that 'popular culture in industrial societies is contradictory to the core'. Much like Tony Bennett (1986:xv–xvi) – who spoke of the popular as a field consisting 'not simply of an imposed mass culture that is coincident with dominant ideology, nor simply of spontaneously oppositional cultures, but . . . an area of negotiation between the two' – his starting point is to note how this contradictory and contested terrain is formed 'at the interface between the products of the culture industries and everyday life' (Fiske, 1989a:25). There are commodities being produced, distributed and sold for profit by manufacturers and retailers in a capitalist market economy – whilst, simultaneously, the consumers of those goods and services incorporate them into their daily lives, constructing certain meanings and pleasures in the process. So far, so good (despite the disappointingly vague definition of 'the people' which is in operation here). Up to now, very little separates Fiske's position from the kind of Gramscian perspective that was employed by Bennett and others at the time. However, whereas Antonio Gramsci had once proclaimed 'pessimism of the intellect and optimism of the will' in political matters, Fiske appears to be declaring optimism all round – putting his faith in subordinated people to always make do with what the system provides, so that everything they touch turns to resistance against 'white, patriarchal, capitalist' structures. He writes about consumers in the same romanticized style which De Certeau used when dedicating *The Practice of Everyday Life* to 'the ordinary man' as 'common hero'. Popular consumption as the tactics of the weak against the strategies of the strong, then, with readers poaching on texts and guerrilla fighters making their raids on places of power.

An example might help us to clarify Fiske's perspective on popular cultural resistance at this stage, and I have chosen to look at his notes on shopping practices because they do present a provocative challenge to the standard Left critique of mass culture – going so far as to suggest that shopping can be an oppositional and empowering activity (he isn't alone in getting excited about shoppers either – see, for instance, some of the postmodernist positions advanced in Shields, 1992). Rather than concentrating on the exploitation of consumers by the retail industry – an approach we could reasonably expect a critical theorist to take – Fiske turns things round by emphasizing the resistant tactics of consumption on exactly those sites where retailers operate. He views the mall and the high street as ideal territory for poachers, 'open invitations to trickery and tenacity' (Fiske, 1989b:17). The main reference point for his bold assertion is an Australian ethnography of young people's 'deviant' behaviour in a shopping centre. These youths use the mall as a space to congregate in large numbers, occupying the place created by retail culture while expressing their own rebellious sense of identity in the process. They are a threatening presence for shop owners and a continual nuisance to the security guards whose job it is to patrol the mall. I have no difficulty in accepting the account as a familiar story of youth resistance, but Fiske (1989b:17) then proceeds to make a massive analytical leap by equating such activity with that of 'lunch hour window shoppers who browse through the stores, trying on goods . . . playing with images, with no intention to buy' or old age pensioners who walk in the warmth of the mall's concourses during the cold winter season. Housewives, too, are seen to exert power and gain pleasure from spending 'their husbands' money' down at the stores. It is this clumsy conflation of very different types of social practice under the common sign of 'the people's tactics' which marks Fiske's major downfall in his analysis of popular culture. The instances of 'shopping' which he describes actually draw more attention to significant divisions and antagonisms than to potential alliances within the terrain of the popular.

Even prior to the adoption of De Certeau's theory of everyday life, Fiske was developing a similar conception of popular resistance and creative consumption in relation to TV texts and audiences. *Television Culture* (1987) is an early introductory overview of the kinds of advance in media theory and research I am concerned with here, although he wraps his commentary there inside a general plan of popular TV that may be at odds with much of the material he talks about (for example, Morley, 1992, strongly disputes Fiske's interpretation of the *Nationwide* project and his inflection of its findings). The general model I refer to is summarized fairly concisely in the final paragraph of *Television Culture*, which begins by arguing that the medium's financial success 'depends upon its ability to serve and promote the diverse and often oppositional interests of its audiences' – and ends with the statement: 'Far from being the agent of the dominant classes, it is the prime site where the dominant have to recognise the insecurity of their power . . . where they have to encourage cultural difference with all the threat to their own position that this implies' (Fiske, 1987:326). His standpoint is already distinctly optimistic. Notions of television as an ideological or hegemonic apparatus, of preferred readings and relative closures, are on the way out. Instead, Fiske foregrounds polysemy and the play of the signifier (the 'producerliness' of texts). In comes the notion of TV cultures as semiotic democracies, obliged to uphold 'readers' rights'. James Curran's recent attack on 'the new revisionism' – aimed too indiscriminately, in my opinion, at a whole body of new work in the cultural studies tradition – does seem to apply to Fiske's perspective on the media. If still dressed in the robes of critical theory, he stands accused of returning to an old-fashioned liberal-pluralism (see Curran, 1990).

Reviewers of Fiske's latest books on television and popular culture, particularly in Britain, have given his writings a cool reception. The coolest by far is Martin Barker's scathing criticism of *Understanding Popular Culture* and *Reading the Popular* (see Barker, 1990). At certain moments, this discussion borders on abuse – with Barker confessing that he 'loathe[s] these two books', calling them both 'bloody dull'. His anger is triggered by what he believes to be 'their profound lack of any interest in history; their transmogrification of theory into hollow and mechanical epithets . . . and their dulling of all politics

... under the guise of advocating "semiotic resistance" ' (Barker, 1990:39). We end up, he says, with a conceptual framework in which 'every bit of popular culture, equally, at all times and places, always combines subordination with resistance ... culture on a vast ironing board'. In short, Barker objects to the undifferentiated commentary on popular practices and the predictably repetitive restatement of a less than original 'people against power bloc' thesis.

Jim Bee (1989) has offered a rather more even-handed assessment of Fiske's position in his critique of the book on TV. He rightly acknowledges the author's achievement in producing an accessible and wide-ranging guide for undergraduate students – a readership which, over the past fifteen years, Fiske and various collaborators have addressed consistently and successfully (at least in terms of sales figures – e.g. Fiske & Hartley, 1978; Fiske, 1982; O'Sullivan *et al.*, 1983). Ultimately, though, Bee finds that the arguments being advanced are 'theoretically confused and politically disabling'. Like Barker, he also finds the analysis somewhat flat and placeless: 'There is no sense of any specific social formation. Australia, Britain and the USA, and by implication any "western" nation, are assumed to be homogeneous for Fiske's analysis. There is no attempt to understand and intervene in a political conjuncture' (Bee, 1989:358). This may, of course, be a problem caused by the increasing demands of the publishing industry for internationally marketable texts – a pressure I am well aware of myself!

The shortcomings identified by Bee can be narrowed down to two principal objections – that there is a lack of any tight definitions of a number of the book's central theoretical concepts such as producerliness and popularity, and that 'for all its rhetoric of resistance, it endorses a politics of quietism' (Bee, 1989:357). Firstly, then, if we examine the idea of the television text as 'producerly', a series of important questions remain unanswered by Fiske. Is producerliness the same as semiotic 'openness'? Are all popular texts producerly to the same degree? What might the opposite of producerly be? And does popular TV always lead to the production of resistant readings? The final query is particularly pertinent because Fiske tends to map the text–reader relation directly on to a power/struggle pairing. If the study of mass communication has long oscillated between the alternative poles of domination and resistance, 'Fiske is probably as far over to the resistance pole as anyone could be' (Bee, 1989:357). He appears oblivious to reactionary elements within popular culture, so that one of his selected examples of consumer productivity reads to me as a profoundly sexist activity: 'the kids who sang jeeringly at a female student of mine as she walked past them in a short skirt and high heels, "Razzmatazz, Razzmatazz, enjoy that jazz" '. As Fiske (1989a:31) puts it, these boys are playfully using the jingle from a pantyhose advert 'for their own cheeky resistive subcultural purposes' – but surely what the kids are 'activating' here is patriarchal ideology. Secondly, pursuing the political implications of his perspective a little further, Bee suggests there can be problems with an overly 'consumptionist' focus on culture (and see McGuigan, 1992). To be fair, the point applies to other work as well as Fiske's – including several of the audience research projects covered in my previous chapters. Bee (1989:357) asks whether the current orientation towards active consumers is directing us away from intervening at the moment of cultural production too: 'Now it seems to me that if feminists have shown we do not all have to be patriarchs, this has not been achieved by waiting for popular television to lead the way but by some women struggling to make interventions' (for instance, challenging sexist images of the female body in advertising or film). Despite its limitations, a 1970s approach like 'screen theory' did at least call for changes in the representations available to people – and media studies in the 1990s now needs a reconstituted form of institutional and textual criticism to sit alongside developments in audience ethnography.

Style, Meaning and Youth Subculture

Another strand of work which has investigated the semiotic resistances of creative consumers – a strand that stretches back much further than the present De Certeauian trend in cultural theory – is the study of spectacular British youth subcultures which took shape at the Birmingham CCCS two decades ago. A crucial publication at that time was the *Resistance through Rituals* collection (Hall & Jefferson, 1976), containing essays by several young researchers who were later to become established figures in the cultural studies field – Paul Willis, Angela McRobbie, Iain Chambers, John Clarke and Dick Hebdige amongst them. Along with Hebdige's own subsequent book, *Subculture: The Meaning of Style* (1979), it served to define a distinctive approach to youth lifestyles that highlighted the social processes through which subcultural groups appropriate and rearticulate the significance of existing objects and commodities. The opposition to the dominant values of their parents' generation was, so the explanation went, expressed primarily (but not exclusively) by symbolic means in the sphere of leisure and consumption. Although it occasionally suffers from a few of the same difficulties as Fiske's writings, I believe this work is preferable precisely because of the historical and social specificity of its analysis – exploring the emergence of certain musical or dress codes within particular generational subgroupings at specific conjunctures during the post-war period in Britain.

   If there is a pivotal concept that informs this inquiry into the practices of various youth subcultures, then – most evidently in Hebdige's text – it is the theory of 'bricolage' (a term De Certeau was also to employ on occasion in his book on everyday life). Drawn from the discipline of anthropology, bricolage refers to the active construction of meaning through an improvised and creative combination of prior discursive elements. Clarke (1976) calls it a 'reordering and recontextualisation of objects to communicate fresh meanings'. Elaborating on that basic definition, he refers us to a fundamental principle of social semiotics: 'Together, object and meaning constitute a sign . . . within any one culture, such signs are assembled, repeatedly, into characteristic forms of discourse. However, when the bricoleur relocates the significant object in a different position . . . a new discourse is constituted, a different message conveyed' (Clarke, 1976:177). For Hebdige, the principle advanced here offers a valuable way of understanding the formal experimentation and 'intentional communication' of youth stylists. Their subversive signifying practices could be compared, he says, with the radical aesthetics of early twentieth-century modernist art – especially with the anarchic collage techniques of Dada or surrealism, where familiar images and objects are juxtaposed in startlingly novel combinations, or else are torn out of context as in Marcel Duchamp's famous 'ready-mades'. Teds, mods, rastas, punks and so on are understood as aesthetic and communicative innovators, and the rather romanticized view of 'life as art' which we found in Fiske and De Certeau is clearly a recognizable feature of Hebdige's perspective on subculture.

'In this way,' writes Hebdige (1979:104), 'the teddy boy's theft and transformation of the Edwardian style revived in the early 1950s by Savile Row for wealthy young men about town can be construed as an act of bricolage' – as can the mod's ripping of a whole range of commodities out of their previous cultural locations (and consult Hebdige, 1976). The suit, collar and tie, short hair, chemists' pills, metal combs, parka anoraks, Italian motor scooters and Union Jack flags were subject to a skilful appropriation and given quite different connotations to the ones they originally had in mainstream society. We might see the 1960s mod look, in fact, as a perfect example of 'la perruque' in the realm of youth subculture. Hebdige (1979:52) notes how they 'invented a style which enabled them to negotiate smoothly between school, work and leisure . . . they were fastidiously neat and tidy . . . pushing neatness to the point of absurdity . . . a little too smart, somewhat too alert, thanks to amphetamines'. Often doing menial office jobs, their disguised leisure identities were to be lived fully in the spaces 'in between' – at 'weekenders', 'all-nighters' and on official holidays.

Subculture is concerned not just with white working-class youth, but with black British subcultures too. Indeed, it proposes an intimate connection between the two. White subcultural forms are readable as 'deep structural adaptations which symbolically accommodate or expunge the black presence from the host community', so that a kind of 'phantom history of race relations since the war' has been played out on the surfaces of youth style in Britain (Hebdige, 1979:44–5). This attempt to chart the underpinnings of particular styles in the social relationships brought about by concrete patterns of historical change – accelerated migration trends and the 'decline of empire' (see also Centre for Contemporary Cultural Studies, 1982) – is an important, if largely undeveloped, aspect of Hebdige's case. It begins to situate the creativity of young bricoleurs within wider structural pressures and determinations, without ever simply reducing agency to structure.

When he comes to interpreting a black musical form such as reggae, and the Rastafarian culture in which it is embedded, Hebdige points to the existence of bricolage tactics that pretty much parallel those used by white counterparts. The most surprising 'theft' in this instance is of themes from 'the white man's Bible' – a text which had previously been used to justify colonial exploitation (Hall, 1986a:54, was to cite it later as an illustration for his theory of articulation). The narrative supplied 'peculiarly appropriate metaphors for the condition of poor, black working class West Indians (Babylon, the suffering Israelites) and a complementary set of metaphorical answers to the problems which define that condition (delivery of the Righteous, retribution for the Wicked, Judgment Day, Zion, the Promised Land)' (Hebdige, 1979:33). These themes appear continually in reggae lyrics of the 1970s, following their translation via the oral culture of Jamaica. Meanwhile, somewhere 'between Trenchtown and Ladbroke Grove', Hebdige (1979:43) notes that a new style code was emerging – with hair plaited into 'locks' or 'knots', and with army surplus stores providing 'battle dress and combat jackets, a . . . wardrobe of sinister guerrilla chic'. A direct modern-day equivalent for black youths in the UK and US would be the rearticulation of sportswear – baseball caps, tracksuits, trainers – as street-corner and dancefloor clothing.

The final example I want to discuss from Hebdige's book is that of punk rock – possibly the most spectacular of all post-war subcultures – and a useful case study because of its eventual reincorporation by the dominant order, as well as its initial symbolic struggle against mainstream British culture. Punks, for Hebdige (1979:107), were collage artists and bricoleurs *par excellence*: 'unremarkable and inappropriate items – a pin, a plastic clothes peg, a television component, a razor blade, a tampon – could be brought within the province of punk (un)fashion'. Objects from some unlikely and often sordid contexts served as confrontational decoration – pornographic bondage gear as street style, lavatory chains as necklaces, or the standard plastic bin liner worn as 'outcast' clothing. The intention was to shock and, for a while, punk succeeded in doing so, giving rise to yet another 'moral panic' in the media. However, by the summer of 1977 'punk clothing and insignia could be bought mail order . . . and in September of that year, *Cosmopolitan* ran a review of Zandra Rhodes' latest collection . . . which consisted entirely of variations on the punk theme' (Hebdige, 1979:96). The magazine's accompanying article declared that 'to shock is chic', heralding the subculture's inevitable decline – and Hebdige's argument about cycles of resistance and reincorporation is a necessary counter to over-optimistic readings of youth rebellion. We are perhaps left to ponder whether, on its own, a 'revolt in style' can actually amount to very much in terms of social and political opposition.

Just a year after the influential *Subculture* was published, McRobbie's paper 'Settling Accounts with Subcultures' (1980) mounted a forceful critique of his work from a feminist stance. A fellow contributor to the *Resistance through Rituals* book (see McRobbie & Garber, 1976), she now turned to address her former male collaborators – also targeting Willis's *Learning to Labour* (1977) (a classic ethnographic study of working-class 'lads' which I touched on briefly in Chapter 3). McRobbie recognized the undoubted insights of these cultural analysts, referring to their key writings as 'sophisticated accounts' of youth lifestyles. Nevertheless, when reading the texts they produce, she is concerned with significant absences or silences as opposed to what is present and spoken there. Her contention was that both Hebdige and Willis had implicitly assumed subcultures to be masculine arenas of social activity, failing to ask in any detail about the everyday practices and positionings of the young men's sisters or girlfriends. Even on occasions when Willis's lads do themselves talk about girls, McRobbie believes he could go further in critically evaluating their sexist attitudes. Of course, there is a problem for the male ethnographer in this situation – particularly when he has to try to 'get in' with his subjects and picture the world through their eyes. The feminist researcher, though, may well see and identify differently. Attempting to fill some of the absences detected in subcultural studies, McRobbie had investigated the phenomenon of 'teeny boppers' (McRobbie & Garber, 1976:219–21) and she went on to co-edit a useful collection of essays on issues of gender and generation (McRobbie & Nava, 1984).

She might have been marginally more impressed by Frank Mort's recent reflections on young men and style, if only because Mort (1988) explicitly raises questions about the social construction of masculinities. He is interested in the relationship between contemporary high street fashion and advertising on the one hand, and possible shifts in masculine identity on the other. Controversially, given his left-wing politics, Mort (1988:197) asserts that the best hope for transforming the vocabulary of masculinity lies in 'the marketplace, the fashion house and the street' rather than in the 'men's group' approach which he argues is 'narrowly class specific and highly eurocentric' (for a personal account of a men's group, see Tolson, 1977). His position is curiously close to Fiske's – notably when he states that 'popular cultures of consumption are . . . deeply contradictory . . . the point where the market meets popular experience and lifestyles on the ground' (Mort, 1988:215) – and he insists that this is necessarily a two-way process. Yes, young males are being sold goods and interpellated by advertising hype – yet the images or looks they consume can still 'rupture traditional icons of masculinity'. As these commodities and representations get imaginatively incorporated into everyday cultures, new masculine structures of feeling and ways of relating to the body are emerging, says Mort. But whilst his enthusiasm for changing fashion codes is infectious, I feel unable to share the same sense of optimism over shifting identities. To be convincing, his project would have to develop a far greater emphasis on ethnographic inquiry because, as Mort (1988:215) himself admits, 'the hardest thing of all to crack is what's going on inside young men's heads'.

Somebody who continues to put his faith in ethnography as a method of investigation is Willis, whose *Common Culture* (1990) presents us with an interpretation of wide-ranging qualitative data on young people's cultural activities. The material was gathered by an experienced team of researchers from around Britain recruited to contribute to a year-long project funded by the Gulbenkian Foundation. Willis had been required to focus on the topic of young people and 'the arts', although he chose to define his brief in broad terms – by paying careful attention to the artful practices of daily living in contrast to the operation of official arts institutions. His perspective is evidently descended from the subculture tradition discussed above – the book's central concept, 'symbolic creativity', has a lot in common with Hebdige's notion of bricolage – but Willis now believes that the idea of subcultures is redundant because all youngsters (not just selected spectacular groupings) are seen to be involved in the active construction of meaning, identity and lifestyle. They are credited, through their consumption of popular TV, film, advertising, music and clothes, with creating a vibrant and resonant culture. Of course, he recognizes that there are structural determinations to be negotiated: 'Identities do not stand alone above history, beyond history.' However, those sociohistorical 'locations and situations are not only determinations – they're also relations and resources to be discovered, explored and experienced. Memberships of race, class, gender, age and region are . . . lived and experimented with' (Willis, 1990:12). This is a promising formulation. It holds on to both creativities and constraints in everyday life, even if we ultimately find ourselves leaning towards the former in Willis's latest study. His theory of 'grounded aesthetics' also connects up particularly well with the concerns of critical audience ethnography, paving the way for further investigations of contextually embedded consumer practices.

Creativities and Constraints in Everyday Life

In this final chapter, my discussion of perspectives on cultural consumption has deliberately been organized around a certain set of themes and oppositions. It is by no means an exhaustive account of the available writings on consumer culture – for instance, I have decided to steer clear of the postmodernist proclamations made by theorists such as Jean Baudrillard (see Baudrillard, 1988; and Bocock, 1992, for a commentary and comparison with Bourdieu). Nor is it the only possible way of delineating the range of different approaches to consumption (e.g. see Featherstone, 1990). My purpose was to identify a productive tension between those cultural analysts who are primarily concerned with structured patterns of distinction, segmentation and social reproduction – and those preferring to acknowledge the creative practices of 'poaching', bricolage and social resistance. The first of these positions, as exemplified by Bourdieu, tends to lead to a political pessimism – while the second, typified by De Certeau or Hebdige, is much more optimistic about what it sees as the tactical evasion of power by subordinate groups in society. To repeat my earlier characterization of the split, I understand it to be a 'constraint versus creativity' debate.

Although the main protagonists on each side of the debate put forward cases which have considerable merit, I would contend that neither position in isolation can allow us to theorize cultural consumption adequately. The challenge for future work in this area is to find a way of combining insights from both camps – elaborating a model of consumer cultures which recognizes creativities and constraints operating simultaneously, and which manages to hold them together within a coherent conceptual framework. Bourdieu's sociology of culture is perhaps the closest thing we have to the model I am proposing here – because he has spoken consistently over the years about transcending the 'subjectivist/objectivist' divide in social theory (see several of the interviews and essays collected in Bourdieu, 1990). It is disappointing, then, that *Distinction* – his major statement on practices and patterns of consumption – is unable, finally, to resolve these matters satisfactorily (remember the criticisms of Garnham, Williams and Jenkins that were summarized in the second section of this chapter). Elsewhere, however, he does point us in precisely the right direction by looking to long-standing disputes between sociologists about the relative influence of human agency or social structure in the shaping of cultures. A return to those fundamental disputes in the social sciences is needed in order to appreciate what is at stake in the study of media and cultural consumption.

Broadly speaking, the discipline of sociology has traditionally divided along a fault line between theories of action and theories of structure (for introductions, see Giddens, 1979; Craib, 1992). Symbolic interactionists, ethnomethodologists and phenomenologists address themselves chiefly to problems of agency and meaning in micro-social situations, leaving the various 'structuralisms' in modern social theory – Marxism, Durkheimian sociology, as well as newer perspectives derived from structural linguistics – to deal more with questions of determination, reproduction and power at the macro-level. This is, of course, a rather oversimplified explanation of a highly complex field, but it helps to illustrate the general parameters of debate. In cultural studies, Hall's well known classification of different approaches as either 'culturalist' or 'structuralist' (Hall, 1986b) bears at least some similarities – with one of these paradigms focussing on the lived experience and sensuous activity of purposeful historical agents, and another stressing the institutional processes that go on 'behind men's backs' and which constitute them as subjects – though we must avoid drawing too direct a parallel here (because there are Marxist thinkers in both paradigms, and culturalists like Williams or Edward Thompson would presumably have been horrified to hear their work compared with, say, symbolic interactionism). Still, just as Hall encouraged us to supersede the culturalist/structuralist divide via Gramsci's ideas, so Anthony Giddens's theory of 'structuration' (see especially Giddens, 1984) might provide a route out of the agency/structure dilemma – and, by extension, a resolution of the arguments over creativity and constraint in everyday consumer cultures.

'Crucial to the idea of structuration,' writes Giddens (1984:25), 'is the theorem of the duality of structure' – his realization that 'agents and structures are not two independently given sets of phenomena, a dualism, but represent a duality . . . the structural properties of social systems are both medium and outcome of the practices they recursively organize'. According to this view, neither action nor structure can be taken as primary – each is given roughly equal weighting in an attempt to escape the problems of previous dichotomies. The British sociologist of culture, Janet Wolff (1981), has applied Giddens's assertions about the 'duality of structure' in her excellent volume, *The Social Production of Art*. As the title implies, she is mainly interested in the moment of cultural production rather than that of consumption – and yet her notes on the concept of creativity in art are of the utmost relevance to our concerns here. Wolff is rightly dismissive of myths about the artist or author as an individual creative genius unfettered by historical and social circumstances, but she also remains reluctant to accept the poststructuralists' complete decentring of subjectivity (think back to my discussion of Lacan) and the related 'death of the author' in certain areas of literary or cultural criticism. Like Giddens, she is unwilling to condone any simple 'disappearance of the subject' – understanding artistic creativity as an active and sometimes innovative practice always carried out within situated contexts of action and definite material or ideological limitations.

The theoretical position which Wolff sets out, then, is exactly the kind of model I believe we ought to be adopting in research on cultures of consumption. Indeed, if we reflect on the best of the ethnographic audience studies covered in previous chapters of this book – such as the work of David Morley or Janice Radway – those projects have consistently sought to account for the interpretative agency of actual viewers and readers whose constructions of meaning are nevertheless subject to physical and symbolic 'resource constraints', including the limits imposed by prior processes of textual production. These investigations contain the vital ingredients for an adequate theory of constrained cultural creativity and a proper method of interpretative cultural study (it is worth noting that Thompson, 1990, refers to Morley and Radway when outlining a general 'methodology of interpretation' for sociological inquiry). An added attraction of their work has been its emphasis on the spatial and temporal contexts of media reception – also a feature of my own qualitative research on early radio and satellite TV consumers – and, making the link with Giddens once again, I have suggested recently that we may now want to pursue the interest in time–space relations of consumption (production and distribution too) by developing a fully fledged 'human geography' of media cultures (Moores, in press b; and see Morley, 1992:40–1). At any rate, when casting an eye forward to potential advances in our field, I hope readers of this text will at least be persuaded of the necessity for a critical ethnographic perspective in future forms of cultural analysis.

References

Adorno, Theodor & Max Horkheimer (1977) 'The Culture Industry : Enlightenment as Mass Deception', pp. 349–83 in James Curran, Michael Gurevitch & Janet Woollacott (eds) *Mass Communication and Society*. London: Edward Arnold.

Althusser, Louis (1984) *Essays on Ideology*. London: Verso.

Anderson, Benedict (1983) *Imagined Communities: Reflections on the Origin and Spread of Nationalism*. London: Verso.

Ang, Ien (1985) *Watching 'Dallas': Soap Opera and the Melodramatic Imagination*. London: Methuen.

Ang, Ien (1989) 'Wanted: Audiences. On the Politics of Empirical Audience Studies', pp. 96–115 in Ellen Seiter, Hans Borchers, Gabriele Kreutzner & Eva-Maria Warth (eds) *Remote Control: Television, Audiences and Cultural Power*. London: Routledge.

Ang, Ien (1990a) 'Culture and Communication: Towards an Ethnographic Critique of Media Consumption in the Transnational Media System', *European Journal of Communication*, 5(2/3): 239–60.

Ang, Ien (1990b) 'Melodramatic Identifications: Television Fiction and Women's Fantasy', pp. 75–88 in Mary Ellen Brown (ed) *Television and Women's Culture: The Politics of the Popular*. London: Sage.

Ang, Ien (1991) *Desperately Seeking the Audience*. London: Routledge.

Ariès, Philippe (1979) *Centuries of Childhood*. London: Peregrine.

Asad, Talal (ed) (1973) *Anthropology and the Colonial Encounter*. London: Ithaca Press.

Atkinson, Paul (1990) *The Ethnographic Imagination: Textual Constructions of Reality*. London: Routledge.

Bachelard, Gaston (1969) *The Poetics of Space*. Boston: Beacon Press.

Barker, Martin (1990) 'Review of John Fiske, "Reading the Popular" and "Understanding Popular Culture" ', *Magazine of Cultural Studies*, 1:39–40.

Barrett, Michele & Mary McIntosh (1982) *The Anti-Social Family*. London: Verso.

Barthes, Roland (1973) *Mythologies*. London: Paladin.

Barthes, Roland (1977) *Image – Music – Text*. New York: Hill & Wang.

Baudrillard, Jean (1988) *Jean Baudrillard: Selected Writings* (ed. Mark Poster). Cambridge: Polity Press.

Bausinger, Hermann (1984) 'Media, Technology and Daily Life', *Media, Culture & Society*, 6(4): 343–51.

Bee, Jim (1989) 'First Citizen of the Semiotic Democracy?', *Cultural Studies*, 3(3): 353–9.

Bennett, Tony (1986) 'Introduction: Popular Culture and "The Turn to Gramsci" ', pp. xi–xix in Tony Bennett, Colin Mercer & Janet Woollacott (eds) *Popular Culture and Social Relations*. Milton Keynes: Open University Press.

Bennett, Tony & Janet Woollacott (1987) *Bond and Beyond: The Political Career of a Popular Hero*. London: Macmillan.

Bennett, Tony, Susan Boyd-Bowman, Colin Mercer & Janet Woollacott (eds) (1981a) *Popular Television and Film*. London: BFI.

Bennett, Tony, Graham Martin, Colin Mercer & Janet Woollacott (eds) (1981b) *Culture, Ideology and Social Process: A Reader*. London: Batsford Academic.

Benveniste, Emile (1971) *Problems in General Linguistics*. Coral Gables, Florida: University of Miami Press.

Bhabha, Homi (ed) (1990) *Nation and Narration*. London: Routledge.

Billig, Michael (1992) *Talking of the Royal Family*. London: Routledge.

Birmingham Popular Memory Group CCCS (1982) 'Popular Memory: Theory Politics, Method', pp. 205–52 in Centre for Contemporary Cultural Studies, *Making Histories: Studies in History-Writing and Politics*. London: Hutchinson.

Black, Maria & Rosalind Coward (1990) 'Linguistic, Social and Sexual Relations: A Review of Dale Spender's "Man Made Language"', pp. 111–33 in Deborah Cameron (ed) *The Feminist Critique of Language: A Reader*. London: Routledge.

Blumler, Jay, Michael Gurevitch & Elihu Katz (1985) 'Reaching Out: A Future for Gratifications Research', pp. 255–73 in Karl Rosengren, Lawrence Wenner & Philip Palmgreen (eds) *Media Gratifications Research: Current Perspectives*. Beverly Hills: Sage.

Bocock, Robert (1992) 'Consumption and Lifestyles', pp. 119–67 in Robert Bocock & Kenneth Thompson (eds) *Social and Cultural Forms of Modernity*. Cambridge: Polity Press.

Boston, Sarah (1987) 'Only Television', pp. 41–7 in Philip Simpson (ed) *Parents Talking Television: Television in the Home*. London: Comedia.

Bourdieu, Pierre (1968) 'Outline of a Sociological Theory of Art Perception', *International Social Science Journal*, 20(4): 589–612.

Bourdieu, Pierre (1972) 'The Berber House', pp. 98–110 in Mary Douglas (ed) *Rules and Meanings*. London: Penguin.

Bourdieu, Pierre (1977) *Outline of a Theory of Practice*. Cambridge: Cambridge University Press.

Bourdieu, Pierre (1984) *Distinction: A Social Critique of the Judgement of Taste*. London: Routledge & Kegan Paul.

Bourdieu, Pierre (1990) *In Other Words: Essays towards a Reflexive Sociology*. Cambridge: Polity Press.

Bourdieu, Pierre & Jean-Claude Passeron (1977) *Reproduction in Education, Society and Culture*. London: Sage.

Brannen, Julia & Gail Wilson (eds) (1987) *Give and Take in Families: Studies in Resource Distribution*. London: Allen & Unwin.

Breakwell, Ian & Paul Hammond (eds) (1990) *Seeing in the Dark: A Compendium of Cinemagoing*. London: Serpent's Tail.

Brunsdon, Charlotte (1981) ' "Crossroads": Notes on Soap Opera', *Screen*, 22(4): 32–7.

Brunsdon, Charlotte (1984) 'Writing about Soap Opera', pp. 82–7 in Len Masterman (ed) *Television Mythologies: Stars, Shows and Signs*. London: Comedia.

Brunsdon, Charlotte (1989) 'Text and Audience', pp. 116–29 in Ellen Seiter, Hans Borchers, Gabriele Kreutzner & Eva-Maria Warth (eds) *Remote Control: Television, Audiences and Cultural Power*. London: Routledge.

Brunsdon, Charlotte (1991) 'Satellite Dishes and the Landscapes of Taste', *New Formations*, 15: 23–42.

Brunsdon, Charlotte & David Morley (1978) *Everyday Television: 'Nationwide'*. London: BFI.

Buckingham, David (1987) *Public Secrets: 'Eastenders' and Its Audience*. London: BFI.

Buckingham, David (1990) 'Seeing Through TV: Children Talking about Television', pp. 87–96 in Janet Willis & Tana Wollen (eds) *The Neglected Audience*. London: BFI.

Buckingham, David (1991) 'What are Words Worth?: Interpreting Children's Talk about Television', *Cultural Studies*, 5(2): 228–45.

Burgess, Robert (1984) *In the Field: An Introduction to Field Research*. London: Unwin Hyman.

CACI Market Analysis (1985) *A Classification of Residential Neighbourhoods*. London: CACI Inc.-International.

Cameron, Deborah, Elizabeth Frazer, Penelope Harvey, Ben Rampton & Kay Richardson (1992) *Researching Language: Issues of Power and Method*. London: Routledge.

Cardiff, David & Paddy Scannell (1987) 'Broadcasting and National Unity', pp. 157–73 in James Curran, Anthony Smith & Pauline Wingate (eds) *Impacts and Influences: Essays on Media Power in the Twentieth Century*. London: Methuen.

Centre for Contemporary Cultural Studies (1982) *The Empire Strikes Back: Race and Racism in 70s Britain*. London: Hutchinson.

Charles, Nickie & Marion Kerr (1988) *Women, Food and Families*. Manchester: Manchester University Press.

Chisnall, Peter (1985) *Marketing: A Behavioural Analysis*. London: McGraw-Hill.

Clarke, John (1976) 'Style', pp. 175–91 in Stuart Hall & Tony Jefferson (eds) *Resistance through Rituals: Youth Subcultures in Post-War Britain*. London: Hutchinson.

Clifford, James (1983) 'On Ethnographic Authority', *Representations*, 1(2): 118–46.

Clifford, James (1986) 'Introduction: Partial Truths', pp. 1–26 in James Clifford & George Marcus (eds) *Writing Culture: The Poetics and Politics of Ethnography*. Berkeley: University of California Press.

Clifford, James (1992) 'Travelling Cultures', pp. 96–116 in Lawrence Grossberg, Cary Nelson & Paula Treichler (eds) *Cultural Studies*. New York: Routledge.

Clifford, James & George Marcus (eds) (1986) *Writing Culture: The Poetics and Politics of Ethnography*. Berkeley: University of California Press.

Cockburn, Cynthia (1985) *Machinery of Dominance: Women, Men and Technical Know-How*. London: Pluto Press.

Collins, Richard (1986) 'Seeing is Believing: The Ideology of Naturalism', pp. 125–38 in John Corner (ed) *Documentary and the Mass Media*. London: Edward Arnold.

Collins, Richard (1990) *Satellite Television in Western Europe*. London: John Libbey.

Corner, John (1991) 'Meaning, Genre and Context: The Problematics of "Public Knowledge" in the New Audience Studies', pp. 267–84 in James Curran & Michael Gurevitch (eds) *Mass Media and Society*. London: Edward Arnold.

Corner, John & Kay Richardson (1986) 'Documentary Meanings and the Discourse of Interpretation', pp. 141–60 in John Corner (ed) *Documentary and the Mass Media*. London: Edward Arnold.

Corner, John, Kay Richardson & Natalie Fenton (1990) *Nuclear Reactions: Form and Response in 'Public Issue' Television*. London: John Libbey.

Coward, Rosalind (1984) *Female Desire: Women's Sexuality Today*. London: Paladin.

Craib, Ian (1992) *Modern Social Theory: From Parsons to Habermas*. London: Harvester Wheatsheaf.

Crawford, June, Susan Kippax, Jenny Onyx, Una Gault & Pam Benton (1992) *Emotion and Gender: Constructing Meaning from Memory*. London: Sage.

Crimp, Margaret (1985) *The Marketing Research Process*. London: Prentice-Hall.

Critcher, Chas & Paul McCann (1990) 'Satellite Television: Pie in the Sky?', pp. 81–200 in Noel Williams & Peter Hartley (eds) *Technology in Human Communication*. London: Pinter.

Cubitt, Sean (1984) 'Top of the Pops: The Politics of the Living Room', pp. 46–8 in Len Masterman (ed) *Television Mythologies: Stars, Shows and Signs*. London: Comedia.

Curran, James (1990) 'The New Revisionism in Mass Communication Research: A Reappraisal', *European Journal of Communication*, 5(2/3): 135–64.

Curti, Lidia (1988) 'Genre and Gender', *Cultural Studies*, 2(2): 152–67.

Dahlgren, Peter (1988) 'What's the Meaning of This?: Viewers' Plural Sense-Making of TV News', *Media, Culture & Society*, 10(3): 285–301.

Dahlgren, Peter & Colin Sparks (eds) (1992) *Journalism and Popular Culture*. London: Sage.

De Certeau, Michel (1984) *The Practice of Everyday Life*. Berkeley: University of California Press.

Deem, Rosemary (1986) *All Work and No Play?: The Sociology of Women and Leisure*. Milton Keynes: Open University Press.

De Sola Pool, Ithaniel (ed) (1977) *The Social Impact of the Telephone*. Cambridge, Mass.: MIT Press.

Donzelot, Jacques (1980) *The Policing of Families*. London: Hutchinson.

Eco, Umberto (1972) 'Towards a Semiotic Inquiry into the Television Message', *Working Papers in Cultural Studies*, 3: 103–21.

Ellis, John (1982) *Visible Fictions: Cinema, Television, Video*. London: Routledge & Kegan Paul.

Engel, James & Roger Blackwell (1982) *Consumer Behaviour*. Chicago: Holt Saunders.

Featherstone, Mike (1990) 'Perspectives on Consumer Culture', *Sociology*, 24(1): 5–22.

Featherstone, Mike (1991) *Consumer Culture and Postmodernism*. London: Sage.

Ferguson, Bob (1987) 'Fight the Good Fight', pp. 54–62 in Philip Simpson (ed) *Parents Talking Television: Television in the Home*. London: Comedia.

Fielding, Guy & Peter Hartley (1987) 'The Telephone: A Neglected Medium', pp. 110–24 in Asher Cashdan & Martin Jordin (eds) *Studies in Communication*. Oxford: Blackwell.

Fischer, Claude (1991) ' "Touch Someone": The Telephone Industry Discovers Sociability', pp. 87–116 in Marcel Lafollette & Jeffrey Stine (eds) *Technology and Choice: Readings from 'Technology and Culture'*. Chicago: University of Chicago Press.

Fiske, John (1982) *Introduction to Communication Studies*. London: Methuen.

Fiske, John (1987) *Television Culture*. London: Methuen.

Fiske, John (1989a) *Understanding Popular Culture*. Boston: Unwin Hyman.

Fiske, John (1989b) *Reading the Popular*. Boston: Unwin Hyman.

Fiske, John & John Hartley (1978) *Reading Television*. London: Methuen.

Formations Collective (eds) (1984) *Formations of Nation and People*. London: Routledge & Kegan Paul.

Forty, Adrian (1986) *Objects of Desire: Design and Society 1750–1980*. London: Thames & Hudson.

Foucault, Michel (1980) *Power/Knowledge: Selected Interviews and Other Writings 1972–1977* (ed. Colin Gordon). Brighton: Harvester Press.

Freund, Elizabeth (1987) *The Return of the Reader: Reader-Response Criticism*. London: Methuen.

Frith, Simon (1983) 'The Pleasures of the Hearth: The Making of BBC Light Entertainment', pp. 101–23 in Formations Collective (eds) *Formations of Pleasure*. London: Routledge & Kegan Paul.

Frow, John (1987) 'Accounting for Tastes: Some Problems in Bourdieu's Sociology of Culture', *Cultural Studies*, 1(1): 59–73.

Frow, John (1991) 'Michel de Certeau and the Practice of Representation', *Cultural Studies*, 5(1): 52–60.

Garnham, Nicholas (1979) 'Subjectivity, Ideology, Class and Historical Materialism', *Screen*, 20(1): 121–33.

Garnham, Nicholas (1986) 'Extended Review: Bourdieu's "Distinction" ', *Sociological Review*, 34(2): 423–33.

Garnham, Nicholas & Raymond Williams (1986) 'Pierre Bourdieu and the Sociology of Culture: An Introduction', pp. 116–30 in Richard Collins, James Curran, Nicholas Garnham, Paddy Scannell, Philip Schlesinger & Colin Sparks (eds) *Media, Culture & Society: A Critical Reader*. London: Sage.

Geertz, Clifford (1973) *The Interpretation of Cultures: Selected Essays*. New York: Basic Books.

Geertz, Clifford (1988) *Works and Lives: The Anthropologist as Author*. Cambridge: Polity Press.

Geraghty, Christine (1981) 'The Continuous Serial: A Definition', pp. 9–26 in Richard Dyer, Christine Geraghty, Marion Jordan, Terry Lovell, Richard Paterson & John Stewart, *'Coronation Street'*. London: BFI.

Geraghty, Christine (1991) *Women and Soap Opera: A Study of Prime Time Soaps*. Cambridge: Polity Press.

Giddens, Anthony (1979) *Central Problems in Social Theory: Action, Structure and Contradiction in Social Analysis*. London: Macmillan.

Giddens, Anthony (1981) *A Contemporary Critique of Historical Materialism*. London: Macmillan.

Giddens, Anthony (1984) *The Constitution of Society: Outline of the Theory of Structuration*. Cambridge: Polity Press.

Giddens, Anthony (1990) *The Consequences of Modernity*. Cambridge: Polity Press.

Gillespie, Marie (1989) 'Technology and Tradition: Audio-Visual Culture among South Asian Families in West London', *Cultural Studies*, 3(2): 226–39.

Glaessner, Verina (1990) 'Gendered Fictions', pp. 115–27 in Andrew Goodwin & Garry Whannell (eds) *Understanding Television*. London: Routledge.

Gray, Ann (1986) 'Video Recorders in the Home: Women's Work and Boys' Toys', Paper presented to the Second International Television Studies Conference, London.

Gray, Ann (1987) 'Behind Closed Doors: Video Recorders in the Home', pp. 38–54 in Helen Baehr & Gillian Dyer (eds) *Boxed In: Women and Television*. London: Pandora.

Gray, Ann (1988) 'Reading the Readings: A Working Paper', Paper presented to the Third International Television Studies Conference, London.

Gray, Ann (1992) *Video Playtime: The Gendering of a Leisure Technology*. London: Routledge.

Gunter, Barrie & Adrian Furnham (1992) *Consumer Profiles: An Introduction to Psychographics*. London: Routledge.

Haddon, Leslie (1988) 'The Home Computer: The Making of a Consumer Electronic', *Science as Culture*, 2: 7–51.

Haddon, Leslie (1991) 'The Cultural Production and Consumption of IT', pp. 157–75 in Hughie Mackay, Michael Young & John Beynon (eds) *Understanding Technology in Education*. London: Falmer Press.

Haddon, Leslie (1992) 'Explaining ICT Consumption: The Case of the Home Computer', pp. 82–96 in Roger Silverstone & Eric Hirsch (eds) *Consuming Technologies: Media and Information in Domestic Spaces*. London: Routledge.

Haddon, Leslie & Roger Silverstone (1992) 'Information and Communication Technologies in the Home: The Case of Teleworking', Science Policy Research Unit, Working Paper 17, University of Sussex.

Hall, Stuart (1973) 'Encoding and Decoding in the Television Discourse', CCCS Stencilled Paper 7, University of Birmingham.

Hall, Stuart (1980) 'Recent Developments in Theories of Language and Ideology: A Critical Note', pp. 157–62 in Stuart Hall, Dorothy Hobson, Andrew Lowe & Paul Willis (eds) *Culture, Media, Language: Working Papers in Cultural Studies 1972–79*. London: Hutchinson.

Hall, Stuart (1982) 'The Rediscovery of "Ideology": Return of the Repressed in Media Studies', pp. 56–90 in Michael Gurevitch, Tony Bennett, James Curran & Janet Woollacott (eds) *Culture, Society and the Media*. London: Methuen.

Hall, Stuart (1986a) 'On Postmodernism and Articulation: An Interview with Stuart Hall', *Journal of Communication Inquiry*, 10(2): 45–60.

Hall, Stuart (1986b) 'Cultural Studies: Two Paradigms', pp. 33–48 in Richard Collins, James Curran, Nicholas Garnham, Paddy Scannell, Philip Schlesinger & Colin Sparks (eds) *Media, Culture & Society: A Critical Reader*. London: Sage.

Hall, Stuart (1988) *The Hard Road to Renewal: Thatcherism and the Crisis of the Left*. London: Verso.

Hall, Stuart & Martin Jacques (eds) (1989) *New Times: The Changing Face of Politics in the 1990s*. London: Lawrence & Wishart.

Hall, Stuart & Tony Jefferson (eds) (1976) *Resistance through Rituals: Youth Subcultures in Post-War Britain*. London: Hutchinson.

Harrisson, Tom & Charles Madge (1986) *Britain by Mass Observation*. London: Hutchinson.

Hartley, John (1987) 'Invisible Fictions: Television Audiences, Paedocracy, Pleasure', *Textual Practice*, 1(2): 121–38.

Harvey, Lee (1990) *Critical Social Research*. London: Unwin Hyman.

Haug, Frigga (ed) (1987) *Female Sexualisation: A Collective Work of Memory*. London: Verso.

Hearn, Jeff & David Morgan (eds) (1990) *Men, Masculinities and Social Theory*. London: Unwin Hyman.

Heath, Stephen (1977/8) 'Notes on Suture', *Screen*, 18(4): 48–76.

Hebdige, Dick (1976) 'The Meaning of Mod', pp. 87–96 in Stuart Hall & Tony Jefferson (eds) *Resistance through Rituals: Youth Subcultures in Post-War Britain*. London: Hutchinson.

Hebdige, Dick (1979) *Subculture: The Meaning of Style*. London: Methuen.

Hebdige, Dick (1982) 'Towards a Cartography of Taste, 1935–1962', pp. 194–218 in Bernard Waites, Tony Bennett & Graham Martin (eds) *Popular Culture: Past and Present*. London: Croom Helm.

Hebdige, Dick (1988) *Hiding in the Light: On Images and Things*. London: Routledge.

Hirsch, Eric (1992) 'The Long Term and the Short Term of Domestic Consumption: An Ethnographic Case Study', pp. 208–26 in Roger Silverstone & Eric Hirsch (eds) *Consuming Technologies: Media and Information in Domestic Spaces*. London: Routledge.

Hobson, Dorothy (1978) 'Housewives: Isolation as Oppression', pp. 79–95 in Women's Studies Group CCCS (eds) *Women Take Issue: Aspects of Women's Subordination*. London: Hutchinson.

Hobson, Dorothy (1980) 'Housewives and the Mass Media', pp. 105–14 in Stuart Hall, Dorothy Hobson, Andrew Lowe & Paul Willis (eds) *Culture, Media, Language: Working Papers in Cultural Studies 1972–79*. London: Hutchinson.

Hobson, Dorothy (1982) *'Crossroads': The Drama of a Soap Opera*. London: Methuen.

Hodge, Bob & David Tripp (1986) *Children and Television: A Semiotic Approach*. Cambridge: Polity Press.

Jackson, David (1990) *Unmasking Masculinity: A Critical Autobiography*. London: Unwin Hyman.

Jackson, Stevi (1982) *Childhood and Sexuality*. Oxford: Blackwell.

Jenkins, Henry (1992) *Textual Poachers: Television Fans and Participatory Culture*. New York: Routledge.

Jenkins, Richard (1992) *Pierre Bourdieu*. London: Routledge.

Jensen, Klaus Bruhn (1986) *Making Sense of the News: Towards a Theory and an Empirical Model of Reception for the Study of Mass Communication*. Aarhus: Aarhus University Press.

Jensen, Klaus Bruhn (1990) 'The Politics of Polysemy: Television News, Everyday Consciousness and Political Action', *Media, Culture & Society*, 12(1): 57–77.

Jensen, Klaus Bruhn (1991) 'Introduction: The Qualitative Turn', pp. 1–11 in Klaus Bruhn Jensen & Nicholas Jankowski (eds) *A Handbook of Qualitative Methodologies for Mass Communication Research*. London: Routledge.

Johnson, Lesley (1981) 'Radio and Everyday Life: The Early Years of Broadcasting in Australia, 1922–1945', *Media, Culture & Society*, 3(2): 167–78.

Johnson, Richard (1986) 'The Story So Far: And Further Transformations?', pp. 277–313 in David Punter (ed) *Introduction to Contemporary Cultural Studies*. London: Longman.

Jones, Deborah (1980) 'Gossip: Notes on Women's Oral Culture', *Women's Studies International Quarterly*, 3(2): 193–8.

Jordin, Martin & Rosalind Brunt (1988) 'Constituting the Television Audience: Problem of Method', pp. 231–49 in Phillip Drummond & Richard Paterson (eds) *Television and its Audience: International Research Perspectives*. London: BFI.

Katz, Elihu & Tamar Liebes (1985) 'Mutual Aid in the Decoding of "Dallas": Preliminary Notes from a Cross-Cultural Study', pp. 187–98 in Phillip Drummond & Richard Paterson (eds) *Television in Transition: Papers from the First International Television Studies Conference*. London: BFI.

Katz, Elihu, Jay Blumler & Michael Gurevitch (1974) 'Utilisation of Mass Communication by the Individual', pp. 19–32 in Jay Blumler & Elihu Katz (eds) *The Uses of Mass Communications: Current Perspectives on Gratifications Research*. Beverly Hills: Sage.

Kopytoff, Igor (1986) 'The Cultural Biography of Things: Commoditisation as Process', pp. 64–91 in Arjun Appadurai (ed) *The Social Life of Things: Commodities in Cultural Perspective*. Cambridge: Cambridge University Press.

Kotler, Philip & Alan Andreasen (1987) *Strategic Marketing for Nonprofit Organisations*. Englewood Cliffs, New Jersey: Prentice-Hall.

Kuhn, Annette (1984) 'Women's Genres', *Screen*, 25(1): 18–28.

Lacan, Jacques (1977) *Ecrits: A Selection*. London: Tavistock.

Lapsley, Robert & Michael Westlake (1988) *Film Theory: An Introduction*. Manchester: Manchester University Press.

Leal, Ondina Fachel (1990) 'Popular Taste and Erudite Repertoire: The Place and Space of Television in Brazil', *Cultural Studies*, 4(1): 19–29.

Lewis, Justin (1983) 'The Encoding/Decoding Model: Criticisms and Redevelopments for Research on Decoding', *Media, Culture & Society*, 5(2): 179–97.

Lewis, Justin (1985) 'Decoding Television News', pp. 205–34 in Phillip Drummond & Richard Paterson (eds) *Television in Transition: Papers from the First International Television Studies Conference*. London: BFI.

Lewis, Justin (1991) *The Ideological Octopus: An Exploration of Television and its Audience*. New York: Routledge.

Liebes, Tamar & Elihu Katz (1990) *The Export of Meaning: Cross-Cultural Readings of 'Dallas'*. New York: Oxford University Press.

Longhurst, Derek (1989) 'Science Fiction: The Dreams of Men', pp. 192–212 in Derek Longhurst (ed) *Gender, Genre and Narrative Pleasure*. London: Unwin Hyman.

Loudon, David & Albert Della Bitta (1988) *Consumer Behaviour: Concepts and Applications*. New York: McGraw-Hill.

Lovell, Terry (1981) 'Ideology and "Coronation Street" ', pp. 40–52 in Richard Dyer, Christine Geraghty, Marion Jordan, Terry Lovell, Richard Paterson & John Stewart, *'Coronation Street'*. London: BFI.

Lull, James (1980) 'The Social Uses of Television', *Human Communication Research*, 6(3): 197–209.

Lull, James (1982) 'How Families Select Television Programmes: A Mass Observational Study', *Journal of Broadcasting and Electronic Media*, 26(4): 801–11.

Lull, James (ed) (1988) *World Families Watch Television*. London: Sage.

Lull, James (1990) *Inside Family Viewing: Ethnographic Research on Television's Audiences*. London: Routledge.

Lusted, David (ed) (1991) *The Media Studies Book: A Guide for Teachers*. London: Routledge.

MacCabe, Colin (1974) 'Realism and the Cinema: Notes on Some Brechtian Theses', *Screen*, 15(2): 7–27.

MacCabe, Colin (1985) *Theoretical Essays: Film, Linguistics, Literature*. Manchester: Manchester University Press.

McGrath, John (1981) *A Good Night Out. Popular Theatre: Audience, Class and Form*. London: Methuen.

McGuigan, Jim (1992) *Cultural Populism*. London: Routledge.

Mackay, Hughie & Gareth Gillespie (1992) 'Extending the Social Shaping of Technology Approach: Ideology and Appropriation', *Social Studies of Science*, 22(4): 685–716.

MacKenzie, Donald & Judy Wajcman (1985a) 'Introductory Essay', pp. 2–25 in Donald MacKenzie & Judy Wajcman (eds) *The Social Shaping of Technology: How the Refrigerator Got Its Hum*. Milton Keynes: Open University Press.

MacKenzie, Donald & Judy Wajcman (eds) (1985b) *The Social Shaping of Technology: How the Refrigerator Got Its Hum*. Milton Keynes: Open University Press.

McQuail, Denis, Jay Blumler & John Brown (1972) 'The Television Audience: A Revised Perspective', pp. 135–65 in Denis McQuail (ed) *Sociology of Mass Communications*. London: Penguin.

McRobbie, Angela (1980) 'Settling Accounts with Subcultures: A Feminist Critique', *Screen Education*, 34: 37–49.

McRobbie, Angela (1982) 'The Politics of Feminist Research: Between Talk, Text and Action', *Feminist Review*, 12: 46–57.

McRobbie, Angela & Jenny Garber (1976) 'Girls and Subcultures', pp. 209–22 in Stuart Hall & Tony Jefferson (eds) *Resistance through Rituals: Youth Subcultures in Post-War Britain*. London: Hutchinson.

McRobbie, Angela & Mica Nava (eds) (1984) *Gender and Generation*. London: Macmillan.

Malinowski, Bronislaw (1978) *Argonauts of the Western Pacific: An Account of Native Enterprise and Adventure in the Archipelagoes of Melanesian New Guinea*. London: Routledge & Kegan Paul.

Marcus, George & Michael Fischer (1986) *Anthropology as Cultural Critique: An Experimental Moment in the Human Sciences*. Chicago: University of Chicago Press.

Masterman, Len (1984) 'The Battle of Orgreave', pp. 99–109 in Len Masterman (ed) *Television Mythologies: Stars, Shows and Signs*. London: Comedia.

Masterman, Len (1985) *Teaching the Media*. London: Comedia.

Matrix Collective (1984) *Making Space: Women and the Man-Made Environment*. London: Pluto Press.

Meyrowitz, Joshua (1985) *No Sense of Place: The Impact of Electronic Media on Social Behaviour*. New York: Oxford University Press.

Miller, Daniel (1987) *Material Culture and Mass Consumption*. Oxford: Blackwell.

Mishler, Elliot (1986) *Research Interviewing: Context and Narrative*. Cambridge, Mass.: Harvard University Press.

Montgomery, Martin (1991) ' "Our Tune": A Study of a Discourse Genre', pp. 138–77 in Paddy Scannell (ed) *Broadcast Talk*. London: Sage.

Moores, Shaun (1985) 'Capturing Time and Space in the Home: Early Radio and Everyday Life', Paper presented to the International Sociological Association Conference on 'Communication and Lifestyles', Ljubljana.

Moores, Shaun (1986) 'Towards an Oral History of Audiences', *Media Education Journal*, 5: 50–2.

Moores, Shaun (1988) ' "The Box on the Dresser": Memories of Early Radio and Everyday Life', *Media, Culture & Society*, 10(1): 23–40.

Moores, Shaun (1991) 'Dishes and Domestic Cultures: Satellite TV as Household Technology', Paper presented to the Fourth International Television Studies Conference, London.

Moores, Shaun (in press a) 'Satellite TV as Cultural Sign: Consumption, Embedding and Articulation', *Media, Culture & Society*, 15(4).

Moores, Shaun (in press b) 'Television, Geography and "Mobile Privatisation" ', *European Journal of Communication*, 8(3).

Morley, David (1974) 'Reconceptualizing the Media Audience', CCCS Stencilled Paper 9, University of Birmingham.

Morley, David (1980a) *The 'Nationwide' Audience: Structure and Decoding*. London: BFI.

Morley, David (1980b) 'Texts, Readers, Subjects', pp. 163–73 in Stuart Hall, Dorothy Hobson, Andrew Lowe & Paul Willis (eds) *Culture, Media, Language: Working Papers in Cultural Studies 1972–79*. London: Hutchinson.

Morley, David (1981a) 'Interpreting Television: A Case Study', pp. 40–68 in *U203 Popular Culture*. Unit 12, Milton Keynes: Open University Press.

Morley, David (1981b) 'The "Nationwide" Audience: A Critical Postscript', *Screen Education*, 39: 3–14.

Morley, David (1986) *Family Television: Cultural Power and Domestic Leisure*. London: Comedia.

Morley, David (1988) 'Domestic Relations: The Framework of Family Viewing in Great Britain', pp. 22–48 in James Lull (ed) *World Families Watch Television*. London: Sage.

Morley, David (1991) 'Where the Global Meets the Local: Notes from the Sitting Room', *Screen*, 32(1): 1–15.

Morley, David (1992) *Television, Audiences and Cultural Studies*. London: Routledge.

Morley, David & Roger Silverstone (1990) 'Domestic Communication: Technologies and Meanings', *Media, Culture & Society*, 12(1): 31–55.

Morris, Meaghan (1990) 'Banality in Cultural Studies', pp. 14–43 in Patricia Mellencamp (ed) *Logics of Television: Essays in Cultural Criticism*. Bloomington: Indiana University Press.

Mort, Frank (1988) 'Boy's Own?: Masculinity, Style and Popular Culture', pp. 193–224 in Rowena Chapman & Jonathan Rutherford (eds) *Male Order: Unwrapping Masculinity*. London: Lawrence & Wishart.

Moss, Gemma (1989) *Un/Popular Fictions*. London: Virago.

Moyal, Ann (1989) 'The Feminine Culture of the Telephone: People, Patterns and Policy', *Prometheus*, 7(1): 5–31.

Moyal, Ann (1992) 'The Gendered Use of the Telephone: An Australian Case Study', *Media, Culture & Society*, 14(1): 51–72.

Mulvey, Laura (1975) 'Visual Pleasure and Narrative Cinema', *Screen*, 16(3): 6–18.

Murdock, Graham (1989) 'Class Stratification and Cultural Consumption: Some Motifs in the Work of Pierre Bourdieu', pp. 90–101 in Fred Coalter (ed) *Freedom and Constraint: The Paradoxes of Leisure*. London: Routledge.

Murdock, Graham, Paul Hartmann & Peggy Gray (1992) 'Contextualising Home Computing: Resources and Practices', pp. 146–60 in Roger Silverstone & Eric Hirsch (eds) *Consuming Technologies: Media and Information in Domestic Spaces*. London: Routledge.

Negrine, Ralph (ed) (1988) *Satellite Broadcasting: The Politics and Implications of the New Media*. London: Routledge.

Nightingale, Virginia (1989) 'What's "Ethnographic" about Ethnographic Audience Research?', *Australian Journal of Communication*, 16: 50–63.

Oliver, Gordon (1986) *Marketing Today*. London: Prentice-Hall.

O'Sullivan, Tim (1991) 'Television Memories and Cultures of Viewing, 1950–65', pp. 159–81 in John Corner (ed) *Popular Television in Britain: Studies in Cultural History*. London: BFI.

O'Sullivan, Tim, John Hartley, Danny Saunders & John Fiske (1983) *Key Concepts in Communication*. London: Methuen.

Oswell, David (1991) 'The Place of Children's Viewing, 1946–1960', Paper presented to the Fourth International Television Studies Conference, London.

Pahl, Jan (1989) *Money and Marriage*. London: Macmillan.

Pahl, Ray (1984) *Divisions of Labour*. Oxford: Blackwell.

Palmer, Patricia (1986) *The Lively Audience: A Study of Children around the TV Set*. Sydney: Allen & Unwin.

Palmer, Patricia (1988) 'The Social Nature of Children's Television Viewing', pp. 139–53 in Phillip Drummond & Richard Paterson (eds) *Television and its Audience: International Research Perspectives*. London: BFI.

Parkin, Frank (1972) *Class Inequality and Political Order*. London: Paladin.

Paterson, Richard (1980) 'Planning the Family: The Art of the Television Schedule', *Screen Education*, 35: 79–85.

Pegg, Mark (1983) *Broadcasting and Society 1918–39*. London: Croom Helm.

Perelberg, Rosine Jozef & Ann Miller (eds) (1990) *Gender and Power in Families*. London: Routledge.

Philo, Greg (1990) *Seeing and Believing: The Influence of Television*. London: Routledge.

Postman, Neil (1982) *The Disappearance of Childhood*. New York: Delacorte.

Provenzo, Eugene (1991) *Video Kids: Making Sense of 'Nintendo'*. Cambridge, Mass.: Harvard University Press.

Radway, Janice (1987) *Reading the Romance: Women, Patriarchy and Popular Literature*. London: Verso.

Radway, Janice (1988) 'Reception Study: Ethnography and the Problems of Dispersed Audiences and Nomadic Subjects', *Cultural Studies*, 2(3): 359–76.

Rakow, Lana (1992) *Gender on the Line: Women, the Telephone and Community Life*. Urbana: University of Illinois Press.

Rath, Claus-Dieter (1985) 'The Invisible Network: Television as an Institution in Everyday Life', pp. 199–204 in Phillip Drummond & Richard Paterson (eds) *Television in Transition: Papers from the First International Television Studies Conference*. London: BFI.

Robins, Kevin (1979) 'Althusserian Marxism and Media Studies: The Case of "Screen" ', *Media, Culture & Society*, 1(4): 355–70.

Rogge, Jan-Uwe & Klaus Jensen (1988) 'Everyday Life and Television in West Germany: An Empathic-Interpretive Perspective on the Family as a System', pp. 80–115 in James Lull (ed) *World Families Watch Television*. London: Sage.

Root, Jane (1986) *Open the Box: About Television*. London: Comedia.

Said, Edward (1978) *Orientalism*. London: Routledge & Kegan Paul.

Sarup, Madan (1992) *Jacques Lacan*. London: Harvester Wheatsheaf.

Scannell, Paddy (1988) 'Radio Times: The Temporal Arrangements of Broadcasting in the Modern World', pp. 15–31 in Phillip Drummond & Richard Paterson (eds) *Television and Its Audience: International Research Perspectives*. London: BFI.

Scannell, Paddy & David Cardiff (1982) 'Serving the Nation: Public Service Broadcasting before the War', pp. 161–88 in Bernard Waites, Tony Bennett & Graham Martin (eds) *Popular Culture: Past and Present*. London: Croom Helm.

Scannell, Paddy & David Cardiff (1991) *A Social History of British Broadcasting, Volume One 1922–1939: Serving the Nation*. Oxford: Blackwell.

Schlesinger, Philip, Rebecca Emerson Dobash, Russell Dobash & Kay Weaver (1992) *Women Viewing Violence*. London: BFI.

Shields, Rob (ed) (1992) *Lifestyle Shopping: The Subject of Consumption*. London: Routledge.

Silverstone, Roger (1989) 'Let Us Then Return to the Murmuring of Everyday Practices: A Note on Michel de Certeau, Television and Everyday Life', *Theory, Culture & Society*, 6(1): 77–94.

Silverstone, Roger (1990) 'Television and Everyday Life: Towards an Anthropology of the Television Audience', pp. 173–89 in Marjorie Ferguson (ed) *Public Communication: The New Imperatives*. London: Sage.

Silverstone, Roger (1991) 'From Audiences to Consumers: The Household and the Consumption of Information and Communication Technologies', *European Journal of Communication*, 6(2): 135–54.

Silverstone, Roger (in press) 'Television, Ontological Security and the Transitional Object', *Media, Culture & Society*, 15(4).

Silverstone, Roger & David Morley (1990) 'Families and Their Technologies: Two Ethnographic Portraits', pp. 74–83 in Tim Putnam & Charles Newton (eds) *Household Choices*. London: Futures Publications.

Silverstone, Roger, David Morley, Andrea Dahlberg & Sonia Livingstone (1989) 'Families, Technologies and Consumption: The Household and Information and Communication Technologies', Centre for Research into Innovation, Culture and Technology, Discussion Paper, Brunel University.

Silverstone, Roger, Eric Hirsch & David Morley (1991) 'Listening to a Long Conversation: An Ethnographic Approach to the Study of Information and Communication Technologies in the Home', *Cultural Studies*, 5(2): 204–27.

Silverstone, Roger, Eric Hirsch & David Morley (1992) 'Information and Communication Technologies and the Moral Economy of the Household', pp. 15–31 in Roger Silverstone & Eric Hirsch (eds) *Consuming Technologies: Media and Information in Domestic Spaces*. London: Routledge.

Simpson, Philip (ed) (1987) *Parents Talking Television: Television in the Home*. London: Comedia.

Skirrow, Gillian (1986) 'Hellivision: An Analysis of Video Games', pp. 115–42 in Colin MacCabe (ed) *High Theory/Low Culture: Analysing Popular Television and Film*. Manchester: Manchester University Press.

Sless, David (1986) *In Search of Semiotics*. London: Croom Helm.

Smythe, Dallas (1981) *Dependency Road: Communications, Capitalism, Consciousness and Canada*. Norwood, NJ: Ablex.

Spigel, Lynn (1986) 'Ambiguity and Hesitation: Discourses on Television and the Housewife in Women's Home Magazines, 1948–55', Paper presented to the Second International Television Studies Conference, London.

Spigel, Lynn (1989) 'The Domestic Economy of Television Viewing in Post-War America', *Critical Studies in Mass Communication*, 6(4): 337–54.

Spigel, Lynn (1992a) *Make Room For TV: Television and the Family Ideal in Post-War America*. Chicago: University of Chicago Press.

Spigel, Lynn (1992b) 'Installing the Television Set: Popular Discourses on Television and Domestic Space, 1948–1955', pp. 3–38 in Lynn Spigel & Denise Mann (eds) *Private Screenings: Television and the Female Consumer*. Minneapolis: University of Minnesota Press.

Thompson, Edward (1967) 'Time, Work-Discipline and Industrial Capitalism', *Past and Present*, 38: 56–97.

Thompson, John (1988) 'Mass Communication and Modern Culture: Contribution to a Critical Theory of Ideology', *Sociology*, 22(3): 359–83.

Thompson, John (1990) *Ideology and Modern Culture: Critical Social Theory in the Era of Mass Communication*. Cambridge: Polity Press.

Thompson, Paul (1978) *The Voice of the Past: Oral History*. Oxford: Oxford University Press.

Tolson, Andrew (1977) *The Limits of Masculinity*. London: Tavistock.

Tomlinson, Alan (1990) 'Home Fixtures: Doing-It-Yourself in a Privatised World', pp. 57–73 in Alan Tomlinson (ed) *Consumption, Identity and Style: Marketing, Meanings and the Packaging of Pleasure*. London: Routledge.

Tomlinson, John (1991) *Cultural Imperialism: A Critical Introduction*. London: Pinter.

Turkle, Sherry (1988) 'Computational Reticence: Why Women Fear the Intimate Machine', pp. 41–61 in Cheris Kramarae (ed) *Technology and Women's Voices*. New York: Simon & Schuster.

Urry, John (1990) *The Tourist Gaze: Leisure and Travel in Contemporary Societies*. London: Sage.

Van Maanen, John (1988) *Tales of the Field: On Writing Ethnography*. Chicago: University of Chicago Press.

Volosinov, Valentin (1973) *Marxism and the Philosophy of Language*. New York: Seminar Press.

Wajcman, Judy (1991) *Feminism Confronts Technology*. Cambridge: Polity Press.

Walkerdine, Valerie (1986) 'Video Replay: Families, Films and Fantasy', pp. 167–99 in Victor Burgin, James Donald & Cora Kaplan (eds) *Formations of Fantasy*. London: Methuen.

Walkerdine, Valerie (1990) *Schoolgirl Fictions*. London: Verso.

Wallman, Sandra (1984) *Eight London Households*. London: Tavistock.

Westwood, Sallie (1984) *All Day Every Day: Factory and Family in the Making of Women's Lives*. London: Pluto Press.

Willett, John (1978) *The New Sobriety: Art and Politics in the Weimar Period 1917–33*. London: Thames & Hudson.

Williams, Raymond (1974) *Television: Technology and Cultural Form*. London: Fontana.

Williams, Raymond (1989) *Resources of Hope: Culture, Democracy, Socialism*. London: Verso.

Willis, Paul (1977) *Learning to Labour: How Working Class Kids Get Working Class Jobs*. Aldershot: Saxon House.

Willis, Paul (1978) *Profane Culture*. London: Routledge & Kegan Paul.

Willis, Paul (1980) 'Notes on Method', pp. 88–95 in Stuart Hall, Dorothy Hobson, Andrew Lowe & Paul Willis (eds) *Culture, Media, Language: Working Papers in Cultural Studies 1972–79*. London: Hutchinson.

Willis, Paul (1982) 'The Motorbike and Motorbike Culture', pp. 284–93 in Bernard Waites, Tony Bennett & Graham Martin (eds) *Popular Culture: Past and Present*. London: Croom Helm.

Willis, Paul (1990) *Common Culture: Symbolic Work at Play in the Everyday Cultures of the Young*. Milton Keynes: Open University Press.

Wolff, Janet (1981) *The Social Production of Art*. London: Macmillan.

Women's Studies Group CCCS (eds) (1978) *Women Take Issue: Aspects of Women's Subordination*. London: Hutchinson.

Worpole, Ken (1987) 'Reduced to Words', pp. 80–9 in Philip Simpson (ed) *Parents Talking Television: Television in the Home*. London: Comedia.

Wynne, Derek (1990) 'Leisure, Lifestyle and the Construction of Social Position', *Leisure Studies*, 9(1): 21–34.

Index